Breaking Out of the
POVERTY TRAP

Case Studies from the Tibetan Plateau in
Yunnan, Qinghai and Gansu

Breaking Out of the
POVERTY TRAP

Case Studies from the Tibetan Plateau in Yunnan, Qinghai and Gansu

Editors

Luolin WANG • Ling ZHU

Chinese Academy of Social Sciences, China

World Century

Published by

World Century Publishing Corporation
27 Warren Street, Suite 401-402, Hackensack, NJ 07601

Library of Congress Control Number: 2013936934

British Library Cataloguing-in-Publication Data
A catalogue record for this book is available from the British Library.

BREAKING OUT OF THE POVERTY TRAP
Case Studies from the Tibetan Plateau in Yunnan, Qinghai and Gansu

Originally published in Chinese.

Copyright © 2013 by World Century Publishing Corporation.

Published by arrangement with SCPG Publishing Corporation.
All Rights Reserved.

ISBN 9781938134074

English Proofreader: Adam Lacey
In-house Editor: Lee Xin Ying

Typeset by Stallion Press
Email: enquiries@stallionpress.com

Printed in Singapore.

Members of the Chinese Academy of Social Sciences' Research Team

Wang Luolin	Adviser of the CASS; Professor
Zhu Ling	Professorial Fellow, Institute of Economics
Yang Chunxue	Professorial Fellow, Institute of Economics
Wei Zhong	Professorial Fellow, Institute of Economics
Zhu Hengpeng	Professorial Fellow, Institute of Economics
Zhou Ji	Professorial Librarian, Institute of Economics
Zhaluo	Associate Research Fellow, Institute of Ethnology and Anthropology
Yao Yu	Associate Research Fellow, Institute of Economics
Jin Chengwu	Associate Research Fellow, Institute of Economics

Contents

Preface

This book is divided into 12 chapters. Except for the introductory chapter, the rest of the chapters are all reports based on the each of the subtopics. The following section provides an overview of the book beginning from the second chapter.

Against the background of economic marketization and globalization, one of the main ways that poor farmers and herdsmen can break through the poverty trap is to enhance their competence in production management and increase their incomes through market trading. However, these rural families usually live in geographical locations far from cities and towns and with poor infrastructure. Additionally, the markets for agricultural products are relatively unstable and risky. Indeed, it is impossible for this group to remove the barriers preventing them from entering the market, by only relying on "the market". Instead, it requires the government to invest in public infrastructure and assist with effective policies that help to build market institutions. In our previous research, our research team has done special studies on government investment in rural roads, drinking water and the agricultural infrastructure in Tibetan regions. In this stage of the research, taking a "micro" perspective, we focus on how farmers and herdsmen enter the market and increase their incomes by adapting to a marketized socioeconomic environment while optimizing their resource allocation. The second chapter of the book takes a theoretical approach, exploring the prerequisites required in order to change the old ways of thinking prevalent in the farmer and herdsmen populations, while questioning the claim that these people have rather "backward ideas and ways of thinking". The third chapter examines the market structure of regions where we did research and the participation of farmers and herdsmen in the market.

In the Tibetan Plateau, certain kinds of mushrooms that grow at an altitude higher than 3,000 meters above sea level have become the major source of cash income for rural families who live in the area. In the high-altitude forests of Diqing, one can find "tricholoma matsutake", a natural specialty. In some of the pastures found in Yushu and Guoluo, high-quality Chinese caterpillar fungus (cordyceps sinensis) has gained a widespread reputation. The seasonal harvesting and selling of these mushrooms is thus an extremely important task in these areas. Using the framework of industrial chain analysis, the fourth and fifth chapters of this book examine respectively the impact of collecting tricholoma matsutake and caterpillar fungus on the employment and income of farmers and herdsmen, the distribution of profits and risks among those involved in the industrial chain, and the damage to the eco-environment, as a result of the profits made from these two specialties.

The delicate ecology of the Tibetan Plateau is an important environmental factor that must be taken into account when considering the regional economic development. Over the past few decades, as a result of natural climatic conditions and human activity, large-scale pastures at the source of the Yangtze River, Yellow River and Lancang River have been degraded and in some cases have even become desertified; whereas glaciers, snow mountains, lakes and wetlands are now shrinking and in some instances have even dried up, resulting in a sharp reduction in water resources. In order to protect the ecological integrity of the area, the central and provincial governments of Qinghai have carried out a number of eco-migration and environmental protection projects in the area, investing 7.5 billion *yuan* in the process. The focus of the sixth chapter is to look at whether the eco-migration projects can assist migrant families to integrate into a new social and economic environment, while continuing to earn a sustainable income. This is of course extremely important for the welfare of the herdsmen, and is also a determining factor as to whether the project is a success.

A marked feature of the poor in these areas is that they seem to find it difficult getting employment or undertaking business activities on their own initiative. Even if they own some capital, it seems that they are unable to avoid poverty, due to an inability to manage their resources in a business context and deal with risk. Therefore, the government should work to improve human resources by investing in health, training and education of the poor, so as to enhance their well-being, knowledge and skills. This will not only help to alleviate current levels of poverty, but also reduce and indeed prevent it in the future. Based on such a belief, the seventh chapter explores means to stop intergenerational transmission of poverty by actions such as improving the healthcare provision for pregnant women. The theme of the eighth chapter is the investment in resources to assist young adults, such as compulsory and vocational education. In addition to formal education books, radio and television are discussed as alternative means for the public to absorb knowledge and information. The ninth chapter takes a look at the impact of radio and TV on the cultural life of farmers and herdsmen.

Anti-poverty plans are targeted at poor people who are still capable of work, whereas social assistance is aimed at the poor who are incapable of work or have lost the ability to work (for example, those who are elderly or severely disabled), and those who have been struck by unexpected disasters which have rendered them incapable of meeting their own basic needs. Experience from China and abroad suggests that any social assistance system needs to be designed so as to specifically target groups and thereby ensure its sustainability. The criteria must be based around the nature of the disaster he or she suffers, as well as the social exclusion he or she encounters.[1] Based on this perspective, the last three chapters explore respectively the role of social assistance and disaster relief systems in poverty alleviation.

The tenth chapter focuses on the means to get government and non-government aid to those who have lost the capability to work and those who suffer from severe and chronic poverty. To date, the minimum living standard guarantee system ("minimum guarantee") has been widely introduced in regions in which we conducted research, and has been warmly welcomed by both farmers and herdsmen. By relying on the minimum guarantee subsidies and medical aid, the target families are able to meet their needs with respect to food as well as address some of the difficulties associated with seeing a doctor. In addition, local temples provide those who are recognized as extremely poor with both material assistance as

---

[1] See Burgess and Stern (1991).

well as spiritual comfort. However, the coverage and the amount of aid that can be distributed as a result of the existing minimum guarantee system, depends on the financial resources of the local government and their ability to distribute financial resources for different uses.[2] The provincial Tibetan regions are plagued by limited financial resources. Education and administrative costs take up the majority of fiscal expenditure, leaving only a very limited amount of resource that can be put into social expenditure, especially social assistance. Therefore, it is not possible to guarantee basic living standards for all of those that qualify as "poor" unless the central government is prepared to take on more responsibility with regards to the funding of social assistance.

Due to the frequent natural disasters in the Tibetan Plateau, the production and daily lives of the local farmers and herdsmen are frequently disturbed by disasters such as droughts, floods, heavy hail storms, mud avalanches and snowstorms. In agricultural areas, the disasters usually result in a poor harvest and in some cases no crops whatsoever. At the very least these disasters can lead to short-term difficulties. However, by relying on government subsidies and their supplementary non-agricultural incomes, production in the following year will not be affected. In pastoral areas, a single snowstorm can deprive some herdsmen of the ability to produce in the second year. This is because after a snow disaster, they often end up as "families without livestock", or "families with few livestock". Indeed, a severe snowstorm is enough to drive the non-poor into poverty and intensify the poverty of those who are already poor. In this sense, the prevention of snowstorms, as well as the implementation of effective aid and rehabilitation efforts after the disaster, plays a key role in preventing and relieving poverty in pastoral areas. Taking these facts into account, the eleventh and twelfth chapters explore respective solutions to the tough problems of snowstorm prevention, disaster relief and after-disaster rehabilitation in pastoral areas by tracing changes in technologies and policies.

Since 1949, the government has consistently encouraged herdsmen to improve their disaster prevention and alleviation methods by making regulations, promoting snowstorm prevention technologies and investing

---

[2] See Ravallion (2009).

in infrastructure construction in pastoral areas. However, due to a number of factors including a sharp increase in population, overgrazing of the pasture lands, pasture degradation, the effects of global warming and increased frequency of heavy snowfall, herdsmen are increasingly prone to the risks associated with snowstorms, and snowstorm prevention remains a tough problem, which has yet to be solved. Thus, it is imperative that the government change existing disaster relief and after-disaster rehabilitation plans, to include useful steps such as ensuring livestock are insured and establishing relief funds to be used in the event of a heavy snowstorm.

Moreover, by helping herdsmen to find new sources of income, the government can help to reduce the cases of disaster-related poverty. With nationwide industrialization and urbanization, some farmers and herdsmen may turn to other industries in order to find a way to increase their income. Those who continue staying in the agricultural areas would voluntarily resort to birth control as a response to the increased living costs. As a result, there would be a decrease in the population of farmers and herdsmen and an increase in income thanks to the improvement in the "quality" of the population and transformation of production modes. This can be understood as an inevitable trend and part of social and historical developments. Thus, one fundamental way to reduce the damage caused by snowstorms is by following the trend and gradually reducing the number of herdsmen and livestock living on the pastures to ensure recovery of the latter while restoring the balance between resources and population.

The practices described above also make up an important part of anti-poverty schemes in agricultural and pastoral areas. For herdsmen living in high-altitude pastoral areas, it means that a large number of them will have to face a significant change in terms of their modes of production, lifestyle, as well as cultural changes. Historical experience has shown that a transformation in the socioeconomic structure will give rise to new social conflicts, which will present a tough challenge to governments, non-governmental organizations, communities, families and the individuals involved. To ensure a smooth transformation, the government should make a long-term investment in the material and institutional infrastructure in the regions involved. Additionally, they should help the herdsmen adapt to an industrialized and urbanized socioeconomic environment.

Moreover, it is also necessary to develop social undertakings in public health, education, training and cultural information by aiming precisely at the needs of the population that will undergo the transformation. The logical thread of this analysis takes us back to the starting point of the research.

In research on the aforementioned topics, most authors happened to mention the same problem, that is, insufficient public investment. In 2010, the budget allocated to the housing project in Yushu (after the earthquake in the area) was as much as 9.6 billion *yuan*.[3] Over the course of the 5th Tibet Work Forum, the central committee approved another list of key construction projects in Tibet.[4] The central committee has also drafted policies on the investment of public finance in the provincial Tibetan regions. It can be expected that in the next five to ten years, there will be a new wave of developments in industries supported by these plans. What needs to be pointed out is that the studies of our research team have shown that the developments of matching "software" in institutions and management is still somewhat underdeveloped despite the swift improvements in "hardware" facilities in specific industries thanks to public investment. In some cases, the improvements even surpass certain stages in the application of technology. Examples include introducing mobile communication facilities to regions with no telecommunications infrastructure or constructing highways in regions inaccessible by roads. Due to the inconsistencies between the development of "software" and "hardware" facilities, the use of "hardware" by the farmers and herdsmen in recipient regions is still limited due to obstacles that could not be overcome in the short term. It is also impossible to realize the goal of improving the quality of human resources and eliminating poverty in one simple step. Unfortunately, the development of human resources is a historical process that takes time, and it is thus more feasible to facilitate the progress than to make a "Great Leap Forward".

When visiting the poor families and anti-poverty organizations in India twice during the 1990s, Zhu Ling learned that it requires at least three generations for a farming household, who has lost land and moved

---

[3] See Yushu Government (2010).
[4] See Xinhua News (2010).

to a city, to overcome poverty and integrate into an urban social, economic and cultural existence. In the past 30 years, it has become common knowledge to understand the hardships faced by Han "rural migrant workers" who move to cities seeking a better life. If farmers and herdsmen in minority-inhabited regions make the same decision, they will be faced with even more barriers. For example, there are the difficulties in overcoming both language and cultural barriers. For issues such as the institutional barriers faced by the rural migrants, the inevitable discrimination from urban residents towards the migrants, as well as the incidents of contradiction between employers and their migrant employees — if handled improperly — they could trigger serious social conflict. Moreover, if different ethnic groups are involved, the social conflict would easily develop into an ethnic conflict. Therefore, it would be better for the government to adopt gradually progressive strategies to allow enough time and opportunities for different groups participating in the transformation to adapt to and learn from each other for mutual development. In other words, the sustainability of the gradual transformation is indeed better than administrative forces that push the process forward. This is a fact that has not only been proved by China's experience in economic reforms, but is also a conclusion that our research team has drawn from the studies on the development of Tibetan regions over the past decade.

Wang Luolin and Zhu Ling

Bibliography

Burgess, Robin and Nicholas Stern, 1991, "Social Security in Developing Countries: What, Why, Who, and How?", In *Social Security in Developing Countries*, Ahmad Ehtisham, Jean Drèze, John Hills, and Amartya Sen (Eds.), Oxford: Oxford University Press, pp. 41–80.

Ravallion, Martin, 2009, "Do Poorer Countries Have Less Capacity for Redistribution?", *Policy Research Working Paper Series 5046*, The World Bank.

Xinhua News, 2010, "The Existence of 'Two Conflicts' Requires Tibet to Promote Leap-Forward Development and Lasting Stability and Peace", http://big5.xinhuanet.com/gate/big5/tibet.news.cn/xwzt/2010–03/21/content_19360290.htm, downloaded on July 22, 2010.

Yushu Government, 2010, "Eight Questions on Yushu: Exclusive Interview by Xinhua Reporter on Luo Huining, Head of After-Earthquake Recovery and Restoration Team in Yushu, Qinghai Province", July 24, 2010, http://www.qhys.gov.cn/yushuxian/html/451/49289.html, downloaded on August 3, 2010.

CHAPTER 1

Introduction

WANG Luolin and ZHU Ling

Abstract

One of the key objectives of China's anti-poverty policies is to alleviate severe and chronic poverty, while also eliminating temporary poverty. The poor rural residents of the Tibetan Plateau suffer from severe poverty, which requires the government to take comprehensive, multi-dimensional measures, to help them break through the poverty trap. Apart from implementing a policy aimed at guaranteeing a minimum standard of living, the government should also invest in infrastructure, information provision, skills training, market organization development, technical support, education, improvements in public health and the provision of other social services.

Keywords: Rural Tibetan Regions; Poverty Alleviation; Development Policies.

I Background and Objective of the Study

Most of the Tibetan population in China is scattered around the Tibetan Plateau, and nearly half of them live in the Tibetan Autonomous Region (TAR). The rest live in the ten Tibetan Autonomous Prefectures under the jurisdiction of Qinghai, Gansu, Sichuan and Yunnan Provinces.[1]

---

[1] According to the 1990 and 2000 nationwide population censuses, the total Tibetan population was 4.593 million and 5.416 million respectively. After the 2010 nationwide population census, China's National Bureau of Statistics has still not released a

1

These areas have a cold climate, high mountains, deep valleys and poor infrastructure. The Tibetan-inhabited regions have also historically lagged behind the national average, in terms of social and economic development. This gap has still not been bridged. In the Tibetan-inhabited regions, about 70% to 80% of laborers make a living through planting crops, undertaking pastoral activity, collecting and other temporary jobs. The incidence of poverty among the farmers and herdsmen is noticeably higher than the national average.[2]

Because of these factors, the Tibetan-inhabited regions have become a key area where the nation's regional development policies and anti-poverty programs are being carried out. Since the 1950s, China's central government has implemented policies including financial transfers to the TAR, as well as direct investment into local infrastructure and public services. The local finance and public services in other Tibetan regions are mainly funded by their provincial governments. However, all of these provinces are found in underdeveloped regions in western China, especially Qinghai and Gansu, whose provincial finances rely heavily on subsidies from the central government. Therefore, there are very limited resources available to these provincial governments to provide for the development of the Tibetan-inhabited regions.

Since the market-oriented economic reforms, the gap has got even larger in terms of the amount of aid available for Tibetan-inhabited regions, under the jurisdiction of different administrative divisions. In 1980, 1984, 1994 and 2001, the central government has held four Tibet work forums, in which it laid down a number of special promotion

---

breakdown of population by ethnicity. The population census communiqué released by the TAR Bureau of Statistics shows that in 2010 there were three million permanent residents in the whole region, of which 2.716 million are Tibetan (www.chinatibet-news.com/xizang/2011-05/07/content_693534.htm, downloaded on October 15, 2011).

[2] In 2009, the nationwide rural poverty line was set at an annual net income of 1,196 *yuan* per capita, with a poverty incidence of 3.8% in rural areas. The poverty incidence ranged from 5% to 18.7% in TAR, Qinghai, Gansu and Yunnan Provinces. Of the poor population, 52.9% lives in mountainous areas (Department of Rural and Social Economic Survey of National Bureau of Statistics, 2010, p. 8.).

policies aimed at boosting Tibetan development.[3] However, it is also the case that the provincial Tibetan regions have not all been treated equally. Even in the provinces neighboring TAR, there are fewer financial resources available and the standard of welfare provided to the residents is much lower than that found in the TAR. For these reasons, the local governments have been appealing to the central government to change its policies. In the fifth Tibet work forum held in 2010, the central government eventually responded to their demands. In the newly drafted plan on regional development, it has not only increased the provision of financial aid and the number of direct investment projects in the TAR, but has also included the public investment of central finance in the Tibetan regions of Sichuan, Yunnan, Qinghai and Gansu.[4] Yet the investment made by the central government still differs among administrative divisions, which means that Tibetan regions under the jurisdiction of different administrative divisions will still experience differing policies.

Few foreign economists have probed into the development of anti-poverty policies in the Tibetan-inhabited regions. Foreign scholars who have looked at this area of research are mostly anthropologists.[5] On the other hand, domestic research tends to focus on five separate areas. The first group tends to focus on the Tibetan economy or the development of an industrial economy, with no analysis of the impact of economic development on different social groups.[6] The second group focuses on the impact of history, geographical location and development policies, on the whole Tibetan population. This type of research lacks an analysis of the social structure in the same area and in the same community.[7] The third group focuses on social relations among various communities in the process of social and economic development, yet fails to probe into the

---

[3] In the White Paper "Sixty Years since Peaceful Liberation of Tibet" released by the State Council Information Office of the People's Republic of China on July 11, 2011, it reveals that the financial aids to TAR from the central government during 1952 to 2010 have reached 300 billion *yuan*, with an annual increase of 22.4%. Over the past 60 years, the central government's direct investment in TAR has exceeded 160 billion *yuan* (http://news.xinhuanet.com/politics/2011-07/11/c_121652482.htm, downloaded on October 16, 2011).

[4] China Broadcasting (2010).

[5] For more details, refer to the works of Melvyn Goldstein and June Teufel Dreyer.

[6] See Sun (1999).

[7] See Bai (2004); Ran and Li (2003) and Xu and Zheng (2000).

marginal groups.[8] The fourth group turns its eye to the living conditions
of the poor and explores ways and means to eliminate regional poverty
that has come about because of the vast differences in income, yet fails
to observe poverty from a multi-dimensional perspective.[9] The fifth
group takes a multi-dimensional perspective, discussing the means by
which poor farmers and herdsmen can escape poverty, but it only touches
upon one of the Tibetan Autonomous Prefectures.[10]

Over the past decade, the research team from the Chinese Academy
of Social Sciences (CASS) on Tibetan development has undertaken
comprehensive studies on the following key questions by taking advantage of collaborative work among scholars from multiple disciplines.
Firstly, what are the most urgent living and development needs of the
poor who live in Tibetan regions? What kind of aid are they most in need
of? Secondly, what impact has existing anti-poverty and regional development policies had on the poor in these regions? Thirdly, in carrying out
anti-poverty and development plans, what institutional innovations
have these regions witnessed that can help the poor break through the
poverty trap and prevent poverty from being passed onto the next
generation?

The so-called "poverty trap" refers to the phenomenon of chronic
poverty. To explain, the hardships the poor have to endure at each stage
of their lives turn out to have a negative impact that only intensifies their
poverty. These factors interact with each other and form a vicious cycle,
consequently trapping individuals or families in a sad predicament with
no way for them to get out.[11] The "intergenerational poverty transmission" refers to the fact that children from poor families inherit the predicament from their parents when they grow up and are likely to pass on
this poverty onto the next generation. For example, if a family lacks a
secure source of food, this would inevitably result in the malnutrition of

[8] See Ma and Danzeng (2006).
[9] Refer to the research by the Socioeconomic Research Institute of the China Tibetology
Research Center (1996) and Luorong (2002).
[10] See Cao *et al.* (2011).
[11] For more details, refer to the research by Partha Dasgupta in 2007 (http://www.ifpri.org/
sites/default/files/publications/beijingbrief_dasgupta.pdf, downloaded on 14 January 2013).

their children, which in turn affects their ability to acquire knowledge and skills. Furthermore, it is quite likely that these same children would be less capable in a work environment once they have grown up, and thus their meager income may well result in them suffering from a lack of food. And so the cycle continues, as they pass on the same problems to their own children.

To better understand the causes and processes that have resulted in those Tibetan farmers and herdsmen becoming impoverished, our research team has done the following fieldwork in the TAR and the provincial Tibetan regions, successively, from the perspectives of economics, law, sociology, ethnology and religion, with a focus on the aforementioned key issues. From 2000 to 2001, we did a case study in the Tibetan region in Yunnan Province on the theme "Choice of Development Mode in Regions Lagging Behind"[12]; from 2002 to 2004, we did a study on the development of TAR under the theme "Marketization and Grass-Root Public Services"[13]; from 2004 to 2005, we did research in the Tibetan areas in Sichuan and Changdu on the theme "Eliminating Barriers to Development"[14]; from 2006 to 2007, we did research in the rural Tibetan regions of Qinghai, Gansu and Yunnan Provinces on the theme "Study on Anti-Poverty and Development Policies in Northwest Frigid Mountainous Areas".[15] In 2011, our research team revisited Tibetan areas found in Sichuan and Changdu to survey the role of public services and social protection policies aimed at reducing the extreme poverty suffered by many farmers. This piece of research allowed us to compare the changes in different regions, as well as the changes within a specific region, over different periods of time.

The content of this book is based on fieldwork that our research team conducted from 2006 to 2007 in Qinghai, Gansu and Yunnan. There

[12]See Wang and Zhu (2002).
[13]See Research Team of Chinese Academy of Scocial Sciences (CASS) (2004) and Wang and Zhu (2005).
[14]See Research Team of CASS (2005).
[15]See Research Team of CASS (2007; 2008) and Wang and Zhu (2010).

are three purposes behind the writing of the book. Firstly, based on a multi-dimensional study on poverty, it provides a reference point for the central and local governments to improve anti-poverty programs and design long-term development strategies in the Tibetan regions. Secondly, by producing a theoretical framework that can work in line with practical research results, it provides a decent amount of material as well as useful conceptual material that other developing countries and societies undergoing a transformation can learn from. Thirdly, by illustrating our discoveries with stories that occurred in regions involved, the book aims to attract non-academic readers to these issues and aims to enrich their knowledge of the current developments in rural Tibetan regions.

II Research Approach

Our research team is composed of members from different ethnic backgrounds, who have received training in varied disciplines. Each member is responsible for a sub-topic, which include areas such as the rural household economy, education, health, social assistance and disaster relief. The basic methodology that the team has adopted is that of using case studies. Each member of the team collected firsthand data by doing interviews with government officials (of varying ranks and in different regions), providers of basic public services and other state-owned institutes, members of village committees, family members found in rural communities, laborers and businessmen, lamas in temples, laymen, as well as local and migrant entrepreneurs.

The research sites are scattered across three provinces and nine counties. The first research site is Xiahe and Zhuoni Counties in South Gansu Tibetan Autonomous Prefecture, and the neighboring areas of Linxia and Hezheng Counties in Linxia Hui (Moslem) Autonomous Prefecture. The second area is Shangri-La County in Diqing Tibetan Autonomous Prefecture of Yunnan. The third is Maqin and Dari Counties of Guoluo Tibetan Autonomous Prefecture of Qinghai, as well as Yushu and Chengduo Counties of Yushu Tibetan Autonomous Prefecture. Among these areas, both the incidence of poverty and the poverty recurrence rate in rural Gansu are the highest in the nation, reaching 21.3%

province-wide in 2008.[16] Both Linxia and Hezheng are agricultural areas dominated by crop farming. These areas feature an arid climate, a large population and limited farmlands. As a result, a large number of male laborers have left these counties in order to engage in trade, mainly in Qinghai and the TAR. Xiahe and Zhuoni are semi-agricultural and semi-pastoral areas. Due to a rapid increase in the population, the local residents have reclaimed land in order to grow crops so as to meet the growing demand, which in turn, has caused the deterioration of the eco-environment.

The counties in Qinghai Province where we did our research are located at the "Source of the Three Rivers" (the source of the Yangtze River, Yellow River and Lancang River). The average altitude of Guoluo and Yushu, two Tibetan Autonomous Prefectures, is 4,200 meters and 4,400 meters respectively, and most residents make a living by grazing their animals on the land all year around. Dawu, the prefecture capital of Guoluo, is 440 kilometers away from the provincial capital, Xi'ning; whereas Jiegu, the prefecture capital of Yushu, is 800 kilometers away. Yet the transport infrastructure, specifically the quality of the roads in Guoluo, is much worse than those found in Yushu. A cold climate, frequent natural disasters, remoteness (in terms of geography) and poor public transportation not only characterize the region, but also account for a number of major factors that have led to its lagging behind other areas in terms of social and economic development (when making a comparison at provincial level). According to the information provided by Qinghai Bureau of Statistics, the region's absolute poverty line is set at an annual net income of 800 *yuan* per capita, whereas the low-income line is set at an annual net income of 1,000 *yuan* per capita. In 2006, Guoluo had a total population around 154,000, with a poverty incidence of 12.5% (which does not include their "low-income population" which is around 14,348)[17]; the total population of Yushu at the time was around 303,000, with a poverty incidence rate as high as 14.8% (again, this does not include their "low-income population" which is around 39,337).[18]

---

[16] See China News (2010).
[17] Bureau of Statistics of Guoluo Prefecture (2007).
[18] Bureau of Statistics of Yushu Prefecture (2007).

Compared to the Han-inhabited regions, the regions where we did our research have distinct peculiarities in terms of geography, history, society, economy, population and ethnic culture. Particularly, for regional development and poverty alleviation, it has significance both in terms of theoretical value as well as policy making in that it helps to identify the causes of poverty, understand the effectiveness of previous poverty alleviation policies, and to explore the ways of solving the issue of poverty traps by taking into account these peculiarities. In recent years, Diqing Tibetan Autonomous Prefecture of Yunnan has taken some quite remarkable steps in poverty alleviation. An important site we visited in Diqing is the agricultural area in Shangri-La (originally called Zhongdian), a county we took as a reference point in our research to identify policy tools that are effective in reducing the incidence of poverty found in the poor Tibetan population.

Bibliography

Bai Tao, 2004, *From Tradition to Modernity: Strategic Choice of Rural Tibet*, Lhasa: Tibet People's Publishing House.

Bureau of Statistics of Guoluo Prefecture, 2007, "Statistical Communiqué of Guoluo Tibetan Autonomous Prefecture on the 2006 National Economic and Social Development", http://www.qh.stats.gov.cn/show.aspx?id=763&cid=47, downloaded on August 19, 2007.

Bureau of Statistics of Yushu Prefecture, 2007, "Statistical Communiqué of Yushu Tibetan Autonomous Prefecture on the 2006 National Economic and Social Development", http://www.qh.stats.gov.cn/show.aspx?id=859&cid=47, downloaded on August 19, 2007.

Cao Hongmin, Wang Xiaolin, Lu Hanwen, 2011, *Multi-Dimensional Survey on an Intervention in Poverty of Special Poor Regions: Case Study on Aba Tibetan and Qiang Autonomous Prefecture in Sichuan Province*, Beijing: China Agricultural Publishing House.

China Broadcasting, 2010, "Jia Qinglin Requires Putting the Spirit of the Central Fifth Tibet Work Forum into Practice", July 7, 2010, http://china.cnr.cn/gdgg/201007/t20100707_506699096.html, downloaded on July 22, 2010.

China News, 2010, "Gansu's Poverty Incidence Rate and Recurrence Rate Highest in the Nation, Heavy and Hard Responsibilities to Help the Poor",

March 15, 2010, http://www.chinanews.com.cn/gn/news/2010/03-15/2170685.
shtml, downloaded on July 31, 2010.

Department of Rural and Social Economic Survey of National Bureau of Statistics, 2010, *Monitoring Report of Poverty in Rural China*, Beijing: China Statistical Publishing House.

Luorong Zhandui, 2002, *Study on Poverty and Anti-Poverty in Tibet*, Beijing: China Tibetology Publishing House.

Ma Rong, Danzeng Lunzhu, 2006, "Survey Report of Migrant Population in Lhasa", *Studies on Northwest Ethnic Groups*, 04, 124–171.

Ran Guangrong, Li Tao, 2003, *Studies on Peculiarities of Tibetan Autonomous Region and Other Tibetan Regions in Western China Development*, Harbin: Heilongjiang People's Publishing House.

Research Team of the Chinese Academy of Social Sciences (CASS), 2004, "Observations on Tibetan Society and Economy", *Loose-Leaf Selections on the Economy*, Issue 4, Beijing: China Financial Economic Publishing House.

Research Team of the CASS, 2005, "A Social Study in Kangba Tibetan Region", *Loose-Leaf Selections on the Economy*, Issue 10, Beijing: China Financial Economic Publishing House.

Research Team of the CASS, 2007, "A Social Economic Study in Rural Gansu Tibetan Region", *Loose-Leaf Selections on the Economy*, Issue 4, Beijing: China Financial Economic Publishing House.

Research Team of the CASS, 2008, "Breaking Through the Poverty Trap in Yunnan and Qinghai Tibetan Regions", *Loose-leaf Selections on the Economy*, Issue 7, Beijing: China Financial Economic Publishing House.

Socioeconomic Research Institute of the China Tibetology Research Center, 1996, *Changes Over Forty Years of Tibetan Families*, Beijing: China Tibetology Publishing House.

Sun Yong, 1999, *Tibet: Development and Reform in a Non-Typical Dual Structure*, Beijing: China Tibetology Publishing House.

Wang Luolin, Zhu Ling (Eds.), 2002, *Choice of Development Mode in Regions Lagging Behind: Case Studies from the Tibetan Plateau in Yunnan Province*, Beijing: Economic Management Publishing House.

Wang Luolin, Zhu Ling (Eds.), 2005, *Marketization and Grass-Root Public Services: Case Studies from the Tibetan Autonomous Region*, Beijing: Ethnic Publishing House.

Wang Luolin, Zhu Ling (Eds.), 2010, *How to Break Through the Poverty Trap: Case Studies from the Tibetan Plateau in Provinces of Yunnan, Qinghai and Gansu*, Beijing: Economic Management Publishing House.

Xu Ping, Zheng Dui, 2000, *Life of Tibetan Farmers*, Beijing: China Tibetology Publishing House.

CHAPTER 2

The Rational Behavior of Tibetan Farmers and Herders

YANG Chunxue*

Abstract

Market-oriented socioeconomic transformation in China is challenging conventional rules and the norms of Tibetan farmers and herders, who are adapting their conventional rational behavior to a market environment. They are making the most of market opportunities, optimizing their use of labor, contracted land and pastures in diverse ways. Despite having a limited ability to take risks, their preference towards risk aversion has not prevented them from using new breeds and applying new technologies suited to the local environment. As a result of the decline in arable land per capita, the fall in the capacity of pasture lands, a rising cost of living and increased competition in migrant work, farmers and herders have reduced the number of children they have. Although religion is still a big part of their lives, they have made rational adjustments to the time they allocate and the amount of money they spend on religious activities.

Keywords: Rational Behavior; Living Environment; Risk Aversion Preferences.

* The author settled on this topic based on a mixture of feelings and observations during his two surveys in Tibet. The first survey (2005) was conducted in the counties of Batang, Tibetan Mangkang, Zuogong, and Changdu, as well as in Lhasa. The second survey (2006) was completed in the counties of Zhuoni, Xiahe and Linxia. During the process of writing this chapter, the author benefited from the assistance and research outcomes of other members of the research panel who conducted extensive surveys across almost all of the areas in Tibet, together with the research outcomes from other scholars.

I Introduction

Looking at the evidence produced from our survey, interviews, and other relevant research material, we regularly find some scholars or government officials attributing poverty to the preferences or behaviors of the poor people themselves. They would always identify a "backward mindset" as a major cause of the problems afflicting poor areas. This explanation can be seen in both government reports and scholarly discussions.

Among government reports obtained from the areas surveyed, one particularly typical example can be found in a document (produced in 2005) from Zuogong County in the Changdu area: *"Under the dominance of the natural economy, most of the farmers and herders are old-fashioned in their thinking, conservative, agrarian, unaware of the market economy, and unproductive. It is therefore hard to improve their living standards. Some of them are satisfied with their current situation and reluctant to strive for something better. They are unable or unwilling to properly schedule their daily life and remain idle despite their ability to work. With poor education, a lack of health-related knowledge, as well as the negative influence of their religious beliefs, these individuals raise too many children, causing a reduction in the available labor force, an increase in the dependency ratio, a decline in per capita resources, which results in the population exceeding the natural capacity of their immediate environment. This is a particularly serious problem in Meiyu Township, where animal husbandry is the only industry. Under the influence of their religious beliefs, the local people are reluctant to kill and sell livestock. As a result of their desire to have an excessive number of livestock, the pastures have been degraded. Moreover, they are unaware or unwilling to comply with and even flatly reject family planning. This has caused the township's population to increase rapidly, whilst per capita livestock and resources are declining, keeping the population in poverty."*[1]

Among scholars, the views expressed by Yang Xiaomei[2] are typical: *"Tibet is an autonomous region inhabited by ethnic minorities and under the deep influence of Buddhism. In farming and herding areas, more than 90% of*

---

[1] Zuogong County Poverty Relief Office (2005, p. 8). We obtained this document during a survey we conducted in the Kangba Tibetan area in 2005. We also surveyed Meiyu Township, which is also mentioned in this chapter.
[2] See Yang (2008).

the people are Buddhists. They firmly believe in samsara, or the cycle of birth, death and rebirth, and pray for happiness in the afterlife. Therefore, a great number of people are quite conservative in their thinking, agrarian, risk averse, easy to satisfy, and reluctant to strive for wealth and endure hardship. Many of them would rather accept government relief funds and food, than to work to escape poverty."

If we draw upon these government reports and scholarly conclusions, the following picture appears to emerge: After 30 years of market-oriented reform, the farmers and herders in Tibetan areas still have a "backward mindset" and most of their behaviors appear irrational.

From an economics perspective, behavioral differences cannot be explained by "value concepts" or preferences, and should instead, be explained by looking at environmental constraints. "Rational behavior" means that people's behavior, when it comes to choice, are based on cost-benefit calculations. However, it is true to state that such calculations may not lead to optimal results. Scholars tend to evaluate rational behavior based on their own understanding, and without considering the specific social background of the subjects of their research. That is why some of the behaviors exhibited by the farmers and herders have been interpreted as irrational. But various site surveys indicate that there are great differences in an individual's behavior, which is due to disparate socioeconomic environments. Putting these behavioral differences into a specific context, we find that these behavioral differences are only different manifestations of rational behaviors.

Based on our survey conducted in Tibetan areas and surveys completed by other scholars, this chapter attempts to reveal the fact that there is a significant and widespread learning process among farmers and herders in the surveyed regions, i.e. there is a process in which people have learned and continue to learn from the market economy in a systematic manner. They are breaking various conventional rules, adapting to the market-oriented socioeconomic environment and shifting conventional rational behaviors to those that are more compatible with a market-based economy. This transition of rational behaviors is applicable to all behaviors.

The regions we surveyed are confined to villages close to the road networks, making them quite accessible. Developments in transportation, telecommunications, television and broadcasting have brought these villagers closer to the colorful and different world outside. To some extent, the surveyed regions have closer and more regular contact with the outside world and may not represent behaviors found in more remote areas. However, our findings in the former area will be applicable to the future of the latter. In this sense, the people in our surveyed areas represent the mainstream trend of changing behaviors among farmers and herders.

II Rational Behaviors of Farmers and Herders

Farmers and herders in Tibetan areas care about their own situation and their children's future and wish to lead happy lives, just like the people who live in more developed areas. In fact, their aspirations are even stronger. There is nothing special about this preference. In addition, they also work hard to achieve things in their lives. In the new environment shaped by market-oriented reform, the desire to lead a life of subsistence will be replaced and reinforced by growing impulses towards prosperity, engendering an inevitable learning process, which comprises the following elements: learning how to communicate with non-local businessmen, learning how to undertake migrant work and emulating the behaviors of successful local people.[3] The results of such a learning process are widely seen in various specific behaviors.

Due to environmental constraints, they failed to fully realize their aspirations. An assessment of whether their behaviors are rational or not must be based on an in-depth analysis of the details of their decision-making environment in order to reach objective conclusions.

1. *Resource allocation and utilization*

If we want to understand the underlying causes for the economic behavior of farmers and herdsmen in Tibetan areas, we need to understand the reform of the household contract system. The result of these reforms is that households have become the basic livelihood unit, and the allocation of resources is conducted exclusively within households.

---

[3]Wang and Zhu (2005) and the CASS Task Team (2007) have many cases to prove the existence of such learning behaviors.

For farmers and herders, their most important resources are time, con-tracted land and the pastures, which begs the question, how do they make use of these resources? In our survey, we have seen significant efforts made by farmers and herders to improve their resource allocation. The evi-dence is outlined below.

First, each household is already making effective use of the contracted pastures and land resources according to their own specific conditions. Tibetan herding areas have kept, for a long time, the practice of "public ownership of the pastures and the private ownership and management of livestock". Under the practice of public ownership and use of the pas-tures, herders cared most about how to increase the number of their own livestock and rarely undertook actions aimed at the protection of the pasture lands. As a result, the pastures suffered from the "tragedy of the commons". But we know that the "tragedy" of collective irrational behav-ior is not a result of a "backward mindset" but an inevitable consequence of public ownership and use of the pastures. Looking at the problem from an economics perspective, the logic is extremely straightforward. Each herder benefits directly from raising livestock, but only suffers part of the costs arising from the degradation of public pasture lands. This provides an incentive for them to increase the number of their livestock.

However, once there was reform to contract pastures out to households, the rational behaviors of herders underwent a substantive transition. In regions that carried out the reform, there is a common phenomenon of "pasture contract transfer" among herders. In order to resolve the contra-diction between private ownership of livestock and public ownership of pastures, in 1999 the Naqu area in Tibet carried out a process of reform of the contract system. By 2007, about 364 million *mu* (1 *mu* = 0.667 hec-tares) of pastures were contracted out to households, which account for 90.1% of the usable pasture lands. Over the course of this process, herders began to explore new models of operation such as shareholding coopera-tives with the sharing of pastures and livestock, trusteeship of livestock, pasture leasing and transfer. In some areas, people organized the collective grazing of livestock from various households, and households with few livestock or no livestock subcontracted pastures to major livestock keepers in exchange for cash and other benefits in kind. Households with few livestock but large pasture lands leased these pastures to other herders in exchange for rent. Households whose livestock exceeded their pasture's capacity leased excess livestock to those who have surplus pasture lands but few or no livestock.

In order to protect their own pastures and ensure the welfare of their children, many herders practiced rest-grazing and rotational grazing measures. They also improved pasture lands, prevented over-grazing, the borrowing of sand and earth and the construction of illegal roads. According to rough estimates, some 19,000 herders in the Naqu region raised about 50 million *yuan* by 2007, which together with national funding, was used to purchase 12,000 meters of fence for 24 million *mu* of natural pasture land. More than 15,700 herders grew 62,600 *mu* of grass in the front and backyards of their homes. Moreover, more than 23,600 herders undertook protection methods against fire, pests and over-grazing of 9.288 million *mu* of pasture lands.[4]

Secondly, all farmers and herders tried to diversify their household's economic activities to optimize their labor allocation. In contrast to the past, many farmers and herders no longer focus on the land as a means to secure a subsistence existence. They are now more inclined to try and find work opportunities outside of their hometowns. It has already become a common practice of farmers and herders to utilize their most abundant resource — labor. This is particularly common in farming and semi-farming/herding areas. Even for households with few laborers, strong and healthy men will leave the family for a period of some months (though this does not occur during the farming season). Most of the Tibetan farmers and herders work in infrastructure construction such as building roads, and some, who choose to work in touristy areas, are engaged in services such as horse harnessing and peddling.

The earnings accrued as a result of migrant work has become a major source of income for Tibetan farmers and herders. Between 1985 and 2003, though household business income was dominant, salary income also increased. It increased from 5.83% in 1985 to 28.39% in 2003.[5] In 2006, according to analytical results produced by the Statistics Bureau of the Tibetan Autonomous Region, the per capita household net business income

---

[4]See Ci'ren (2007).
[5]See Yang (2005).

of Tibetan farmers and herders was 1,505 *yuan*. This was 401 *yuan* more than the figure for 2002, representing an increase of 36.3%, and accounting for 61.8% of total annual net income. Net salary income (mainly from migrant work) reached 568 *yuan*. This was 333 *yuan* more than their net salary income in 2002, representing a 1.4 times increase, and accounting for 23.3% of annual net income. Net transfer and property income was 362 *yuan*. This was 98.9% more than the figure for 2002, accounting for 14.9% of their annual net income.[6]

Third, the local farmers and herders seek to utilize local special resources and market opportunities. In addition to migrant work, another source of cash income for the farmers and herders is the collection of caterpillar fungus, fritillary, matsutake and wild mushrooms. In regions that are rich in undergrowth, during the harvest season almost all house-holds collect matsutake in the surrounding mountains. Young men would often carry their own clothes, possessions and sufficient dry food in order to collect the fungus in the more remote mountains. In these regions, collection of the fungus has become a major source of cash revenue for farmers and herders. Some regions have even officially recognized the "caterpillar fungus vacation", when primary and middle schools tempo-rarily close so that their students can go home and help their family collect caterpillar fungus.

According to an estimate produced by a research specialist in 2006, around 200,000 farmers and herders in Naqu and 450,000 farmers and herders in Changdu depend on collecting caterpillar fungus as their main source of income. In addition, almost 100,000 farmers and herders in other sub-producing areas also rely on collecting caterpillar fungus. In these areas, *"over a third of per capita net income for farmers and herders is not from agriculture and animal husbandry, but from the collection of caterpil-lar fungus"*.[7]

In general, the argument that "Tibetans have poor market awareness" is wrong. The farmers and herders in Tibetan areas are no worse than people in more developed regions in terms of improving resource allocation and making use of market opportunities. The only difference is

---

[6]See De and Bianba (2008).
[7]Quoted from Luorong and Dawa (2006).

their ability to seek out and grasp opportunities. For instance, there are many herders who do not speak Mandarin very well and lack the necessary skills to undertake certain modern jobs. This makes it impossible for them to find jobs in the Mainland. The farmers and herders we surveyed live in closed and remote areas found in China's western region. Compared with rural populations in more developed regions, they have a poorer understanding of how to live and to become more prosperous. But the problem, as it stands, mainly rests with a lack in individual capabilities and access to the right information, rather than their preferences or a certain kind of mindset.[8] Moreover, it has nothing to do with whether their behavior is rational or not.

2. Attitudes towards new plant types and new technologies: Risk averse

In Tibetan areas, there is indeed a somewhat aloof and wait-and-see attitude towards new methods of increasing agricultural productivity. But if we properly understand the unique effect of risk and uncertainties in subsistence agricultural economies, we would not make the mistake of defining "risk aversion", "reluctance to engage in new business ventures", "short-sightedness" or even "ignorance" as a common characteristic of farmers and herders. Moreover, we should not regard their suspicion towards new technologies and new plant types as some form of "ignorance". Compared to more developed regions, the advancement of technology in the farming and husbandry sectors in Tibetan areas is indeed very slow. But it is still an open question as to whether the problem can be attributed to the irrational behavior of farmers and herders.

In fact, there has always been technological progress in the agriculture and animal husbandry industries in Tibetan areas. Such progress is less visible because it is manifested in the simplest form, such as occasional improvements in farming and grazing, the application of new chemical fertilizers and pesticides, and the use of new and improved plant types.

---

[8]We can make an assessment on capability gaps based on the following statistics: The illiteracy ratio is 43.6% among young farmers and herders in Xiahe County, and this figure is 62.4% for townships where animal husbandry is predominant (in the year 2005).

Many forms of technological progress that may seem initially insignificant, are in fact very practical and useful for farmers and herders. For instance, leather bags or wooden buckets are often used as rather conventional containers for ghee. It takes time to make the ghee and physical strength to carry it around. In the 1990s, a milk separator emerged in Tibetan herding areas and became popular among many households. The separator is both easy to use and repair, and can reduce the work intensity of women in farming and herding areas, leaving them with more free time for other activities. For example, the "little prodigy" washing machine, which has a ghee-making function, can make ghee in three hours. This is equivalent to three days of work for an average young woman.[9]

The introduction of new types of crop and livestock, as well as the construction of livestock sheds, are obvious forms of major technological progress. Such progress has been realized almost exclusively because of the leadership and drive of government. Since the reform and opening up of China in the late 1970s, the introduction and roll-out of most new technologies and new breeds were and continue to be realized through the setting up of "model households", which have access to government sponsorship and loans. This is extremely important given the limited financial resources of most farmers and herders.

Superficially, the fact that the government is providing leadership could seem to imply a lack of enthusiasm among farmers and herders towards new technologies and new breeds of animals and plants. However, this is not the case. The reason behind the fact that very few farmers and herdsmen have taken the initiative to introduce new breeds and new technologies is due to very poor risk-taking capabilities and the harsh Qinghai–Tibet plateau environment. The harshness of the environment means that it is difficult for new breeds to grow and thrive. Under high degrees of risk and uncertainty, it is natural for farmers and herders to be unwilling to replace familiar conventional production technologies and breeds with potentially more productive but riskier new technologies and breeds, no matter if the threat is real or perceived. When maintaining an output that leads to your family's subsistence is your primary goal, it is more important to avoid a bad year than to

---

[9]See Su (2009).

maximize output in better years. Using terminology found in economic statistics, risk-averse farmers and herders tend to use conventional technologies, although average yield per *mu* is relatively less, the square error is also smaller (deviation from average output is small), and thus they are unwilling to adopt new technologies and breeds that can increase the average yield but have a greater amount of risk.

In this sense, their behavioral preference towards risk aversion is consistent with basic economic theory. Due to poverty, the consequence of uncertainties often puts farmers in a situation where they are finely balanced between subsistence and hunger. It is a difficult choice, and the safest option of livelihood is undoubtedly the most reasonable. Considering other constraints (particularly constraints of the capability of understanding and wealth), we can see the rational nature behind such behaviors. This is the main reason why poor households are slow to adopt new breeds and technologies.

This at least explains that the reason why poor farmers adopt new technologies and breeds far later than might be expected, and that this behavior is not due to a "backward mindset", but their fragile economic circumstances which limit their ability to take risks. Otherwise, it would be very difficult to explain why the rich and poor in the same region and even in the same village treat risky new products in very different ways. We cannot attribute this phenomenon to an intrinsic difference of mindset, as they all live in the same social and cultural environment.

Under the pressure of having to maintain a subsistence existence, farmers and herders often display a preference for risk aversion. But this does not mean that they will not accept risky business opportunities or new things. They are actually very happy to accept new technologies and breeds that have been proven to be suitable to the local natural conditions. Otherwise, there is no basis to explain the new technological improvements that have already been implemented in Tibetan areas.

III Reproductive Behavior: Birth Rate and Family Size

Compared with other regions, the population growth rate in Tibet's farming and herding areas is relatively high. According to China's fifth census, which was carried out in 2000, the region's total population was

2.62 million (excluding the migrant population). This is an increase in population of 42.03 million (19.1%), compared with the fourth census ten years ago. The census also showed that there was an annual average increase of 40,700 people (an annual average growth rate of 1.7%), which is higher than the national average. The population growth mainly occurred in the farming and herding areas. The population growth rate in the former was higher than that found in the latter. With a large number of "extended families", the average household population was relatively high.

How should one look at the "population phenomenon" found in Tibetan areas? The truth is not in line with what many people believe, i.e. that they have a "backward mindset" and are "ignorant".

Looking at the issue from a historical point of view, a large number of local men, influenced by Tibetan Buddhism, became monks and consequently lowered the reproduction rate of the Tibetan population. According to historical records, Tibet had a population estimated at about two million during the 1720–1730s. In 1951, the Tibetan local government estimated that their population was just 1.2 million. In other words, the Tibetan population fell over this period of time.[10]

Considering the historical facts and the decline in population, the central government did not implement compulsory family planning policy in Tibetan areas. In addition, improvements in medical and living conditions have pushed up the natural population growth rate in these areas.

From a microscopic point of view, there is an underlying rationale causing the high fertility rates. A more specific explanation is provided in a sample survey in 1994 (see Table 1).

Looking at the results of the survey, it is clear that Tibetan farmers and herders, much in the same way as people from other areas, have numerous reasons for why they decide to reproduce, and each reason has its intrinsic rationality.[11]

First, "to increase the labor force" is listed as one of the most important reasons why farmers and herders decide to reproduce. The decision is based

---

[10] See Lang (2006); Yang and Chen (2005).
[11] See Lü and Chen (2005).

Table 1:   Reproductive Purpose (unit: % in surveyed households).

	Continue the family line	Want to bring up sons to support their parents in old age	Add to the labor force	Natural law	Not yet considered
Banjuelunbu Village in Jiangzi County	23.3	74.4	11.6	2.3	2.3
Yaoqia Village in An'duo County	34.9	86	23.3		

Notes: Banjuelunbu Village is a farming area while Yaoqia Village is a herding area. In both areas, the researchers who conducted the survey took a sample of 43 households. Most of the households chose multiple reasons for why they wanted to reproduce.
Source: Socioeconomic Research Institute of the China Tibetology Research Center, 1996, p. 475.

on the inherent relationship between family size, the way a family business operates, as well as the division of labor.[12] In fact, since reform and opening up, labor force status in farming and herding areas has become a determinant of a household's economic status and income. In this regard, the author of the report quoted above provided useful analytical insights and a sound summary: "*After reform and opening up, the increase in the local population, caused by a growing demand for labor in an increasingly diversified household operation, meant that families could not only manage a large area of land and livestock which was effectively contracted to households, but also utilize labor in sideline activities such as running transportation, businesses etc, rather than engaging in agriculture and animal husbandry.*"[13]

Second, in my opinion, "carrying on the family line" is a fairly sound rationale, because it is a prerequisite for the reproduction of human beings. Thus, the argument made by some scholars that Tibetans do not want to carry on their family line is absurd. In every nation, people have the desire to produce offspring, though they may differ in the intensity of their endeavors. Perhaps the truth is that the Tibetans lack the same "intensity" as their Han counterparts.

---

[12] Wang and Zhu (2005, p. 200).
[13] Socioeconomic Research Institute of the China Tibetology Research Center (1996, p. 399–400).

Third, the fact that farmers and herders put "raising children to support them in their old age" as the most common response is inevitable when social welfare and security are not available. Parents without a regular income, medical or social security can only rely on their children. This is very different from the collective economy era when the social security system was both sound and sophisticated. For the poor families, children can be seen as capital goods with an expected revenue. These families easily fall into the "Malthusian Poverty Trap" not only because of their low living standards but also because they lack the basic social security. As a result, their freedom to choose an ideal family size has been limited by poverty and economic uncertainty.

Although some families prefer to have more children, most of the families are aware of the adverse consequences of this preference, a fear that has originated from very practical considerations. Despite the vast size of its territory and the scarcity of its population, Tibet has very few areas of arable land and pastures. Moreover, per capita arable land area decreased when the latest generation's children got married and settled down, as pastures were degraded as a result of excessive grazing. On the other hand, the rising costs of living, setting up a new family, as well as the increased competition in migrant work, are all factors that have caused many families to limit the number of children they conceive. Therefore, since the mid-1990s, more women have voluntarily adopted birth control measures.[14] The speed of this change is indeed astonishing.

As a result of this rational choice, actual fertility rates in Tibetan areas declined despite the absence of a compulsory family planning policy. The fertility rate of Tibetan women rose from 3.02 in 1950s to 5.36 in the early 1980s. Since 1982 there has been a decline in the fertility rate, and a significant drop (from 2.97 to 1.85) occurred during the period 1995–2000.[15]

IV Consumer Behavior and Religion

There were murmurs of discontent when the discussion turned towards the topic of how Tibetan Buddhism influences the behavior of farmers

---

[14]Quoted from Goldstein *et al.* (2003).
[15]See He and Li (2006).

and herders. There are questions about their superstitious behavior and their excessive spending on religious activities, when they cannot even meet their basic needs, in terms of items such as food and clothes. A typical argument is as follows: Tibetan Buddhism "guided people to the pursuit of an afterlife" and this had a negative impact on their attitudes towards the present; strong religious emotion induces the believers to spend their hard-won property in a form of religious consumption, where for example they release captive animals, provide donations, construct temples, give food to the monks or renovate their churches. This form of "religious consumption" not only seriously affects the living standards of the majority of farmers and herders, but has also resulted in a huge negative effect on the sustainable development of agriculture and animal husbandry.[16] So, given the inconsistencies shown above, what is the real situation?

1. Structure of consumption expenses and religious expenses

First, we need to establish exactly how much farmers and herders spend on religious activities. Do they spend a large proportion of their capital on such activities? To clearly answer these two questions, we need to draw a clear line between what happened in the past and what happens now.

Over the course of Tibet's history, religion has seriously obstructed economic development. According to the results of a survey and some statistics, in 1694 there were 97,528 monks in Tibet and the Hekang region. By 1737, the number of monks had grown to 319,270. It is assumed that the total population of Tibet and the Hekang region was 2.5 million by 1737. At that time monks accounted for around 13% of the population and approximately 26% of the male population became monks. In 1956, there were 114,103 monks and nuns in Tibet, about 10% of the total population. We can imagine how much it would have cost in terms of social and economic resources to support these monks and nuns.

The situation changed significantly after the "democratic reforms", a movement launched after the founding of the People's Republic of

---

[16]See Tang and He (2002).

China in 1949. For policy reasons, most of the monks were forced to return to secular life, thus, each family only spent a small amount of their income on religion. However, after the implementation of new ethnic and religious policies in the late 1970s and as the economic situation improved, there was a rush to construct new temples and for lay people to become monks and nuns. During the early stages of the revival (particularly in the 1980s), farmers and herders spent a lot of money on religious activities.

However, since the 1990s, the lifestyles of the farmers and herders have changed in accordance with the new environment, which has been shaped by market-oriented reforms. More people make a living away from home and thus, with the exception of large-scale religious activities, religious activity in general has reduced significantly. In addition, only a small segment of people still regard being a monk as an ideal life. Accordingly, the amount of money people spend on religious activities is steadily declining.

What is the exact ratio of funds spent on religious activities? We have seen sporadic cases in almost all the existing literature, which have lots of limitations as it may contain some unusual expenses. For example, the amount of expenses incurred by a believer's family will obviously be increased when they hold ceremonies like weddings, funerals and *pravrajana* (becoming a monk or nun). If a family member plans to worship at distant places (e.g. Lhasa, Ta'er Lamasery), then costs will be much higher.

There is some academic literature devoted to covering the topic of religious expenditure, such as a piece of research done by Muchi Yundengjiacuo[17], which focused on a number of cases in Qinghai. According to his research, farmers' and herders' expenditure on religion was quite high in the 1980s. For example, in Dari County, at a religious site, a donation of 70,000 *yuan* was made in 1986. This accounted for 14.62% of the total revenue of the county and was a per capita allocation of 50 *yuan*. However, the proportion of religious expenses fell sharply as a result of reduced enthusiasm and increased household income. For example, in 1998, the financial burden of religious people in Guide, Gonghe and Tongde Counties accounted for only 1.9%, 2.2% and 2.2%

---

[17]See Muchi (2002).

of total revenue respectively; while in Longwu, Qukuhu and Huang Naihai Counties the figures were also quite low, 4.3%, 4.8% and 3.8% respectively.

According to a survey completed in 2006 in Xiahe County, annual per capita total expenditure amounted to 2,014 *yuan* in the grazing district and 1,524 *yuan* in half-farming, half-grazing districts (in 2005, the per capita net income of farmers and herders in the County was 1,640 *yuan*). The structure of the expenditure was broken down in the following way: production costs (7.6%), religious activities (8.4%)[18] and the cost of living (84%) (i.e. food, clothing, medical care and tuition fees, not including medical expenses and housing).[19]

The above data shows that religious expenditure varies significantly over time, by region and by household. However, in general, the expenditure over the last ten years is not as high as people had imagined.[20]

A fundamental question is how we should look at their religious expenditure. According to some analysts, it is irrational to spend money on religious activities when the believers themselves are in poverty. In fact, as long as we admit that property alone does not ensure happiness and there is a specific value to religion, then we can discern that there is a rational side to their behavior. According to Bruno Frey and Alois Stutzer[21], religion offers an "interpretative framework", which can instill life with meaning and purpose. The feeling of being close to God and the belief in an afterlife provide existential certainty and are sources of happiness. Happiness also depends on one's personal attitude. With stronger religious consciousness, there is a natural, positive and unique intrinsic relationship between the Tibetan Buddhists and happiness. Naturally, different types of expenditure have different religious meanings. Some religious activities add value and meaning to the lives of farmers and herdsmen. For example, the routine family religious practices enable Tibetans to feel that they are able to communicate directly

---

[18] 8.4% also includes hidden expenses such as dispute resolution.
[19] Data from the Poverty Relief Office of Xiahe County, *Survey Report on Special Types of Poverty*.
[20] In general, the younger generation does not regard being a monk as an ideal lifestyle.
[21] See Frey and Stutzer (2006, p. 67).

with God, which provides some form of psychological benefit. Attending collective religious activities constitute an important part of Tibetans' social activities, where they feel emotions and converse about their beliefs with conviction. It is not only an enjoyable process but it also gives the believers a way to gain social recognition and respect.

Second, the entertainment value of some religious activities is more important than the underlying religious meaning. After the "reform and opening up" in 1992, the religious enthusiasm of farmers and herders has been re-released. However, the meaning behind their religious activities has changed significantly. In particular, the vast majority of young people are taking part in religious activities because they find them entertaining, and not because of any underlying religious meaning. Even so, religious activities are being replaced by television and other recreational activities.

Third, when monks were invited to undertake religious rites when someone is sick, it can be viewed as a form of "mental therapy". The following case proves that some Tibetans are aware of this.

Case 1 Ren Ji is a village doctor found in New Pagui Village of Jiangre Town, Jiangzi County. He was working away from home when we conducted this survey in 2003. His sister Gui Sang is a nun and she returned home to take care of her ailing mother. Gui Sang believes that chanting will alleviate her mother's pain. Other villagers go to the hospital when they get sick and also ask Gui Sang to chant for them. Gui Sang practices chanting 1–2 times a month and is paid 5 yuan each time. It seems that Tibetans tend to view disease as being both a physical and spiritual phenomenon; therefore, Ren Ji and Gui Sang provide both of these aspects.[22]

Fourth, the biggest one-off expense a villager may need to deal with is the costs associated with the special religious activities that take place when a loved one passes away. We may understand its function from the lyrics of "Celestial Burial", i.e. to face death calmly: "*Silently wave to you, leaving the fate of our reincarnation; eagles summoned from heaven, please take away the glory of my life; gently pass my house, remember the oath to never*

---

[22]Taken from Wang and Zhu (2005, p. 307–308).

change over thousands of years; eagles summoned from heaven, please open my *sunshine path to heaven, so peaceful and serene, what a wonderful and magical* *time, death is disappearing and life is flying on the wings."* Here, death is no longer a terrible thing, but a declaration of the ultimate value of life.

Therefore, as a result of what Weber calls "value rationality" and "witchcraft", religious activities became an integral part of a Tibetan's life. Minorities, whose religious beliefs are still rather backward, obtain this value and sense of belonging from ancestor worship. Those Tibetans with a more advanced form of religious belief obtain life's value and a sense of belonging from the divinity of their religion.

2. Religion and individuals' economic behavior

Again, let us look at the religious influence on the behavior of the farmers and herders. Regarding religious influence, Banban Duojie's interpretation is the most exemplary: *"The superstition created by religion has clouded* *the Tibetans' thinking and value orientation away from that found in a modern* *society which features competition, commodity consciousness and openness."*[23] However, I do not agree with his judgment.

Before there can be "democratic reform", the socio-political system requires a unification of the state and church. Therefore, all of the behaviors of the farmers and herders were branded with religion. When the farmers and herders were impoverished, they were exploited, and lived desperate lives. It was then quite natural for them to place their hopes and dreams on religion. Consequently, all of their social and economic behavior were seen as being heavily influenced by religion.

However, after the "democratic reform" — especially the market-oriented reform over the last few decades — the situation has changed significantly. There is a growing tendency of secularization among Tibetan Buddhists. Encouraged by the government policy of "self-reliance", temples started running companies, hotels, shops, clinics and began to compete with other secular rivals. For example and Labu Temple in Yushu Prefecture runs a number of grocery shops and luxurious hotels in Jiegu Town. It also runs department stores in three counties in the Yushu Prefecture.[24]

---

[23] See Banban (2001).
[24] See Huare (2009).

The Tibetan Buddhist Temple undertakes some profit-making initiatives. For example, some monks make additional money from chanting for third parties. Moreover, this behavior is permitted provided that the monks and the monastery share the revenue. This behavior is essentially a form of economic activity. Monks provide services to believers in exchange for income, while the believers pay for their faith.[25]

The market economy not only changed the behavior of the monastery and the monks, but also the economic behavior of ordinary people. After seeing the monastery and the monks control the populations of insects and other pests with chemicals, farmers and herders have abandoned the practice of chanting in order to dispel the insects.[26] Similarly, when the profit-making behavior of monasteries and monks prevails, farmers and herders will never regard doing business as some form of misconduct. Although some farmers and herders are weak in terms of their understanding of the market, this has nothing to do with religion.

Most importantly, farmers and herders have been able to rationally coordinate the time they allocate to religious activities. Case 2 is a superb example. When economic activity clashes with religious activity, people will make rational choices, i.e. they will make a decision that allows them to take part in religious activities, without negatively affecting the family's economic activities. In fact, people have got involved in a variety of economic activities, leaving them less energy to devote to religious activities.

Case 2 Doji is the head of a composite family of nine members in Qucai Village, Ningzhong Town, Dangxiong County. In winter, Doji's three sons go to a town called Naqu, where they undertake various activities including selling meat, leather, cashmere and yaks. In the other seasons, fathers and sons work away from home. This year is the animal year of Namco — the Tibetan Year of the Water Goat — and large festivals will be held by the lake. However, only three of Doji's family members (the Doji couple and their six-year-old grandson) will attend the activity. When asked why his son and daughter-in-law do not want to join them, he said in a rather straightforward

---

[25] See Chapter 8 of Wang and Zhu (2005).
[26] See Wu (2001).

manner that they do not have enough time. Similarly, other families in the village only send elderly relatives and children, because the young people are far too busy.[27]

Our explanation does not mean that religion has no negative impacts on Tibetans. Just like any other religion, Tibetan Buddhism also faces the challenge of how to adapt to the changing socioeconomic environment.

V Conclusions

Adam Smith once said: "*Each nation has a rotten thing*", which is either reflected in their ideas and concepts or in individual behavior. Nevertheless, we should pay attention to the positive side. This is the fundamental basis for the future of the Tibetan farmers and herders.

This chapter would like to stress that, in many cases, Tibetans cannot be said to have a "backward mindset". Instead, the observed behaviors are due to uncertainty and the risk aversion of the individuals, limited capacity, or the special structure of the system. Regardless of the exact details of the behavior, it can be seen as largely rational. In making this statement, we are not denying that there is a "backward element" to some of the behaviors, but would like to emphasize that there needs to be a massive effort to reduce the impact of these factors on the poor. Moreover, we do not believe a "backward mindset" is the key variable that is preventing the poor from becoming rich. Neither do we insist that the existing rational behavior is perfect, instead, we believe that rational behavior itself has its own process of evolution.

I am convinced that the following argument by Theodore William Schultz also applies to Tibetan farmers and herders: "*The world's farmers are economic people and they calculate the costs, benefits and risks of any action, and are good entrepreneurs in their own fields.*"[28]

Since the basic mode of the farmers and herders' economic behavior is rational, why are they still in poverty? This is a classic question of economics. An individual's rational behavior may lead to collective irrationality, i.e. a "social dilemma". The results of this collective irrationality can

---

[27]Taken from Wang and Zhu (2005, p. 88–89).
[28]Quoted from Schultz (1999[1979], p. 411).

be expressed in a variety of forms. Families tend to have more children which pushes up the birth rate of the entire Tibetan region and impedes social and economic development. In this scenario, given that the pastures are publicly-owned and shared, each herder will maximize the number of cattle they own, which will lead to the degradation of the pastures. Farmers and herders showed a strong preference of "risk aversion" with regards to applying new breeds and new technologies. This behaviorism will result in slow technical progress in the Tibetan agriculture and animal husbandry industries, etc. All of these phenomena are, in fact, a reflection of the classic question above; they could not be regarded as evidence of personal irrational behavior. The emergence of this phenomenon has much to do with the entire socioeconomic development level and the system.

The solution to this kind of "social dilemma" lies in the specific design of the system. If we want to help the poverty-stricken areas, we need to pay more attention to rational incentives and policies. In fact, relatively effective policy needs to follow the logic above. For example, young farmers and herders need to obtain the necessary skills through vocational training. Once that is achieved, the farmers and herders will be more aware of the risks of introducing new breeds through government-backed demonstration actions, etc. In some cases, with a good system, farmers and herders will naturally respond to the adverse consequences of certain acts. The significant change in behavior after contracting pastures to individual households is a good example.

Bibliography

Banban Duojie, 2001, "Buddhist Values and Modern Transition of Tibetan Mindset", *World Religious Research*, 02.

CASS Task Team, 2007, *Socioeconomic Survey on Farming and Herding Areas of Gansu Province*, Beijing: China Finance and Economics Publishing House.

Ci'ren Luobu, 2007, "Ninety Percent of Pastures in Naqu Contracted to Households", *Tibet News Network*, November 21, 2007, http://www.chinatibetnews.com/xizang/2007-11/21/content_120806.htm, downloaded on 14 January, 2013.

De Ji and Bianba Ci'ren, 2008, "Revenue of Tibetan Farmers and Herders Tends to be Diversified", *Xinhua News*, http://news.xinhuanet.com/newscenter/2008-04/13/content_7969460.htm, downloaded on 14 January, 2013.

Frey, Bruno S. and Alois Stutzer, 2006, *Happiness and Economics — Influence of Economics and Institutions on Human Happiness*, Beijing: Peking University Press.

Goldstein, Melvyn C, Ben Jiao, Cynthia M Beall, Phuntsog Tsering, 2003, "Development and Change in Rural Tibet." *Asian Survey*, 43(5): 758–779.

He Jingxi, 1995, "Change in China's Tibetan Population — Research on the Ethnic Composition in Main Tibetan Autonomous Regions", *China Social Sciences*, 04, 105–116.

He Jingxi, Li Ailin, 2006, "Discussion on Demographic Dividend in Tibet's Demographic Transition — Opportunities and Challenges from the Perspective of Demographic Development", *Tibet Research*, 03, 112–117.

Huare Duojie, 2009, "Secularization and Motivations of Tibetan Buddhism", *China Tibetology*, 02, 45–50.

Lang Weiwei, 2006, "Protection of Rights of Childbirth and Development for Tibetans in China's Demographic Policy from the Perspective of Tibetan Demographic Changes", *Tibetan Studies*, 02, 83–93.

Luorong Zhandui, Dawa Ci'ren, 2006, "Research Report on Tibetan Caterpillar Fungus Resources and Its Influence on the Income of Farmers and Herders", *China Tibetology*, 02, 102–107.

Lü Zhaohe, Chen Ying, 2005, "Analysis on the Childbirth Behaviors of China's Ethnic Minority Villages and Rational Choice", *Ethnicity Research*, 01, 27–35.

Mei'erwen Ge'ersitan, Banjue, Xinbiya Bi'er, Pingcuo Ciren, 2003, "Tibet Survey: Childbirth and Family Planning in Rural Tibet", China Tibet Information Center, http://www.tibetinfor.com.cn/news/2003-5-22/N032003522163403.htm, downloaded on 14 January, 2013.

Muchi Yundengjiacuo, 2002, "History and Current Situation of Religious and Economic Burdens among Tibetan Buddhists", *Tibet Research*, 01, 44–49.

Schultz, Theodore William, 1987[1964], *Transforming Traditional Agriculture*, translated by Liang Xiaomin, Beijing: Commercial Press.

Schultz, Theodore William, 1999[1979], "The Economics of Being Poor", in *Works of Nobel Laureates: Economics*, translated by Luo Han, Shanghai: Shanghai People's Press.

Socioeconomic Research Institute of the China Tibetology Research Center, 1996, *Forty Years of Change in Tibetan Households — Research Report on 100 Tibetan Households*, Beijing: China Tibetology Press.

Su Faxiang, 2009, "Influence of Milk Separators on the Conventional Herding Life of Tibetans — Case Study of Technology and Tibetan Social Change", *China Tibetology*, 04, 70–73.

Tang Zhangquan, He Xiaoping, 2002, "Modernization of Lifestyle among Tibetan Herders", *Tibet University Journal*, 17(4), 37–41.

Wang Luolin, Zhu Ling, 2005, *Modernization and Grassroots Public Services*, Beijing: Nationality Press.

Wang Xiaoqiang, Bai Nanfeng, 1986, *Prosperous Poverty*, Sichuan: Sichuan People's Press.

Wu Yuncen, 2001, "History, Current Situation and Countermeasures of Tibet Monastery Economy", *Journal of Tibet College of Nationalities*, 22(2), 42–49.

Xiahe County Poverty Relief Office, 2006, "Survey Report on Special Types of Poverty".

Yang Huajun, Chen Changwen, 2005, "History and Analysis of Tibetan Demographic Statistics", *China Tibetology*, 03, 136–143.

Yang Minghong, 2005, "Evolutionary Patterns of Tibetan Farmer Economy: Empirical Analysis Based on Survey Information of Rural Households", *China Tibetology*, 03, 72–81.

Yang Xiaomei, 2008, "How to Improve Employment Skills of Rural Surplus Labor in Tibet", *Tibet Agricultural Technology*, 30(3), 45–48.

Zhang Juan, 2007, "Survey on the Transformation of Social Lifestyle in Tibetan Zuogai Duoma Township of Herding Areas in South Gansu Province", PhD thesis, Northwest University of Nationalities.

Zuogong County Poverty Relief Office, 2005, "Evaluation Report on Poverty Relief and Development in the 10th Five-Year Plan Period of Zuogong County", June 16, 2005.

CHAPTER 3

How Do Farmers and Herdsmen Participate in the Market?

ZHU Hengpeng

Abstract

Though market development in Tibetan areas is restricted by unfavorable natural conditions, there have been many cases of farmers and herdsmen participating in market activities. Moreover, examples of their participation can be found from a long time ago. Meanwhile, marketization in inland areas has accelerated the same process in Tibetan-inhabited areas, allowing Tibetan farmers and herdsmen to trade more extensively. However, due to the small size of the local market, all products sold by farmers and herdsmen are at the bottom of the industrial chain and thus, are susceptible to large price fluctuations. With little bargaining power, individual farmers or herdsmen have unstable income streams. In addition, only a limited number of farmers and herdsmen can get hired in the traditional handicraft industry, and few can find jobs in other areas, such as retail or working in restaurants and hotels.

In the service sector, the only local competitors of the small trade companies founded by migrants are companies run by temples. Their comparative advantage lies in the fact that they are a neatly-organized entity, with educated workers (i.e. lamas) and have regular contact with the local consumers. Presently, to enhance the bargaining power of local farmers and herdsmen, the only way is to improve their alignment and promote better cooperation. Even in developed economies, for

individual farmers to achieve economies of scale, the best
option is to form a cooperative. For one, it allows them to compete with larger companies. Moreover, traditional community-
based culture and mutual assistance in Tibetan areas serve as
the foundation for sales and credit cooperatives in the modern
market economy.

Keywords: Farmers and Herdsmen; Markets; Cooperatives.

Compared with inland areas, most Tibetan areas are located in high altitudes. The population is far smaller than that of the inland rural areas.
Because of natural conditions, it is obvious that the Tibetan market lags
far behind inland rural areas, both in terms of maturity and size. However,
the marketization process in Tibetan areas has already commenced, exert-
ing a profound impact on how goods are produced and the lifestyle of
farmers and herdsmen. Given the fact that the market economy has
already become dominant in China, it is unthinkable that Tibet, a part of
the Chinese economy, would stagnate by persisting with a social structure
based on legacy.[1] In fact, marketization of the Tibetan economy has pro-
gressed well, thanks to the development of the market economy in inland
China, resulting in a steady growth of per capita income, and the integration of the Chinese economy into the global market as a result of economic globalization. This has enabled Tibetan farmers and herdsmen to
join in a wide range of economic activities, having a significant impact
on their economic and social life with substantial improvements to their
living standards.

However, though Tibet has made considerable progress in farming and
livestock breeding over the last few decades, local farmers and nomadic
herdsmen still rely on traditional forms of agriculture and animal husbandry as their dominant means of production. Because of the scattered
population, the market is relatively small. Moreover, with a small population and a limited local market, it is difficult to find opportunities to

---

[1] See Zhu (2005).

promote the division of labor. With a lack of a division of labor, the capacity for market growth is limited. Additionally, market capacity is determined by effective purchasing power, which in turn is determined by the efficiency of production. This factor is of course, dependent upon the division of labor. Therefore, despite the fact that farmers and herdsmen in Tibetan areas have engaged extensively in market activities, the capacity of the local market is still small. Products produced through agriculture, forestry and husbandry, sold by farmers and herdsmen, are all primary products at the bottom of the industrial chain. Dramatic price fluctuations in these products result in drastic changes to the incomes of farmers and herdsmen, especially income derived from hard currency. In addition, considering that farmers and herdsmen live far away from each other, they are far less organized than their counterparts in inland areas when it comes to market activity. Therefore, individual farmers and herdsmen suffer the most from unstable income streams, due to the lack of bargaining power. They are the most vulnerable to price-related risks. When compared to other players in the industrial chains, they often end up bearing the largest natural and market risks. Moreover, since the traditional handicraft industry offers few job opportunities, it is impossible for the handicraft industry to become a major source of employment in the non-agricultural sector for farmers and herdsmen.

The first section of this chapter begins with a detailed description of how farmers and herdsmen participate in market activities, focusing on their disadvantages in the market. By presenting facts, the second section illustrates the important influences of migrant populations, entrepreneurs and temples in the Tibetan areas on the farmers and herdsmen and their market participation.

I Basic Means of Market Participation for Farmers and Herdsmen and Their Roles in the Market

Market participation refers to the fact that farmers and herdsmen exchange what they have produced for money. The trade depends on whether the buyer is willing to purchase the goods, either in the form of products or labor, from the farmers and herdsmen.

1. Opportunities to participate in the market activities for farmers and herdsmen

Currently, the main opportunities for farmers and herdsmen in Tibetan areas to participate in market activities and benefit from them include the following:

Their first option is to sell agricultural, forestry and animal husbandry products, in other words, the commercialization of traditional products or the introduction of new commodity-based by-products. The commercialization of traditional products is possible because those products have a comparative advantage in Tibetan areas. Introduction of new commercial agricultural and animal husbandry by-products has a positive impact in that it encourages the participation of farmers and herdsmen in the market. The part of Nixi Village in Shangri-La County we visited has an altitude of over 2,000 meters with lots of farmland. Local Tibetans' livelihoods are based upon plant cultivation rather than herding animals. Yu Guoxing, the director of Nixi's Agricultural Science Station, told us that the station helped several households grow potatoes in winters of 1999 and 2002. It also acted as a prototype for others. The Agricultural Science Station was responsible for introducing new species and providing technical support to these households. It also continues to offer them some technical equipment at a lower price. When other rural households saw the increase in income in these model households, they adopted the new planting technology. When we visited Nixi in 2007, it had already had an off-season vegetable production base of nearly 2,500 *mu* (or approximately 412 acres). The main products available included potatoes sowed in winter, tomatoes, hot peppers and Chinese cabbage. No chemicals but natural fertilizers were used to grow these vegetables. Nowadays, the potatoes and hot peppers that grow in Nixi have become a well-known brand in Diqing in the Tibetan Autonomous Region. Moreover they have gained the trust of local consumers as a pollution-free and safe product. The potatoes and hot peppers are now sold in areas as far as Changdu.

At present, the biggest challenge in promoting off-season vegetable planting comes from sales of these vegetables. The current practice is that all farmers sell vegetables by themselves. Vendors come to the farms or farmers transport the vegetables to the town and sell them at a booth in a market. Farmers do not work cooperatively with each other when it comes to selling their products. In 2006, the government at county and village levels set up a Vegetables Association in Nixi County. However, that association was not structured correctly and failed to organize the farmers so that they could sell their products as a group.

Economic growth in inland China and its integration into the global market has sped up the marketization of the Tibetan economy. It has encouraged farmers and herdsmen to participate more extensively in market activities. This in turn has had a profound impact on their economic and social life, and has improved their living standards significantly. A typical example is the trade of tricholoma matsutake in Shangri-La in the Yunnan Province.

Their second option is to engage in a secondary industry, such as producing household handicraft products or goods through a household workshop. They sell these products either to contracted buyers or they sell them by themselves (see Case 1).

Case 1 The Wooden Bowl Business in Xingfu Village

Gasong Wenfen, a Xingfu villager who lives in Nixi County, makes wooden bowls. It is a family tradition. They have been making these bowls for five generations. While many families in the village can make wooden bowls, Gasong learned this unique skill from his father. He can paint and draw pictures on the bowls. Due to the increasing number of orders, Gasong started to buy wooden bowls from villagers and focus only on the refinement process. He purchased semi-finished wooden bowls at approximately 30 yuan and sells them for 50 yuan after refining them with various pictures. He always pays on site and never defaults on a payment.

There is no need for Gasong to sell the bowls by himself in the market. Migrant vendors come to his home on a regular basis and purchase the refined bowls. Similarly, they pay him immediately for the painted bowls.

Some villagers have even opened stores in Lhasa and Changdu to sell wooden bowls. Gasong asks acquaintances who are passing by to transport his bowls to the store owners, and pay the driver 50 yuan for each box. The driver will then bring back the money on his return trip. As Gasong said, he has done this for years, and there has never been a mistake. Both the drivers and the store owners are villagers from Xingfu and there is no reason not to trust them.

Another option is to work for enterprises or other institutions in the towns. This means that the farmers and herdsmen left the primary sector and entered into a non-agrarian organization or industry to earn wages for their labor. When the farmers and herdsmen trade agricultural work for work in the secondary or tertiary sector, they need a period of learning and adjustment. Judging from the current situation, the secondary sector in Tibetan areas does not offer farmers and herdsmen many opportunities to get a job. It is even more difficult for local farmers and herdsmen to leave Tibetan areas and work in towns or cities. The flexible and local-grown tertiary industry, however, can be a more effective path for farmers and herdsmen to get employed in the non-agricultural sector. In this case, local tourism and related industries play a significant role in recruiting farmers and herdsmen.

Since China adopted the reform and opening up policy, a large number of inland laborers have migrated to Tibetan areas for a number of reasons. The migrant population has stimulated demand for consumer goods for their daily necessities and has promoted the development of related industries such as transportation, commerce and the service sector. Most of these industries have a low threshold for market entry in terms of capital and technology requirements, thus it is easy to attract laborers from the surrounding and inland areas to either start a new business in Tibet, or work as a migrant there. The inflow of labor, capital and entrepreneurs has given the local farmers and herdsmen more opportunities to learn non-agricultural skills, as well as the chance to cultivate a "spirit of entrepreneurship".

2. *The role of migrant merchants in the market network in Tibetan areas*

To facilitate trade and benefit farmers and herdsmen, the market network plays a crucial role. Hayami Yujiro[2] once pointed out that developing countries must establish a domestic trade network that can easily connect external demand with local producers. Without such a network, rural laborers can do nothing but migrate to the big cities. On the one hand, only factories in the big cities can meet domestic and foreign demand for labor-intensive products. However, it is not possible for Tibetan farmers and herdsmen to work as migrant workers in the big cities in the near future. For them, more practical options are the commercialization of traditional agricultural products, the introduction of modern commodity-featured products, and a focus on gaining local non-agricultural employment. In these cases, a trading network that connects products in Tibetan areas with external demand becomes extremely important.

Currently, agricultural products, handicrafts and natural specialties are still sold in a traditional way, in a loose network of individuals with multi-level agents. The system consists of a large number of individual merchants at different levels. Vendors go to villages to buy agricultural products from farmers. They then sell these products to big merchants in towns or cities, who either sell these products in local markets or transport them to other regions. In this system, the connection between merchants at various levels is rather loose. Those who do business time and again are often from the same community. When it comes to the actual transaction, the buyer usually pays cash for the goods and the seller provides the goods immediately.

Migrant workers, entrepreneurs and external capital play significant roles in the formation of the market network that connects external and internal demand with the products of farmers and herdsmen.

3. *The role of farmers and herdsmen in markets*

However, as mentioned above, due to the small size of the market in Tibetan areas, all agricultural products sold by farmers and herdsmen are

---

[2]See Hayami (2000).

at the bottom of the industrial chain and therefore are susceptible to significant changes in price. Additionally, farmers and herdsmen suffer from
a lack of organizational skills and limited participation in the market
place. This results from the fact that they lack bargaining power and have
an unstable income stream from the goods they sell. Though they are the
least immune to risks when compared to other participants working in
other industries, farmers and herdsmen often end up bearing the greatest
natural and market risks. This can be seen most clearly in the business of
tricholoma matsutake and Chinese caterpillar fungus collection. Therefore,
a new way to increase income needs to be found to help farmers and herdsmen become less dependent on the collecting industry. However, due to
the limited capacity of the market, only a small number of people can find
a job in the traditional handicraft industry. To date, there are already cases
of farmers and herdsmen in Tibetan areas entering into non-agricultural
work and engaging in the service sector. They have been found to work in
areas such as retail, restaurants and hotels, but at this point, their numbers
are still relatively small. While Tibetan farmers and herdsmen have started
to work in the service sector, and some even set up their own businesses,
they are still at a disadvantage, compared to the migrant businessmen
from the inland areas. They need to go through a learning process which
takes some time.

II Contribution of Traditional Tibetan Community to Market Participation of Farmers and Herdsmen

Looking at the whole trading process in Tibetan areas, due to the small
trade volume among the farmers and herdsmen, it is obviously not practical for them to resort to formal legal procedures to ensure that contractual
obligations are met, especially given that the judicial costs involved in
solving conflicts are usually higher than the expected amount of compensation. As Hayami Yujiro[3] pointed out, the industrialization process that
occurred in Japanese rural areas depended largely on the successful application of a community-based system, used to solve the problems arising
from asymmetric information. Likewise, a traditional community system,

---

[3] See Hayami (1998).

as well as common social rules and customs in local Tibetan areas, reduced the number of problems, such as opportunistic behavior from information asymmetry. When the production of traditional agricultural products and modern commodities have not reached economies of scale, local households or communities prove to be more efficient than the large-scale collective organization (see Case 2), as the former considerably reduces the cost of labor supervision. Once opportunistic practices during the sales process have been effectively curbed, it is highly possible to put more local agricultural and handicraft products into the market, and introduce modern market-oriented and commodity-featured products. Rather than hindering the local market economy's development, a traditional community-based system promotes market growth and market economy more generally.

Case 2 Forest Protection System Set Up by the Yihe Cooperative in Jidi Village

While conducting interviews with people from Yihe Cooperative in Jidi Village (Jiantang Town, Shangri-La County), we learned from the villagers about the collective forest protection system. To prevent poorly organized or excessive logging, after discussions with the local villagers, Yihe Cooperative set up some regulations. First, logging is strictly prohibited, unless it is done for building houses for the villagers. This rule is applied stringently, especially in cases where individuals try to sell the logs in local markets. Second, logging is only permitted in the forest farms in Yihe Cooperative and trees can only be cut down by family members who need the wood to build their own house. Third, the household must obtain permission from village committee in order to cut down trees. Moreover, the village collective set a ceiling for the number of trees to be cut down each year. Fourth, the cooperative only permits logging by one household each year. If the household needs more logs than it is entitled to, it needs to wait until the next year before it can further log.

Regulations on logging in another villagers' cooperative (villagers' group) in Jidi are slightly different from those in Yihe Cooperative.

Although the basic principles are the same, the specific rules differ greatly. Due to historical reasons, per capita forest acreage found in that cooperative is several times more than that in Yihe Cooperative. So it divides the forests into parts that can be used for firewood, and parts that can be used for house building. There is an annual villager meeting to discuss matters associated with logging, in particular issues associated with logging in order to build houses. During this meeting, they decide which households can cut down trees in order to build new houses and what the annual ceiling for logging is for each household; however, there is no need to draw lots.

During the investigation into the area, we also learned that many state-owned forests near the villagers' cooperatives are also protected by the locals and treated as if they were their own forests. Regulations set by these cooperatives also apply to the practice of logging and the collection of tricholoma matsutake in these state-owned forests. Moreover, we found during our interviews that although most villagers have no idea what an ecological forest means, they have a long tradition of ecological protection. A few traditional, unwritten rural regulations on ecological protection still apply effectively to villagers, which supports the above rules in real life.

Non-governmental community and related credibility systems can help reduce trading costs, which lower the threshold for farmers and herdsmen to participate in market activities, while expanding the scale of the local market and bringing greater profits. In the aforementioned Case 1, the practice of transporting wooden bowls made in Xingfu Village to Lhasa is a typical illustration of the role played by the traditional community-based credibility system.

In terms of the market participation of farmers and herdsmen, it is highly likely that migrants or local entrepreneurs integrate traditional community rules and customs into modern market organizations, ensuring that the market behaviors of farmers and herdsmen are consistent with traditional social rules, reducing trading costs and risks for farmers and herdsmen in participating in the market (see Case 3).

Case 3 Policies on Private Loans and Bankruptcy in Tibetan
Areas

The village secretary Qu Re (49 years old) of Manzhang in Dari
County told us a number of stories about loans with especially high
rates of interest.

Qu Re told us that it is very difficult for herdsmen to borrow
money from credit cooperatives. They are not only prevented from
borrowing due to the high interest rates, but also due to the requirement for property ownership. However, most of the herdsmen do
not have any property, and assets such as cattle and sheep do not
help them to qualify for a mortgage. Without a mortgage, herdsmen
have to find three guarantors who have a stable source of income.
In Tibetan areas, it seems that only civil servants are qualified to
act as guarantors. But for most herdsmen, it is hard to find three
civil servant friends who are willing to act as guarantors for their
loans.

Therefore, most herdsmen can only borrow money through
private channels, which incur high interest rates. Generally, there
are two ways to calculate the interest rates when going through
such a channel: "Big Three" and "Little Three". "Three" refers to a
monthly interest rate of 3%. For "Big Three", the interest is calculated on a 12-month basis. It adopts a simple interest rule, which
means that interest will not generate additional interest. Therefore,
the annual interest rate of "Big Three" is 36%. For "Little Three", it
is also one year loan, but the interest is calculated on a 10-month
basis. So its annual interest rate is 30%. For emergency loans,
the monthly interest rate can be as high as 5%, but the loan
period is usually less than one year, in most cases, either three
or six months.

A private loan requires a guarantor and an intermediary. This
guarantor is usually a senior person in the village or a tribe, outlin-
ing the details of the loan. We asked Qu Re if there were any
professional usurers; he said there were none. He added that if a
herdsman needed money urgently, he would usually borrow it from
rich villagers.

When we asked what would happen if the debtor could not pay back, we got an interesting answer. When it comes to economic exchanges over a long period of time, local Tibetans have formed a custom very similar to today's law of bankruptcy. If a herdsman cannot pay back his outstanding debts, even after taking into consideration the total value of his or her property, a "policy of bankruptcy" is undertaken. An individual perceived to be of great virtue and held in high esteem by the villagers will send out invitations to all of the creditors as well as other individuals who are important figures in the village and ask them to come to the debtor's house. The debtor then has to take a vow in the presence of all of these people. In the oath, the debtor reports all of his or her property, even small items. The host will then distribute all his property among the creditors, which is calculated roughly on the basis of the percentage of debt they are owed. After the ceremony in which the property is distributed, the debtor becomes a person with no property and no debt. Taking into account the dire position of the individual at this point, the senior person in the tribe will call for tribe members to donate various necessities such as clothes, food and even cattle and sheep to ensure his survival during this difficult period.

Such market organizations and their business activities have existed for a long time in Tibetan areas which serve as a good example for farmers and herdsmen, by demonstrating that anyone can participate in the market activities, showing them how to be successful, and in particular how to manage an organization that functions well in a market and how to cope with the market risks. An excellent example is the shops and hotels run by Jiegu Temple Management Committee and its lamas (see Case 4). In addition, the temple also provides farmers and herdsmen with basic financial services and some public services.

Case 4 Profitable Business in Jiegu Temple

On the morning of July 13, 2007, we visited Jiegu Temple in the town of Jiegu where the prefecture government of Yushu is located. In the afternoon we visited some of the very profitable businesses operated by Jiegu Temple.

Jiegu Temple is a Buddhist temple which has existed for hundreds of years. It has a well-developed asset management system. In this temple, a specialized management committee was founded to manage the business affairs and assets of the temple. The committee members are elected every three years by vote. The committee is made up of lamas, between the ages of 21 and 40, who have at least a middle school level of education and are familiar with both Han and Tibetan cultures and can speak fluent Mandarin. Moreover, they are also required to have strong business acumen. Since having a successful business and ensuring good asset management are important to all lamas in the temple, they broadly share the same interests and select only the capable candidates to sit on the committee. To motivate the committee members and the staff in charge of asset management, the temple has adopted many economic incentives similar to a performance-based pay approach. The religious groups and secular economic organizations are no different in this respect. Our visits to the Jiegu Temple and interviews conducted in the shops and hotels confirm this assumption.

As Jiegu is the premise of Yushu's prefecture government, it is one of the most developed cities in the Tibetan areas found in Qinghai Province. Jiegu Temple runs five stores in the town. Their businesses include selling groceries, tea and Chinese caterpillar fungus. In our interviews, we learned that each store can generate a profit of about 500,000 yuan. All administrators and sales assistants found in the stores are lamas from the temple. Jiegu Temple also owns 3 inns and 13 street stores in the town. All of the stores are rented out to secular people, at a rate of 1,000 yuan per store per month.

We visited two stores and one inn run by Jiegu Temple. In the stores, the lamas served the customers in a friendly manner and were able to use the calculators proficiently. If they changed into ordinary clothes, these lamas looked no different from the Han or Hui shopkeepers found in nearby stores.

III Policy Suggestions

The basic argument of this chapter is to encourage farmers and herdsmen to actively participate in market activities and increase their income.

By leveraging the opportunities presented by the market place, they will be able to raise their standard of living and quality of life. However, since the small-scale rural economy is fragile, it cannot afford the sharp ups and downs of a pure market economy. It requires the local government to take various measures to protect the interests of the farmers and herdsmen and encourage and assist so that they can get involved in the market place. Additionally, given that the incomes of farmers and herdsmen are a lot lower than that of urban residents, it is necessary for the local government to support them with continued investment. This is also a common practice found in developed countries. However, we do not think it is appropriate for the local government to take direct control over the economy and production. During the process of reform and opening up, there is no doubt in our minds that government investment has been an important factor in the economic development of Tibetan areas. However, history has shown us that although government investment in infrastructure and public services is important for an economy, investment in the highly competitive parts of the industry focused on direct production, or excessive intervention in the industry, often results in investment mistakes and a waste of resources. Therefore, market-oriented private investment stands out as the most effective way to nurture industries with potential endogenous growth as well as maintaining stable and sustainable economic prosperity.[4]

Given the current administrative capability of the government at various levels, it can only provide tangible hardware such as infrastructure and public services. However, in terms of software, it is better for the government to grant as much freedom as possible to private entrepreneurs, allowing them to establish private, intangible, and perhaps even an informal, but effective trading system. A good trading environment should have a spontaneous market, where the traditional community plays a larger role. Moreover, innovation from local and migrant entrepreneurs is also important. Typical examples are as illustrated above.

First, government participation in the field of economic activity should focus purely on the provision of infrastructure, such as transport links and communication facilities. It should not get involved in distorting the incentives for market participants.

[4]See Zhu (2005).

Infrastructure developments in transportation and communication, such as roads, railways, power and information technology, help to reduce the costs of production and sales and expand the scope and scale of the market. This allows farmers and herdsmen to participate in markets more extensively, which benefits both the buyers and the sellers. Farmers and herdsmen can sell products at a higher price, whereas urban consumers can purchase commodities at a lower price, thus promoting trade between urban and rural areas. In addition, the reduced costs of transportation and communication help integrate small and scattered markets in remote areas, turning them into large-scale regional markets. As a result, merchants who once monopolized certain small markets now face more intensive competition.[5] With better infrastructure and a lower threshold for market entry, more merchants in other areas will be attracted to local Tibetan markets. This will, in turn, promote competition and eventually benefit the scattered farmers and herdsmen.

When there is intensive competition in the market, private merchants in Tibetan areas have to cut costs and improve efficiency to make a profit. With competitive buyers, scattered farmers and herdsmen can benefit more from trade in the market. Therefore, the government should not allow the markets to be monopolized by buyers, through granting of franchise rights or via special subsidies, loans or resources. Otherwise, the purchaser would shift their business focus to rent-seeking activities rather than on reducing costs and improving efficiency, which would undermine the interests of the scattered farmers and herdsmen. While we recognize the importance of the government's support for, and aid provided to, economic cooperatives for farmers and herdsmen, we do not think it is appropriate for the government to grant special aid to specific cooperatives or associations of farmers and herdsmen. By undertaking such a course of action, the real beneficiary might be the community's political elites, who are in charge of these organizations. In such a case, these elites would focus on rent-seeking activities rather than competing through reduced costs and improved services. More importantly, either in face of buyers or cooperatives, farmers and herdsmen should be given the right to withdraw from the market. The farmers and herdsmen should be

---

[5]See Baulch (1997).

entitled to choose other buyers after fulfilling the terms of their current contract. Otherwise, it is very likely that profit-making firms or non-profit cooperatives will abuse their power by taking advantage of their position as monopolized buyers to suppress and exploit the scattered farmers and herdsmen.

Second, the government should provide training for the farmers and herdsmen as well as intellectual and technological support to enhance their competitive edge in market activities.

Though the local government has made a lot of effort in recent years, they still need to improve their training methodology. When we undertook interviews in Moba Village in Dari County, we met a Tibetan couple who attended a free training program organized by the local government under the identity of ecological migrants. Over the course of the training the husband learned Tibetan costume tailoring and the wife learned wool carpet weaving. However, the tailor shop opened up by the husband had to be closed down shortly after due to a lack of customers. Moreover, the wife did not receive any pay from an indebted government-run wool carpet factory since there is no market for their products. As a result, the couple borrowed a loan of 5,000 *yuan* with an annual interest rate of 40% to open up a roadside store near the Moba government. When we visited their store, they had just paid back the loan of 7,000 *yuan*. Their story of doing business does not sound particularly complicated. They learned from drivers who were passing by as well as local herdsmen about which products were the most popular. The husband also learned how to buy goods in the Dari County from his cousin, who has opened a restaurant near the couple's store and goes to Dari to buy products on a regular basis.

Third, the government should help to nurture markets suitable for farmers and herdsmen, for example, the production and sale of souvenirs, restaurants, hotels, and sports and leisure services such as horse riding, hiking and rock-climbing. With a well-developed tourism industry, Diqing, found in the Tibetan Autonomous Region, leads other Tibetan areas in this sector.

Lastly, the local government should take advantage of the special resources in Tibetan areas to develop environmentally friendly industries, create job opportunities and increase the income of farmers and herdsmen.

For example, in order to protect the ecological environment, most state-owned forests in Diqing are banned from logging for commercial purposes. These areas are transformed into public forests. Mixed with the collectively-owned forests in the same area, the state-owned forest farms have the same natural characteristics as the collective farms. After the state-owned forest farms banned logging in wild forests, their main economic income came from the sale of tricholoma matsutake. The local government therefore can contract the protection rights of state-owned forests to the nearby villagers for a long period of time. This will not change the public nature of these forests, and villagers who take care of these forests can generate some income from the government subsidies, ecological compensation funds and from the collection of natural products. This "state-owned, private-run" model can reduce the government's expenses on human, financial and material resources. On the other hand, it can also motivate the local villagers to take care of the forests. As a result, the government can withdraw from the daily work of operating and managing the state-owned forests, while also providing opportunities to create more jobs and income for the local farmers and herdsmen.

Bibliography

Baulch, Bob C, 1997, "Transfer Costs, Spacial Arbitrage, and Testing for Food Marketing Integration", *American Journal of Agricultural Economics*, 79 (May): 477–487.

Hayami Yujiro, 1998, *Toward the Rural-Based Development of Commerce and Industry: Selected Experiences from East Asia*, EDI Learning Resources Series, Washington, DC: Economic Development Institute, World Bank.

Hayami Yujiro, 2000, "Toward a New Model of Rural-Urban Linkages under Globalization", In *Local Dynamics in an Era of Globalization*, Simon, J. Evenett, Weiping Wu, Shahid Yusuf (Eds.), Oxford: Oxford University Press, pp. 74–83.

Hayami Yijiro, Godo Yoshihisa, 2009, *Development Economics: From Poverty to the Wealth of Nations*, (*Third Edition, in Chinese*). Oxford: Oxford University Press.

Huang Zongzhi, Peng Yusheng, 2007, "Convergence of Three Historical Changes and Prospects of Small-Scaled Agriculture in China", *Chinese Social Sciences*, 04, 74–88.

Schultz, Theodore William, 1964, *Transforming Traditional Agriculture*, Chicago: The University of Chicago Press.

Zhu Ling, 2005, "Impact of External Resources on Marketization of Tibetan Economy", In *Marketization and Grass-Root Public Services — Case Study on Tibet*, Wang Luolin, Zhu Ling (Eds.), Bejing: The Ethnic Publishing House, May.

CHAPTER 4

Sustainable Development of the Tricholoma Matsutake Industry in Tibetan-Inhabited Regions of Yunnan, and Their Participation in the Global Market: Discussions Based on Value Chain Analysis

YAO Yu

Abstract

This chapter probes into the tricholoma matsutake industry by applying value chain analysis. The author argues that the Tibetans found in the areas that produce tricholoma matsutake receive an extremely small portion of the profits from the global market. This is not only disadvantageous to the interests of the Tibetans but also to the protection of tricholoma matsutake resources. Merchants of tricholoma matsutake in China should work together to enhance their role in the global market and bring an end to the current situation in which they are merely passive price-takers, so as to help the Tibetans gain a larger proportion of the overall profits. Meanwhile, local governments should put higher premiums on the regulation and protection of tricholoma matsutake resources. Moreover, various organizations should establish and maintain effective rules on the collection of tricholoma matsutake. Only with multidirectional policies can China's tricholoma matsutake industry follow the path of steady and sustainable development.

Keywords: Trichohoma Matsutake Industry; Sustainable Development.

With a reputation as the "king of mushrooms", tricholoma matsutake is a natural, rare, and edible mushroom that grows in mountains and forest floors. It is found above altitudes of 3,500 meters above sea level, and in areas of cold or temperate climate. Research conducted by botanists show that tricholoma matsutake can be used as a nutritious health supplement. It mainly grows in China, Japan and North Korea. Within China, the plant is found most commonly in northeast China, Yunnan and Tibet. Of these regions, the Tibetan-inhabited region of Shangri-La[1] in Yunnan Province is rich in tricholoma matsutake and there is a great deal of economic activity around the collection of various natural resources, including tricholoma matsutake. The collection of this mushroom has a profound impact on the economic income and social life of the Tibetans in Yunnan. By examining the development of the tricholoma matsutake industry in Diqing and the associated problems, this chapter proposes various solutions for the Tibetans, which aim at integrating this activity into the global market place.[2]

I The Emergence of the Tricholoma Matsutake Industry

Though references to tricholoma matsutake could be found in publications as early as "*Classified Herbs for Emergency from Classics and Histories*" written during the Song Dynasty, people have long paid little attention to the research and industrial development of the plant. Fifty years ago, the locals still referred to this mushroom, which has a faint smell, as the "stinky termite mushroom". The fate of tricholoma matsutake was completely changed by a story. The saying goes that after the atomic bomb hit Hiroshima in August 1945, the only plant that survived was tricholoma matsutake. Ever since then, the consumption of tricholoma matsutake became extremely popular in Japan, where the mushroom was relatively expensive. With the income levels of the Japanese people reaching similar

---

[1] The original name of the county was Zhongdian, but in 2001 the name was changed to Shangri-La County.
[2] The topic under discussion in this chapter, as well as our discoveries, is based on the research our project group did in the Diqing Tibetan Autonomous Region of Shangri-La in 2007.

levels to that found in developed countries, the market for tricholoma matsutake prospered. Indeed, Japan has been importing this product from China since the 1980s. In 2007, when our team undertook some research in Diqing, the technology associated with the cultivation of tricholoma matsutake had not yet been developed, and the product was still collected by hand. In 2007, 1,656 tons of tricholoma matsutake was sold in Japan, of which only 56 tons were produced in Japan and most of the rest was imported from China (amounting to about 90% of the market).

The ex-director of Office of Tricholoma Matsutake in Diqing explained: *"We have been collecting tricholoma matsutake since 1985. In the past, the locals did not enjoy eating it. The mushroom has been sold to Japan since 1985, with sales peaking in 1987 and 1988. Production was high and we sold fresh tricholoma matsutake directly into foreign markets. The only additional process that might have happened in China was a salting of the product. At that time, each of our five leadership teams was responsible for the development of one industry in the county. We chose the biological industry and made policies to oversee and support the industry. We also helped to develop a market for the product by using a few provincial import and export companies to export it. These companies staffed their agencies here to purchase tricholoma matsutake."*

The locals also told us that compared to other mushrooms, tricholoma matsutake is not palatable and they themselves do not like to eat it. They left it to naturally grow in the surrounding forests and mountains. It was only since tricholoma matsutake began to be exported to Japan and became a way of increasing income that activities around the collection of tricholoma matsutake began in earnest. Processing and trading the product has since caught on. A majority of the 1,656 tons of Japan's annual sales of tricholoma matsutake, as we mentioned earlier, comes from China. Moreover, in Shangri-La County alone, the annual export of tricholoma matsutake to Japan is as much as 1,000 tons. Today, money earned from the collection of tricholoma matsutake has become the second most important source of income for local Tibetans, after income earned from working in the city.

The ex-director elaborated: *"There is a huge disparity in wealth between regions where tricholoma matsutake is produced and where it is not. In the first case, a household can make a maximum of 70,000 to 80,000 yuan a year while in the second, the locals have to seek employment outside of the region and*

can only make 5,000 yuan a year at most. The villagers in Jidi became aware
of the benefits, and have began to protect their interests and autonomy. Today,
the locals have made a fortune and would easily spend 300,000 to 400,000
yuan building a new house, often vying with each other over who has the best
house. They also spend vast sums of money (ranging from tens of thousands to
millions of yuan) on jewelry and Tibetan costumes, all of which has been earned
by selling tricholoma matsutake."

II Current Developments of Tricholoma Matsutake Industry

1. Value chain of tricholoma matsutake industry in the global market

If we apply value chain analysis to the tricholoma matsutake industry, all
the economic activity involved in tricholoma matsutake can be summarized by the following stages:

A. The first value-added stage: After collecting tricholoma matsutake,
    farmers then sell it to retailers.
B. The second value-added stage: Retailers sell tricholoma matsutake to
    medium-scale merchants.
C. The third value-added stage: Medium-scale merchants sell tricho-
    loma matsutake to large-scale merchants at a higher price.
D. The fourth value-added stage: Export corporations again increase the
    price of tricholoma matsutake.
E. The fifth value-added stage: In the Japanese market, the Japanese
    once again increase the price of tricholoma matsutake.
F. The sixth value-added stage: The price of tricholoma matsutake is
    raised once more when the product is sold in the Japanese
    supermarkets.

In the above value chain (see Figure 1), fresh tricholoma matsutake
must be delivered to consumers in a timely manner. Therefore, there
can be no delay in each of the stages, all the way from the basic collection of the product, to selling it in the final market. Collecting tricholoma matsutake is extremely hard work. When the season comes, the
villagers start collecting tricholoma matsutake in the mountains before

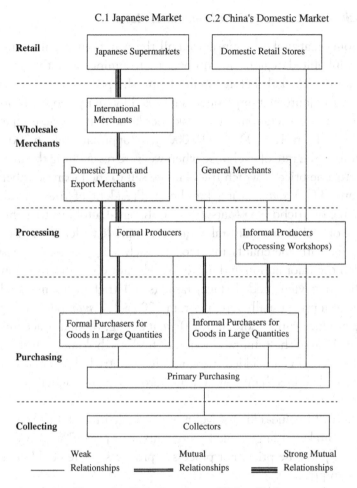

Figure 1: Basic Structure of Value Chain.

5 a.m. each and every morning. They usually work until 8 a.m. or 9 a.m, to ensure that they still have time to sell the mushrooms to retailers, who then sell the produce to medium-scaled merchants, who ensure tricholoma matsutake is transported to Japan. In cases where the merchants have to go to very high mountains or villages that are quite far away from Shangri-La, they have to prepare ice packs to keep the mushrooms fresh. It costs these merchants an extra 30,000 to 40,000 *yuan* to buy these ice packs.

2. Pricing process of tricholoma matsutake

Tricholoma matsutake is transported all the way from the mountains of Tibetan-inhabited regions in Yunnan to Kunming, and then through Shanghai or Bangkok before finally being shipped to Japan. Over the course of the journey, the product is handled by many people. It appears that the price of tricholoma matsutake per kg sold in Japanese supermarkets ranges from 100,000 to 110,000 yen (approximately 6,200 yuan, according to the rate of exchange when we were researching the matter in 2007). Yet the price at which the Chinese sell to the Japanese is between 2,000 and 3,000 yuan. Wang Jianzhong, President of the Chamber of Commerce of Tricholoma Matsutake in Shangri-La told us that the market price of tricholoma matsutake was very unpredictable. After discussing the matter with merchants involved in each stage of the business, we compiled the information and made the relevant comparisons below.

In the first value-added stage, farmers sell tricholoma matsutake to retailers at a price usually ranging from 100 to 200 yuan per kg. Superior quality produce can be sold at 3,000 yuan per kg, though it accounts for less than 10% of the total production of fresh tricholoma matsutake.

In the second value-added stage, retailers sell tricholoma matsutake to medium-scaled merchants at a price around 10% higher than they bought it for.

In the third value-added stage, medium-scaled merchants sell tricholoma matsutake to large-scaled merchants at a price 7% to 8% higher than their purchase price. For processed products, there could be a 15% increase in price.

In the fourth value-added stage, exporters increase the price by another 15%.

In the fifth value-added stage, the Japanese increase the price by another 300% once the products enter the Japanese market.

In the sixth and final value-added stage, there is another 15% increase to the price of tricholoma matsutake sold in the Japanese supermarkets.

The above pricing process looks pretty clear (Figure 2), so this begs the question of why President Wang told us that the market price of tricholoma matsutake was very unpredictable. The reason has to do with a remarkable characteristic of the tricholoma matsutake market in Yunnan,

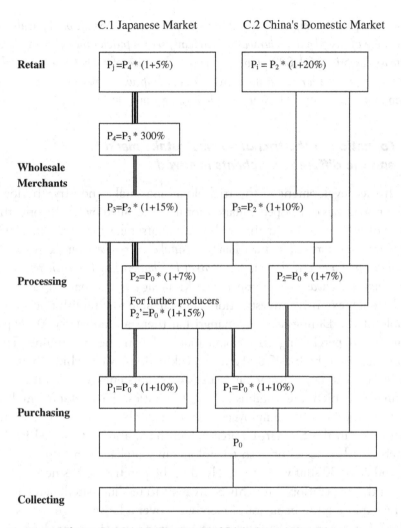

Figure 2: Pricing Processes of Tricholoma Matsutake.

that is, fluctuating prices. Generally speaking, the price of tricholoma matsutake changes every single day and can sometimes change by the hour. The dramatic price fluctuation causes a number of problems to merchants in each stage of the tricholoma matsutake market and has even made some of them bankrupt. President Wang told us: *"A few years ago, there were a few big merchants who purchased a ton of tricholoma matsutake in one day.*

However, prices slumped from 1,000 yuan per kg to 200 yuan per kg within a day. One of my friends, who was a merchant, set his purchasing price on a predicted sales price of 1,000 yuan. However, the price of tricholoma matsutake kept falling by the hour and the merchant ended up with a net loss of 600,000 yuan in just one day. This resulted in him going bankrupt."

3. Formation of the tricholoma matsutake market and the different merchants involved

With the development of the tricholoma matsutake industry, the local government has developed a market for it. As recalled by Li Zhiyong, the CEO of an enterprise in the tricholoma matsutake industry, *"In 1993, there were vendors selling tricholoma matsutake everywhere on the streets of Shangri-La. Later on, there was a market in Shangri-La, from where tricholoma matsutake was to be transported to Kunming and then onto Japan."*

Through extensive investigation, we were able to establish that in the whole of the Diqing area in Shangri-La, there are about 3,000 people engaged in purchasing tricholoma matsutake in the mountains. This figure can be as high as 5,000 during peak periods. Meanwhile, there are about 60 to 70 large- to medium-sized merchants engaged in purchasing businesses which are established in the cities. Each stand employs between four and five employees. In addition, there are five processing companies in the Shangri-La area, which have also participated in the purchasing businesses of fresh tricholoma matsutake. Each company has around 20 to 30 staff who are involved in the purchasing businesses. The size of their operation is roughly equivalent to medium-sized merchants.

By exploring the behavior of merchants over a larger range, we established that in Yunnan Province, there are six engaging in the trade of fresh tricholoma matsutake and six responsible for the finished product. This differs greatly from Sichuan Province, where policies permit merchants to perform as export agencies as long as they have an export license. There are around a dozen tricholoma matsutake processing factories in Sichuan. Apart from processing products such as tricholoma matsutake, they also process other kinds of mushroom.

There were once about 30 merchants purchasing tricholoma matsutake in large quantities in Yunnan Province. Now the number has shrunk to just 20. Some foreign trade companies involved in importing and exporting also came to the county to purchase tricholoma matsutake. There are four or five international merchants from Japan, which rise to a maximum of seven or eight during peak periods, that have tricholoma matsutake businesses both in Yunnan and Sichuan.

Based on value chain analysis, we know that profitability varies among merchants in different stages of the value chain. By examining the number of merchants in each stage, we can get a clear sense of the amount of market control each of them has, and to what extent they can control the market altogether.

4. The labor market in the tricholoma matsutake industry

The prosperous tricholoma matsutake industry has created many job opportunities for the locals. Statistics are not available regarding the exact number of people engaged in jobs related to tricholoma matsutake (see Figure 3 for an overview). There is a common saying that when the season comes, each family member, regardless of gender or age, has to collect tricholoma matsutake in the mountains, except for one member who has to stay at home and do the cooking. Generally speaking, in a village with around 200 people, there are about five small merchants engaged in the trade of tricholoma matsutake. Using this assumption, there should be around 120,000 to 200,000 people collecting tricholoma matsutake in the mountains each year. Using a formal definition of "employment", these people cannot be strictly defined as being employed. Yet they can be viewed as "self-employed workers" in a broader sense. A high proportion of women are involved in the collection stage, especially young women with good eyesight who are particularly efficient at collecting tricholoma matsutake. The category of "self-employed workers" also includes the small merchants (3,000 to 5,000 in number) who engage in the trade of tricholoma matsutake in the mountains, as well as their medium- and large-scale counterparts in the cities. Most of the workers participating in the purchasing stage are male.

Around 500 people are employed by the medium- and large-scale merchants who engage in the purchasing in the cities. There are five processing companies in the region of Shangri-La, each employing over 150 seasonal workers and having a fixed staff of 60 to 70 workers. During the peak season, a factory usually needs to hire over 400 people, all of whom

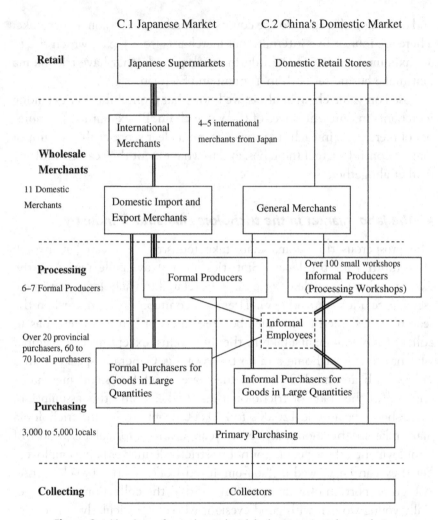

Figure 3: Number of merchants in tricholoma matsutake market.

are seasonal workers and are only employed for three months in a year. These factories also hire some other people, mostly female farmers from nearby villages, to wash tricholoma matsutake. Paid by the hour, they have a flexible schedule, going to work at any time and working for any length of time in any one day, with no need to be on duty every day.

In the processing factories, 70% of the employees are women, who mainly engage in slicing tricholoma matsutake, whereas men work

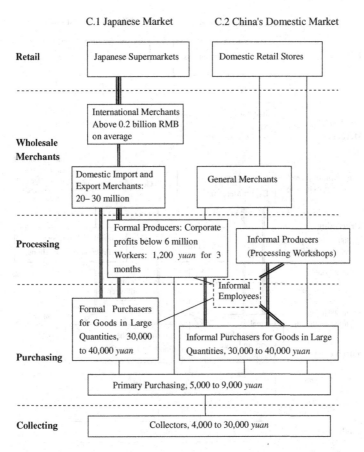

Figure 4:   Profit-Making Ability of Merchants in Tricholoma Matsutake Market.

as porters and packagers. The monthly salary is 1,200 *yuan* and the employees work eight hours a day, earning four *yuan* per hour (Figure 4). Given that slicing requires skill, those who work on this task are paid slightly higher. To ensure timely delivery of the products, the companies usually require employees to work overtime. To meet the production deadline, each employee has to work 13 hours a day, going to work at 8 a.m. in the morning, eating lunch and taking a rest at noon and finishing the day at 10 p.m. Factories provide accommodation for the workers in the factory and cover their living expenses. The actual salary cost of a worker per month is around 1,700 to 1,800 *yuan* and the figure dropped

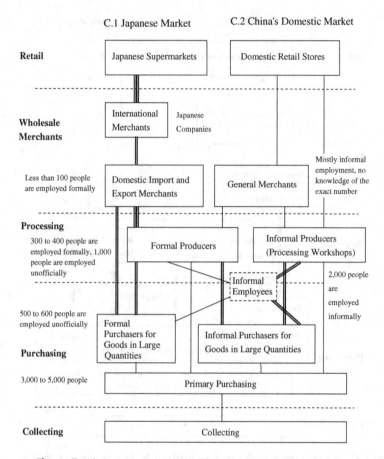

Figure 5: Labor Market in the Tricholoma Matsutake Industry.

to 1,500 *yuan* in 2007. Those who wash tricholoma matsutake can earn four *yuan* per hour, which, according to the locals, is a fair rate of pay for someone working on that kind of a task in the region.

Regarding the processing workshops not operated by formal economic departments, we did not have access to exact statistics, and were only able to visit experts in the industry, who informed us that there are at least 2,000 people engaged in processing tricholoma matsutake (see Figure 5 for more details). Yet most of the tricholoma matsutake that they process falls into the inferior category, i.e. the mushroom has already parachuted or is broken. Moreover, the processed products do not qualify to be exported and are mostly sold to domestic markets found in Shanghai, Yunnan and Guangdong. However, the product is barely sold in other regions. The income of those who work in these workshops is approximately 800 to 1,000 *yuan* per month.

5. The institutional environment's impact on the development of the tricholoma matsutake industry

In order to better support the development of the tricholoma matsutake industry, the local government in each of the producing regions has established institutions like the "Office of Tricholoma Matsutake Industry". On the whole, this kind of institution is temporary in nature and works together with numerous other departments and plays a key role in building the right institutional environment for the development of the industry. Additionally, most members of this association are big bosses in the tricholoma matsutake industry, who have control over companies in the domestic market.

The development of the tricholoma matsutake industry also involves departments such as the Commodity Inspection Department, which, in 2005, began to undertake local inspections. Prior to this, all of the commodities were inspected in Kunming. Local inspection has made it much easier to trade and export tricholoma matsutake, and helps to keep the product fresher by reducing the amount of time involved in trading. This also results in a significant increase in the income of villagers. Beginning in 2004, the tax department no longer imposed taxes on specialties which beforehand had been taxed at eight *yuan* per kg. The value-added tax is four *yuan* per kg whereas income tax is two *yuan* per kg. The products are taxed by the kilogram rather than by the total currency value, because the price of tricholoma matsutake changes by the hour, making it impossible to estimate the actual income of a merchant in any one day. Therefore, the merchant is taxed by the weight of his product. Each year when the season comes, the Commission for Discipline Inspection of the County works alongside the Office of Tricholoma Matsutake, launching a program of tax-collection. The Department of Industry and Commerce does not charge a market administration fee for temporary markets found either in the county or village, for it is impossible to collect the fees even if the department intends to. The business administration fee is also charged by the kilogram. It amounts to 0.5 *yuan* per kg. The Department of Forestry is responsible for overseeing all activities in the mountains which can potentially cause damage to the forests. There are many cases of people arbitrarily cutting down trees when collecting tricholoma matsutake in the mountains.

To illustrate how the institutional environment affects the development of the tricholoma matsutake industry clearly, we have designed Figure 6 to explain the relationships between the departments and institutions related to the development of the industry, as well as to highlight the different stages involved in the collection and sale of tricholoma matsutake.

III Sustainable Development of Yunnan's Tricholoma Matsutake Industry

In Shangri-La, Diqing, collecting and selling tricholoma matsutake is the only source of cash for local households in major tricholoma matsutake

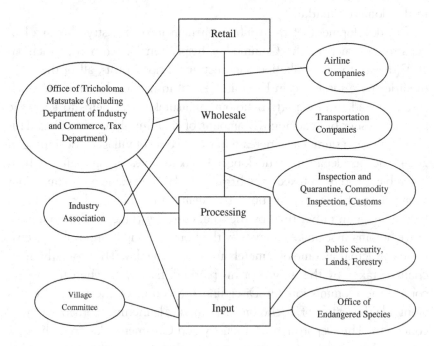

Figure 6: Service Providers and Market Supervisors in the Value Chain of the Tricholoma Matsutake Industry.

producing regions. In 2000, when the market was buoyant, every household earned thousands or even hundred thousands of *yuan* from the collection of tricholoma matsutake. But as output has declined in recent years, the average annual income per household from collecting tricholoma matsutake is at most 20,000 to 30,000 *yuan*. This raises the question: What has caused this dramatic fall in income? According to a local official, collecting tricholoma matsutake is getting harder and harder. There is a great deal of concern about the sustainable development of the tricholoma matsutake industry.

1. Causes for the decline of the tricholoma matsutake resources

The decline of tricholoma matsutake resources is reflected in both quantity and quality. Before discussing the causes, let us take a look at the grading system of tricholoma matsutake. According to the introduction on a website specifically designed to provide trade information relating to tricholoma matsutake (www.songrong.com), the grades for tricholoma matsutake are: 3L, 2L, L, ML, M, HA3L, HA2L, HAL, HA, HB3L, HB2L, HBL, HB, MS, S and P. There are two main grading criteria: whether the mushroom cap has opened and whether its partial veil has disintegrated.[3] Immature tricholoma matsutake is regarded as high-grade; while tricholoma matsutake with a fully opened cap and disintegrated partial veil is regarded as low-grade. Figure 7 shows pictures of tricholoma matsutake across three different grades:

For tricholoma matsutake, a higher grade means a better price. Following this logic, collecting tricholoma matsutake with closed caps generates higher economic returns. But according to botanical knowledge, tricholoma matsutake with a closed cap means that its partial veil has not disintegrated, thus reproductive spores have not fallen out. As time passes, the amount of tricholoma matsutake spores will decline gradually in the producing regions.

The young tricholoma matsutake refers to the little tricholoma matsutake less than 6 centimeters long. In order to protect the young tricholoma matsutake, the county formulated a relevant measure. In essence,

---

[3] For more information, see Song Rong (2007).

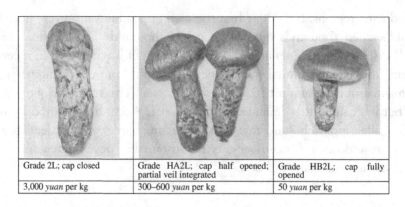

Grade 2L; cap closed	Grade HA2L; cap half opened; partial veil integrated	Grade HB2L; cap fully opened
3,000 *yuan* per kg	300–600 *yuan* per kg	50 *yuan* per kg

Figure 7: Examples of Tricholoma Matsutake of Different Grades.

young tricholoma matsutakes that are less than 3 centimeters long will be confiscated. For young tricholoma matsutakes with a length of 3 to 6 centimeters, a fine of at least 50 *yuan* will be levied. The exact amount of the fine is decided on a case by case basis with an average of 100 to 200 *yuan*. The fine will be imposed on the immediate possessor of the young tricholoma matsutake, regardless of whether the person in question is a villager or a merchant. The *Notice on Enhancing Export Management of Tricholoma Matsutake* by the Office of Endangered Species and General Administration of Customs also stated: "*Tricholoma matsutake is a precious natural resource in our country, which only grows in Yunnan, Sichuan, Tibet, Jilin and Heilongjiang Provinces.*" Tricholoma matsutake is found mostly in regions inhabited by ethnic groups, playing an important role in protecting the forest ecological environment in China and contributing to the region's economic development. After the launching of the Natural Forest Protection Program, protecting tricholoma matsutake has become even more important. In recent years, China exports a large amount of tricholoma matsutake, resulting in severe damage to the tricholoma matsutake stocks and its growing environment. Therefore, enhancing the export management of tricholoma matsutake resources is of great value in terms of protecting the forest environment, restoring the stock of tricholoma matsutake, maintaining the ecological balance and safeguarding the long-term interests of the people in producing regions.

In reality, the retailers have no alternative but to purchase young tricholoma matsutake. According to them, when the price for normal tricholoma matsutake is around 300 *yuan*, they purchase young tricholoma matsutake at 30 to 40 *yuan*, and then sell it at 40 to 50 *yuan* in Shangri-La. They retailers commented: *"The young ones must be hidden well. When the villagers bring the young ones to us, we must purchase them; otherwise they might not sell us the bigger ones. The government banned the collection or purchasing of young tricholoma matsutake, but we have no choice."*

In addition, the decline of tricholoma matsutake stocks is also caused by the lack of a collecting schedule and shiro protection. If tricholoma matsutake grows on one shiro, it still grows the next year, provided the shiro is well protected. However, while collecting tricholoma matsutake, some villagers use inappropriate tools and methods which result in damage to the shiro and a disruption of the tricholoma matsutake's reproduction process.

2. Tibetan farmers at the bottom of the global value chain

The retail price of tricholoma matsutake in Japanese market is as high as 100,000 to 110,000 *yen*, but this hardly benefits the Tibetan people.

This chapter has analyzed the pricing process of tricholoma matsutake using value chain analysis (Figure 8), from which we can see: (1) Profits of tricholoma matsutake are mainly generated from the international market rather than the domestic market, and it is because of the Japanese people's special love for tricholoma matsutake that there is this market in the first place; (2) Japanese dealers have monopolized the Japanese market, making it difficult for Chinese merchants to enter. Under such circumstances, although the local government has formulated some industrial support policies, it cannot change China's tricholoma matsutake industry's position in the global value chain. Chinese merchants remain passive price-takers. Even thought the merchants try to transfer as much benefits as they can to the tricholoma matsutake collectors, their ability to raise the Tibetan people's income is still limited.

3. Dramatic price fluctuations

The high value of tricholoma matsutake is primarily reflected in its price. According to the ex-director of the Office of Tricholoma Matsutake, when the market is good, fresh high-grade tricholoma matsutake can be sold at 3,000 *yuan* per kg, but the price may fall to 50 or 60 *yuan* in the same year. The average price over a year is around 400 *yuan*. The main contributor to the dramatic price fluctuations is not differences in grade but the changing quoted price in the Japanese market. The quoted price may change on a daily basis, sometimes even on an hourly basis.

In Japanese supermarkets, the price of tricholoma matsutake is very high. However, when Chinese merchants sell the product to the Japanese market they only make around 2,000–3,000 *yuan* per kg. President Wang used to lead a delegation to Japan in order to conduct market research. He

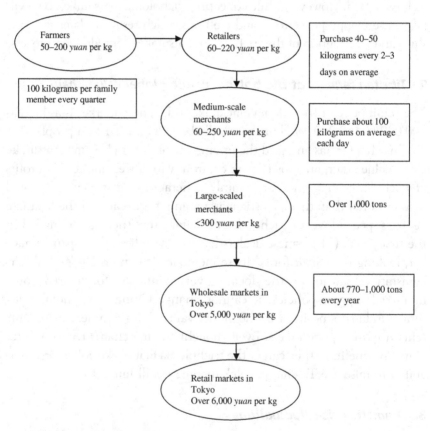

Figure 8: Price of Tricholoma Matsutake at Different Stages (Using Fair to Average Quality Tricholoma Matsutake).

found that the price of tricholoma matsutake in Japanese markets is con-trolled by Japanese trading companies and noted that the retail price of tricholoma matsutake has not changed in the past decade. But in the Chinese market, the purchasing price is lower than that in the 1990s. Compared to the peak price in the 1990s, the current price has fallen more than two-thirds. Taking the most inferior tricholoma matsutake as an example, the price was around 90 *yuan* during the worst period in the mar-ket depression in the 1990s, while the present price is around 20 *yuan.*

On September 4, 2007, just as the delegation finished their market research and returned to Beijing, they found that on September 3, 2007, in a China News article, an official in the Yunnan Provincial Department of Commerce, Kunming, was quoted as saying that since 2007, the vol-ume of tricholoma matsutake exports from Yunnan has fallen signifi-cantly and the value of exports has also fallen. This phenomenon was due to a number of reasons. In August that year, the export price fell to 25 US dollars per kg, accounting for less than 20% of the average price over the past few years.[4]

What makes the price fluctuate so wildly? Who is able to influence the price of tricholoma matsutake? An official from the county government told us that there was no way they can manipulate the price of tricholoma matsutake. Since only fresh tricholoma matsutake can be sold at a good price, domestic companies and government departments made concerted efforts to work well together. At the beginning of the 21st century, tricho-loma matsutake could be delivered from China to supermarkets in Tokyo in just 24 hours. At every stage of the export chain, Chinese companies must keep an eye on the quoted price in the Japanese market. They are also worried about failures in transactions with Japanese companies, as this slows down the process, resulting in products that are far from fresh. Thus, when they eventually sell it to the Japanese market, the price of the ticholoma matsutake will be even lower.

The Japanese government is also able to influence the market price by imposing inspection orders on exported tricholoma matsutake and over-emphasizing issues around pesticide residues. In 2007, some tricholoma matsutake export companies in Jilin Province failed some quality control

---

[4]See Shi (2007).

tests and exported some batches of tricholoma matsutake that exceeded the required pesticide residue levels. The Japanese government then imposed the strictest "inspection order" for imported goods from this company and expanded the inspection order to all tricholoma matsutake from Yunnan. After tricholoma matsutake was put into the "Positive List", the inspection was expanded to 256 items and the inspection fee was 25 times as high. However, both China and Japan have incurred great losses, because tricholoma matsutake is no longer fresh after the inspection and therefore most of its market advantages are lost.

China–Japan relations also influence the tricholoma matsutake price. When tensions occur between the two countries, the Japanese side will almost always release some news reports which have a negative impact on the development of the tricholoma matsutake industry.

4. Over-dependence on foreign markets

A vast majority of China's tricholoma matsutake goes to Japan. In terms of raw materials, out of all of the tricholoma matsutake sold in the domestic market, less than 30% is made from high-grade tricholoma matsutake, while the majority is made from low-grade products. During the first purchasing stage, 80% of tricholoma matsutake products collected are sold to Japan, only a small proportion are sold in the domestic market. Every year China exports approximately 1,000 tons of fresh tricholoma matsutake, and sometimes as much as 1,300 tons. China also exports another 1,000 tons of processed tricholoma matsutake (i.e. frozen, boiled or salted).

Domestic consumption amounts to a total of 600 to 650 tons of tricholoma matsutake. Looking at the breakdown of China's total output of 3,000 tons, Diqing produces around 600 tons, but sometimes as much as 900 tons, ranking top among all producing regions in China. Yunnan Province also produces 300 to 400 tons of processed tricholoma matsutake. Another major producing region of processed tricholoma matsutake is Sichuan Province, to be more exact, the Tibetan regions found in Sichuan.

In order to meet the standard for international long-distance transportation and keep the tricholoma matsutake fresh, Chinese export companies need to use packaging that keeps the product fresh, costing them another 12 to 13 dollars per ton. However, fresh and frozen tricholoma matsutake products enjoy a tax rebate of 15%, and salted tricholoma matsutake a tax rebate of 13%. Some companies take advantage of the tax rebate policies to make profit in order to get orders. Such a situation constitutes a severe challenge to the development of the industry. President Wang of the Chamber of Commerce of Tricholoma Matsutake in Shangri-La keeps emphasizing the need "to urgently start exploring markets outside of Japan".

5. Lack of value-added methods

Tang Xijin, the President of the Yunnan Chamber of International Commerce and Tricholoma Matsutake Commerce, remarked: "*In recent years, tricholoma matsutake is still only a commodity. It lacks scientific content and relies heavily on nature. The farmers (collectors) and merchants in mountainous areas all live on Heaven's produce. Tricholoma matsutake is collected and exported just as it is in the nature. That being the case, we can hardly maintain the share of Yunnan tricholoma matsutake in the international market, let alone increase production.*" The problem he raised is to the point, but there is no workable solution as yet.

On August 4, 2008, a news article on Songrong.com reads: "*According to Nikkei News, the Japanese company Takara Bio Inc. has announced its success in cultivating shiro for tricholoma matsutake. This means that tricholoma matsutake that could only be grown in wild in the past can now be cultivated artificially... the artificially cultivated tricholoma matsutake is said to be of a high grade, and aimed at the high-end market which offers a lot of value-adding opportunities.*"

IV Policy Discussions: Developing the Tricholoma Matsutake Industry

1. Suggestions related to the collection of tricholoma matsutake

(A) *Clarify ownership of tricholoma matsutake resources and emphasize the importance of protecting tricholoma matsutake among locals*

During our research, the villagers told us clearly that tricholoma matsutake resources are better protected in commune-owned forests than in state-owned forests. So what is the underlying difference? Woods in colder regions grow more slowly, therefore investments in these woods take a long time to generate returns and result in somewhat limited income. Additionally, in this region, forest ownership does not only mean the ownership of woods, but primarily the ownership of the cash crops beneath the woods. However, in state-owned forests, much attention is paid to the ownership of woods while management and protection of the cash crops is often neglected. Thus, the characteristics of the local forestry economy should be taken into account during the reform of forest ownership. The government should manage tricholoma matsutake resources, subsidiary resources and encourage local people to protect all forestry resources, including tricholoma matsutake.

(B) *Encourage and help each village to set up their own tricholoma matsutake protection organization and enhance the conservation of shiro*

It is clearly the case that in each village tricholoma matsutake is an extremely valuable resource. Commune-owned forests are a necessary condition to sustain the stocks of tricholoma matsutake. But using different methods may have a different impact on the protection of forestry resources and shiro in each and every village. We found that protection is most effective when there is an organization to manage the work. Organizations built on the basis of a "commune" can take advantage of the multiple interests of the villagers and organize them to conserve the shiro in their village.

(C) *Encourage the Office of Tricholoma Matsutake, an interdepartmental organization, to continue its role as a regulator of the industry*

In the past 20 years, the Office of Tricholoma Matsutake, made up of multiple departments, has played an important role in the regulation of tricholoma matsutake. It has helped to implement the government's tricholoma matsutake policies, collate merchants' opinions and report to the county's foreign trade department for external negotiations. In addition to their work on regulation, the Office should also help with the work of the industry association. The existing Tricholoma Matsutake Industry Association has a rather limited capacity. It is not able to launch tricholoma matsutake research or an extensive publicity campaign. This is where the Office can help to ask for support from relevant government departments.

(D) *Enhance law enforcement and eliminate existing formalism*

It is true that laws are not fully observed nor have they been strictly enforced in the past, but it is impossible to deny the legal validity of the regulations and laws on tricholoma matsutake protection. In the future, the officials should focus on changing their working patterns and enhancing law enforcement.

(E) *Diversify income sources and lower the locals' income dependence on tricholoma matsutake*

Our research found that the wealthiest households in every village did not get rich by collecting tricholoma matsutake. Those who have accumulated their wealth through the collection of tricholoma matsutake are not as well-off as those who have become rich by other means. For example, a household in one village has raised 100 cows and thus does not need to depend on the collection of tricholoma matsutake in order to generate income. If more people chose this route, the pressure on exploiting tricholoma matsutake resources would be lessened.

2. *Suggestions for protecting tricholoma matsutake resources in international trade*

(A) *Establish national standards for tricholoma matsutake products and ban the export of young tricholoma matsutake*

As indicated in the diagrams of the value chain and the institutional environment of the tricholoma matsutake industry, almost all the high-grade tricholoma matsutake products need to pass through customs before they can be exported. Therefore, phytosanitary departments and formal trading companies can serve as a means for government departments to regulate the industry. By establishing clear standards for tricholoma matsutake products, China can ensure the quality of its tricholoma matsutake and its status in the international market. In addition, by establishing export rules and implementing punitive measures against rule-breakers, government departments can stop the collection of young tricholoma matsutake to ensure the sustainable development of tricholoma matsutake stocks.

(B) *Encourage domestic export agencies to establish a price negotiation organization in order to enhance bargaining power in negotiations with Japan*

We acknowledge that Japan is the major buyer in the tricholoma matsutake market. However, as Chinese tricholoma matsutake accounts for an absolute share in the Japanese market, the Chinese government and the industry association can help to establish a unified organization to negotiate the price of tricholoma matsutake with the Japanese side and form a new pricing process.

(C) *Regulate the annual export scale and forbid disorderly competition*

In order to protect tricholoma matsutake stocks, the Chinese government and Tibetan local government can regulate the scale of tricholoma matsutake collection and export. Regulation of the scale of export can also help to form a pricing process of tricholoma matsutake that is to the advantage of the Chinese side.

Bibliography

Shangri-La Wild Food Import & Export Company, 2007, *Grading Standard for Fresh Tricholoma Matsutake*, Company Profile Booklet, http://www.songrong.com/index.htm.

Shi Yu, 2007, "Export Prices of Tricholoma Matsutake Fall Drastically in Yunnan", *China News Agency*, August 4, 2007, http://news.163.com/07/0904/02/3NGVRL0U000120GU.html, downloaded on 15 January, 2013.

Song Rong, 2007, "Grading Criteria of Fresh Tricholoma Matsutake", August 1, 2007, http://www.songrong.com/List_Show.asp?id=2103, downloaded on January 14, 2013.

CHAPTER 5

The Socioeconomic Impact of Cordyceps Sinensis Resource Management in Tibetan-Inhabited Regions of Qinghai

YAO Yu

Abstract

This chapter describes the role that cordyceps sinensis resources[1] plays in the socioeconomic development in Tibetan-inhabited areas of Qinghai Province, emphasizing the importance of protecting the eco-environment as the basis for developing the resources. Reform of the pasture contract system must be intensified in order to grant Tibetan herders resource ownership in their contract pastures as an incentive for them to protect cordyceps sinensis and the eco-environment.

Keywords: Cordyceps Sinensis; Resource Management.

With rising income levels and health awareness in China, there has been a soaring demand for immunity-enhancing health products, which are vigorously advertised by the sellers. Cordyceps sinensis, a precious Chinese herb grown in plateaus, is becoming a favored tonic

---

[1] Known in Tibetan as *yartsa gunbu* or *yatsa gunbu*, caterpillar fungi are the result of a parasitic relationship between the fungus and the larva of the ghost moth genus *Thitarodes*, several species of which live on the Tibetan Plateau (Tibet, Qinghai, western Sichuan, southwestern Gansu and northwestern Yunnan, all in China, and the Himalayas in India, Nepal, Bhutan). The fungus germinates in living organisms (in some cases the larvae), kills and mummifies the insect, and then the fungus grows from the body of the insect (http://en.wikipedia.org/wiki/Ophiocordyceps_sinensis, downloaded on 23 November, 2012).

and even regarded by some as a panacea. Known as a main area for cordyceps sinensis production, Yushu and Guoluo, both in the Tibetan Autonomous Prefectures of Qinghai, began to issue provincial regulations on the restricted collection of cordyceps sinensis in 2004. The local legislation has exerted a far-reaching influence on various processes, from the collection of the product to its sale. Our survey team developed a full understanding of the policies currently in place in the cordyceps sinensis industry and the status of policy implementation through presentations given to us by local officials, site observations and visits to individual households. This chapter provides a report on our survey.

I Cordyceps Sinensis Has Become a Major Source of Income for Local Farmers and Herders

Cordyceps sinensis is grown in alpine pastures from between 3,500 meters and 5,000 meters in altitude. Under the climatic conditions found at this altitude, farming and animal husbandry activities are extremely inefficient. Not only is crop farming difficult, but the breeding of cattle and sheep is also particularly slow. In addition, Tibetan people are not very sensitive to indexes such as the "livestock take-off rate".[2] Therefore, alternative industries were developed in order to increase the local population's income. The price of cordyceps sinensis has soared over the past decade, and thus, local farmers and herders have swarmed to collect cordyceps sinensis and even non-local laborers are attracted to this "gold rush".

Our survey uncovered that in the areas that produce cordyceps sinensis, every household has at least someone actively engaged in collecting cordyceps sinensis and whole families even stay on the mountain day and night during the harvest season, collecting cordyceps sinensis. Children are an important source of labor because of their good

---

[2] During our survey in Dari County, we were told by Mr. Qu Ning from the county's "three-river source" protection office that it takes five years for local herders to raise a calf into an adult yak. Since the end of 1970s, these local Animal Husbandry Bureaus have preferred to use the index of breeding stock over the index of livestock take-off rate in their assessments.

eyesight and quick reactions, while those people who are around 50 years of age, despite their age, also stay on the mountains to search for cordyceps sinensis. The harvesting season generally lasts for 40 days from May to June. Except for the women, who are not skilled in collecting cordyceps sinensis, and would otherwise stay home to take care of cattle and prepare food, those who are strong and active, as well as elderly men and school-age children, all go to the mountains to collect cordyceps sinensis.

In the Tibetan-inhabited areas of Yushu and Guoluo, animal husbandry provides a major source of income for the herders. The average household will raise between 20 to 30 yaks to provide food, while income from collecting cordyceps sinensis will generate almost half of a household's annual cash income.[3] For households with individuals who are healthy and strong, income from collecting cordyceps sinensis is around 30,000 *yuan* per year. For those who are less skilled at harvesting, an income of several thousand *yuan* is still achievable. According to village cadres, although more and more people are involved in harvesting cordyceps sinensis, making it less easy to find, prices are still rising and thus their income has not fallen.[4]

II Cordyceps Sinensis Trade Promoted Local Socioeconomic Development

Cordyceps sinensis is the top earner in terms of the foreign exchange in Qinghai. With an average export price of USD 6.51 million/ton,[5] it not only brings important financial revenues to Qinghai, but also opportunities for local economic development as well. This massive increase of labor in a particular region brings numerous opportunities for local businesses. In the Maqin and Dari county seats of the Guoluo Prefecture,

---

[3] See Li (2007).
[4] Zhang Shenglong from the Information Division of the Guoluo Prefecture Government participated in the work of the Caterpillar Fungus Management Office. He told us that although there were less caterpillar fungi over the last few years, the prices had increased and so herders' income has not been reduced.
[5] Sohu Health Channel (2007).

shopkeepers, tailors, grocery owners and catering operators all mentioned that there were significant business opportunities generated by gatherers of cordyceps sinensis. For non-local gatherers, they need to buy food, daily necessities and harvesting tools from the local population. Concentration of gatherers in this region also brings more business to companies and individuals offering a automobile repair service. Cordyceps sinensis buyers and traders are also the key clients for the prosperous local hotel industry. In the past, Guoluo Prefecture had limited tourism and its hospitality industry was underdeveloped. But over the past two or three years, several new hotels appeared in Dawu Town in the Maqin county seat, yet the demand generated by caterpillar traders is still not met. We were told by many caterpillar traders that they often had to rent farmers' houses for security reasons. After trading cordyceps sinensis, the harvesters will use a portion of their income on daily expenditure on new clothes and motorcycles. For non-nomadic herding villages, their biggest piece of expenditure after selling their cordyceps sinensis is to build houses.

Traders of cordyceps sinensis brought both new ways of thinking and new business opportunities. Some of them have found other local business opportunities in the process of trading, such as providing information on the livestock market. After trading cordyceps sinensis, an activity that only lasts for one or two months in a year, they will shift to trade in other goods.

While the business of cordyceps sinensis brings cash income to local farmers and herders, it has also increased their demand for external goods and services. In Dari County, there are more than 40 grocery stores run by people from the Hunan Province. When asked why they open stores in this high-altitude area, they all replied that the locals grew rich from selling cordyceps sinensis, but local commerce is very underdeveloped. They perceive the local residents as not being skilled at business, so they have come from afar to fill this gap. This narrative is consistent with conversations we have had with the local population. We were also told that there were not many shops before and that all the changes took place after the collection of cordyceps sinensis became a profitable industry.

III Challenges in This Industry

The gathering and trading of cordyceps sinensis has developed well as an industry over the past few years. However, as with all industries, it has met with its own challenges and problems, as detailed below.

1. Unclear ownership rights

Cordyceps sinensis grows on the pastures on mountains contracted by household collectives or individual households. According to some legal experts, a core and basic element to contract operation rights under China's *Rural Land Contract Law* is: *"The contractor is entitled by law to use and profit from the contracted land and has the right to independently conduct production, operation and disposal of goods."* Herders are legally entitled to use, profit from and independently control the resources in a contracted pasture. Cordyceps sinensis is a wild plant and should be included in what is defined as pasture resources. If cordyceps sinensis grows on the contracted pasture, herders should surely have the rights to use, profit from and independently control the cordyceps sinensis resources.

But in the *Detailed Provisions of Yushu Prefecture on the Implementation of Provisional Regulations on the Management of Cordyceps Sinensis and Collection in Qinghai Province* issued on January 6, 2005, it is explicitly stipulated that cordyceps sinensis resources are "state-owned". Following this regulation, the local government issued a series of local laws to pro-hibit and restrict the collection of cordyceps sinensis but failed to resolve the confusion surrounding the ownership of cordyceps sinensis. In 2005, there was a large conflict involving more than ten thousand people over a dispute relating to the gathering of cordyceps sinensis. Through our research, we have not been able to find any specific regulations relating to the ownership of cordyceps sinensis in the laws and regulations above the provincial level concerning cordyceps sinensis. In the *Provisional Regulations on the Management of Cordyceps Sinensis and Collection in Qinghai Province*, we only found vague phrases such as *"caterpillar resources are protected by state laws"*. This extremely vague definition of ownership has a profoundly negative effect on the management of caterpillar resources. For instance, over the course of the survey we had conducted, we heard incessant com-plaints from people who had to pay fees to gather cordyceps sinensis in other townships. They were doing this because there were no cordyceps sinensis to be found in their own township. They questioned the legality of the fee charging system since cordyceps sinensis is supposedly state-owned. They also complained that the pasture compensation fees that locals charge non-locals are exorbitant and vary greatly depending on whether they belonged to the person's tribe. On the whole, the fee is 1,000 *yuan* to 2,000 *yuan* for people from the same tribe but 5,000 *yuan* and in some cases even as much as 7,000 *yuan* for people from external tribes for the use of the same pasture. If a local household has rich entomophyte resources in its pasture, it will have a larger number of complaints and members may question the following: On what basis does the Herders' Committee bring outsiders to work on my pasture lands? How come the pasture compensation fees are evenly distributed among households, despite the varying amounts of caterpillar resources on their pastures?

Local government departments who work on issues associated with cordyceps sinensis in Maqin County and Dari County told us that they believe the caterpillar resources are owned by the government. Thus, they can issue local legislation to restrict non-locals from harvesting cordyceps sinensis and punish poachers and those who violate the harvesting regulations. In addition, the county and township governments have the right to distribute caterpillar compensation fees collected by the Herders' Committee. Because the local governments already receive sufficient fees from the Herders' Committee, they are not incentivized, and indeed lack the motivation to collect further taxes. This is not helped by the difficulties of collecting taxes from the collection of cordyceps sinensis in the first place.

2. Market speculations

Cordyceps sinensis has been gathered since ancient times, but why has its collection become such a topical issue in recent times? The main reason is of course, the soaring price of the product. We were not able to find accurate statistics on the price of cordyceps sinensis over time. In our survey, we asked harvesters of different age groups and gained a rough understanding of the changes to cordyceps sinensis prices over the past decades.

The left side of Table 1 shows the primary transaction prices in the areas where cordyceps sinensis is grown. In the main areas where cordyceps

Table 1: Prices of Cordyceps Sinensis Over Time.

Time	Producing area		Sales market	
	Location	Cordyceps sinensis price	Location	Cordyceps sinensis price
1960s	Tibet	One kilogram of cordyceps sinensis could be exchanged for two packets of cigarettes each worth about 30 cents RMB.		
1970s	Qinghai	One kilogram is traded at 21 *yuan* (state purchase price).		
Late 1970s	Yunnan	50 pieces of fresh cordyceps sinensis are traded at 50 cents RMB.		
Late 1970s and early 1980s	Tibet	Five to six *yuan* per 500 grams (the purchase price of a pharmaceutical company in the autonomous region).		
End of 1980s	South Tibet	A piece of garlic could be exchanged for a piece of cordyceps sinensis.		
Early 1990s	South Tibet	Cordyceps sinensis cost about ten *yuan* per 500g. Additional amounts could be given for free if bought from households.		

(Continued)

Table 1: (*Continued*)

Time	Producing area		Sales market	
	Location	Cordyceps sinensis price	Location	Cordyceps sinensis price
1995			Sales market in the eastern region	Around 2,000 *yuan* per kg.
2003			Sales market in the eastern region	The lowest grade of cordyceps sinensis traded at more than 30,000 *yuan* per kg after SARS.
2004	Original producing area in Qinghai	About 2,000 pieces of cordyceps sinensis were traded at 49,000 *yuan* per kg; about 2,500 pieces of cordyceps sinensis was traded at 41,000 *yuan.* per kg; and 3,000 pieces of cordyceps sinensis were sold at over 33,500 *yuan* per kg.		
2005			TCM pharmacy in Beijing and Jinan	Increased from 220 *yuan* to 340 *yuan* per 5 g (lowest grade)

(*Continued*)

Table 1: (Continued)

| Time | Producing area | | Sales market | |
	Location	Cordyceps sinensis price	Location	Cordyceps sinensis price
2006			TCM wholesale market in Guangzhou	About 2,000 pieces of cordyceps sinensis were traded at 100,000 yuan per kg. This was a wholesale price. In December 2006, the price went up by 30–40% or more than 10,000 yuan in a single month.
2006			Retail sales market in Guangzhou	Second grade product was sold at 70–120 yuan per g; first grade product was sold at 130 yuan per g; and top grade product was sold at 269 yuan per g.
2007	Yunnan	80,000 yuan per kg.		
2007	Qinghai	More than 80,000 yuan per kg.	Retail sales market in the eastern region	140,000 yuan per kg. Top grade cordyceps sinensis traded at nearly 300,000 yuan per kg.
2007	Naqu	The standard price for 2,400 pieces of product was 100,000 yuan per kg.		

Sources: 1. People's Daily (2012); 2. Some information provided by senior engineer Yuan Zhengdong from the Forestry Bureau of Shangri-La County, Diqing Prefecture; 3. Information collected by the author.

sinensis is sold, which include China's coastal areas in the southeast and Southeast Asian countries, the prices are 4,000 *yuan* higher than the wholesale prices in the areas where the product is grown.[6] Over the course of completing our survey, we were told that the price was already more than 80,000 *yuan* per kg. But in large cities such as Beijing, Nanjing and Guangzhou, cordyceps sinensis trades at more than 100,000 *yuan* per kg.[7] It is fair to say that the price of cordyceps sinensis is the highest it has ever been. Guangdong is the biggest cordyceps sinensis market in China, and accounts for more than half of the total national consumption. It is thus believed by some that price changes in Guangdong are a barometer which can be used to understand any likely trends in prices across the country.[8]

Soaring cordyceps sinensis prices are a result of an imbalance between supply and demand in recent years. With increasing income levels and living standards, people are paying more attention to their health. As a precious traditional tonic, cordyceps sinensis is increasingly in demand, but its output is dependent on the "forces of nature". So, the general trend over the years has been for prices to rise. Meanwhile, some manufacturers of health products have exaggerated the effects of cordyceps sinensis. They have described the product as a panacea that can improve your immunity, cure SARS, fight cancer, improve male potency, improve one's complexion, inhibit AIDS, and so on. These exaggerated advertisements have helped to fuel the irrational boom in prices already present in the cordyceps sinensis market.[9,10]

---

[6] Wen *et al.* (2004).

[7] In 2007, low-grade old stock traded at 70,000 *yuan* per kg in cities like Beijing, Shanghai and Nanjing.

[8] Zhang (2007).

[9] In the *Supplement to Compendium of Materia Medica* (1765), the Qing Dynasty medical expert Zhao Xuemin also recorded that caterpillar fungus has the same function with ginseng and can cure Qi deficiency and replenish Yin and Yang.

[10] According to modern pharmacology, caterpillar fungus in Qinghai contains 7% cordycepic acid, 25% protein and about 8.4% fat, of which 82.2% are unsaturated fatty acids that are necessary but cannot be synthesized by the human body, and 28.9% carbohydrates. There are 12 types of free amino acids, and 18 types of hydrolyzed amino acid liquids, which include all 8 types of amino acids that are essential for adults and can be acquired from food intake. Other elements include vitamin complex B12, fungisterol, hexose, bio-alkaline, etc. (Xie and Yu, 1996).

Cordyceps sinensis has been transformed from a form of medicine to a health product, and it is now being marketed as a luxury item. The price of this product has completely exceeded that of comparable medicinal products.

There are two other possible reasons for the soaring prices of cordyceps sinensis. The first reason is that the opening of the Qinghai–Tibet Railway has led to a massive increase in sales, and has brought numerous tourists to Qinghai and Tibet whose primary purpose is to purchase cordyceps sinensis. The tourists were more than happy to buy this local specialty. Another version of events is that the real estate speculators in Wenzhou shifted to the speculation around the cordyceps sinensis market. However, both versions lack verifiable evidence.

3. Diminishing cordyceps sinensis resources

Will rampant gathering cause damage to cordyceps sinensis resources? Over the course of conducting our survey, we heard two distinct answers. The first suggests that there would not be any damage, because cordyceps sinensis will become rotten if it is not dug out of the ground and its growth is free from human control. In the same pasture, it is quite possible for cordyceps sinensis to grow in one place this year and another next year. But some old villagers and cadres think that the output of cordyceps sinensis has declined markedly over the last ten years. A native township cadre told me that they used to be able to find cordyceps sinensis at altitudes below 3,800 meters.[11] But, nowadays it is impossible to find any growing at such an altitude. He felt there were two underlying reasons. The first was the effects of global warming, but the second was rampant harvesting. In order to sell more cordyceps sinensis, locals began to collect it before it had matured.

---

[11] According to Mr. Ma Fuliang, Party Secretary of Xialaxiu Township in Yushu County, in present days, we cannot find any fungus in the places where it used to be, and the altitude of distribution is increasing.

We gathered information on how the annual output of cordyceps sin-ensis changed over time (see Table 2). In the survey, we also asked har-vesters of different age groups to recall the difficulty of harvesting, with a record of their replies below (Table 3).

Table 2: Changing Output of Cordyceps Sinensis in China.

Year	Output of cordyceps sinensis in China
1950s	More than 200 tons
Early 1960s	More than 150 tons
1990s	Down to around 80 tons
Today	80–100 tons

Sources: 1. Zhang (2007); 2. Collected by the author of the survey.

We learned over the course of a survey we conducted in June and July that another survey had been conducted on the main areas that produce cordyceps sinensis in Tibet, Qinghai, Sichuan, Gansu and Yunnan. The survey was conducted by a team whose members are a part of the Xishuan

Table 3: Difficulty of Gathering Cordyceps Sinensis Over Time.

Year	Difficulty
1970s	The record high was 102 pieces of cordyceps sinensis in one square meter, and one person could harvest between 600 and 800 pieces a day.
End of 1970s and early 1980s	A primary school student could harvest between 400 and 800 pieces a day.[12]
1980s	Each herder could harvest at least five kilograms and up to dozens of kilograms, over the course of the harvest season.
1990s	Those who are capable could harvest between 300–500 pieces per day.[13]
Today	Those who are lucky can harvest more than 100 pieces a day, and it would be classified as a very good day if you harvested over 40 pieces.[14]

Source: Information collected by author during the course of the survey.

---

[12] Information provided by Mr. Qu Ning from the Three-River Source Protection Office, Dari County.

[13] Information from Tibetan E Ni during a survey in the Maqin County.

[14] General beliefs of Tibetans gleaned from our household visits during our survey.

Banna Tropical Botanic Garden (Chinese Academy of Sciences). The survey team compared their results with information from 25 years ago and found that in most regions, the output of cordyceps sinensis is less than 10% of that found 25 years ago. Moreover, they were unable to locate any cordyceps sinensis in 40% of the areas that used to be very rich in these resources.[15]

4. Negative impacts on the local eco-environment

Harvesting cordyceps sinensis has indeed brought about certain negative impacts on local agricultural production and animal husbandry. Prior to the harvest period, some people arrived in the collection area as much as two months in advance, erected tents and trampled on the grassland. Harvesters also cut down the limited shrubbery on the plateau, generated a lot of domestic waste, and polluted the environment, damaging the fragile ecology of the pasture lands.

Cordyceps sinensis grows deep under the earth. According to local harvesting rules, after cordyceps sinensis is uprooted, the hole in the ground must be filled with mud and dirt. However, non-local harvesters have never followed this rule. Harvesting only one piece of cordyceps sinensis will damage at least 30 square millimeters of turf, while a much larger turf area would be damaged by vehicles. Damage to the vegetation and the holes left in the ground by thousands of people have accelerated soil erosion in the plateau, especially in the rainy season.

According to local technicians, every year there are some 100,000 non-locals who come to harvest cordyceps sinensis in the "three-river source" protection zone. Each person has the capacity to harvest six to ten pieces a day, over the course of 50 days approximately. Roughly 80,000 to 108,000 square meters of turf are damaged each year. The areas that are affected by trampling and cars have a much higher figure. So, in conclusion, there are a few hundred thousands of square meters of pasture lands damaged each year.[16]

---

[15] Wen (2007).

5. An imperfect institutional environment for the protection of cordyceps sinensis

In 2004, the Qinghai Provincial government issued the following regulation, *Interim Regulations on the Management of Cordyceps Sinensis Collection in Qinghai Province*. The regulation stated that in order to protect cordyceps sinensis, the provincial departments of agriculture and animal husbandry should formulate provincial plans for the protection of cordyceps sinensis in light of the findings of the survey. Moreover, competent authorities in charge of cordyceps sinensis at the prefecture and county level should develop local protection plans in line with the provincial plans and together with the relevant departments. The authorities should submit these plans to the same level of people's government, and file a record of their plans with a higher authority in charge of agriculture and animal husbandry. The protection plans should identify the distribution regions, areas and suitable collection areas of cordyceps sinensis. It should also identify pastures with fragile eco-environments, which should be classified as areas where the collection of cordyceps sinensis is prohibited. Annual plans, both on the protection of the pasture lands and the collection of cordyceps sinensis, should have a scientific and rational method for identifying those regions and areas which can be used for harvesting. It should also specify the number of gatherers, the collection period and the areas which are prohibited.

However, there is no statistical information on the quantity of cordyceps sinensis which is collected, nor the number of transactions. Additionally, the distribution of cordyceps sinensis is very difficult to predict. Thus, the above regulations have no realistic relevance in terms of implementation.

So what is the actual situation? During the season when cordyceps sinensis is collected, non-local gatherers swarm to the cordyceps sinensis producing areas, far outnumbering the local households (local gatherers

---

[16] According to the Qinghai News Network (2007), relevant officials with Agricultural and Environmental Commission of the Provincial People's Congress believe that 100,000 *mu* of pasture mountains are damaged each year.

and owners). In order to avoid conflict over the gathering of the product, local governments have all developed systems to prohibit non-locals from harvesting in their jurisdictions. In 2005, a system in which a collection certificate was required for the gathering of cordyceps sinensis, was put in place. This allowed non-locals to enter the producing areas, after they had paid a pasture compensation fee (this fee was normally between 1,000 and 2,000 RMB, but in reality, the difference in cost could be quite substantial, and in some cases non-local harvesters were required to pay as much as 8,000 RMB). From 2006, all non-locals were prohibited from entering the producing areas. Local farmers and herders in non-producing areas were also subject to certain conditions that restricted their access.

However, these regulations are basically disregarded once the collectors enter an area that has cordyceps sinensis. Competition among collectors, trespassing and unlicensed collection are common occurences and pose a serious threat to social stability.

In order to control the non-local population during the harvest season, the county government needs to dispatch a greater number of officials to set up barricades, as well as search and fine non-locals for violations of the code. In a recent harvest season alone, Maqin County mobilized more than 400 cadres to barricade the affected areas and to ensure that the restrictions are followed. Over 1,000 people from the county were involved in this effort. During this period, all the other work in the county and township came to a halt.

IV Policy Recommendations on the Development of the Cordyceps Sinensis Industry

1. *The need to create an industry development plan and protect the plateau's ecology*

Any development plan aimed at resolving the problems inherent in the caterpillar industry should first try to clarify the relationship between the cordyceps sinensis industry and the sustainable development of the plateau's pasture lands and local ecology — this industry is highly dependent on the sustainable development of the plateau. In some sense, protection of the plateau's pasture lands and local ecology will in turn help to protect the cordyceps sinensis resources. However, given the rampant development of the cordyceps sinensis industry, we believe that it is necessary for producing areas to protect the plateau's pasture lands in terms of its ecology and reduce excessive collection. Only on the premise of sound ecological and pasture development will the industry maintain a sufficient stock of cordyceps sinensis.

2. Deepen and further clarify the reform of pasture ownership

As it is a main source of income for farmers and herders in Qinghai Province, there should be legal clarification that caterpillar fungi are owned by local farmers and herders. According to the *Detailed Provisions of Yushu Prefecture on the Implementation of Provisional Regulations on the Management of Cordyceps Sinensis Collection in Qinghai Province*, pasture contract rights are protected by law and cannot be violated by any organization or individual. If someone wants to collect herbs or cut down shrubbery, they must have the prior consent of the owners of the pasture land. Plateau pastures where cordyceps sinensis grows are all contracted to the herders. According to the contract between the herders and the government, herders have the right to possess, use and profit from the pasture resources. This of course includes the cordyceps sinensis which grows on the pastures. When developing local legislation on the management of cordyceps sinensis, prefecture and county governments must follow correct ownership structures and issue policies that provide protection, rather than depriving farmers and herders of their ownership of cordyceps sinensis which is found on their own pasture lands.

Given the contradiction between regulations which protect cordyceps sinensis and pasture contract operation rights, we must first respect the lawful rights of pasture contractors and manage the collection, sales and purchase of cordyceps sinensis by law in accordance with the *Regulations on the Protection of Wild Plants*. For the collection, sale and distribution of cordyceps sinensis, local farmers and herders should also have to apply for purchase licenses.

3. Regulate the advertising market and develop alternative industries

The collection of cordyceps sinensis is still the the main source of income for farmers and herders in Qinghai Province. However, it is becoming increasingly rare. In order to ensure the sustainable development of the industry, we need to create a market based on rational consumption. Despite certain positive effects on the lungs, kidneys, heart, blood pressure and the body's general immune system, the medicinal effects of cordyceps sinensis have been greatly exaggerated in advertisements. Medical experts note that despite the enhancement effect on the immune system, the medicinal mechanism of cordyceps sinensis is very complex, and it is impossible to heal illnesses through the consumption of one or two specimens. Health and improvements to the immune system can be realized through a number of ways such as physical exercise, and cordyceps sinensis is not the only option. In future, the press and advertisement authorities should tighten supervision on advertisements that carry incorrect messages and correct the public's understanding of the benefits of cordyceps sinensis.

On the other hand, artificial planting technology should be encouraged to reduce the pressures on the ecology of the plateau, which has been brought about by the collection of cordyceps sinensis. There are two alternatives: epigamous artificial breeding and asexual breeding. As the former is difficult to implement, most research institutions and professionals have focused on asexual breeding. In the 19 provinces and municipalities including Beijing, Jilin, Shanxi and Shanghai, there are research bases for the fermentation culture and solid culture of mycelium and conidiome as epigamous substitutes of cordyceps sinensis. Some producers have already started mass production of these substitutes. If cordyceps sinensis really has great medicinal value, there should be a lot of potential in the market for its synthetic substitutes.

4. Design protection systems for cordyceps sinensis resources and develop other avenues for income growth

My opinion is that all of the institutions engaged in protecting cordyceps sinensis should comply with this principle: Ensure sustainable income growth for local farmers and herders while protecting the local eco-environment and natural resources. It can be assumed that if the locals find other opportunities to increase their income, the pressures on collecting cordyceps sinensis will be reduced. In the survey, we found that Guoluo and Yushu's prefecture governments have been proactively directing local people to develop other industries. The Yushu Prefecture has made great efforts to develop tourism and has already achieved positive results.

Bibliography

Chen Shijiang, Zhang Guoyue, Ma Kaisen, 2006, "Reflections and Recommendations on the Sustainable Utilization of Precious Cordyceps Sinensis Resources", *Chongqing Journal of Research on Chinese Drugs and Herbs*, 54(2), 8–10.

Guoluo Prefecture Government, 2007, *Opinions on the Protection and Management of Cordyceps Sinensis Resources in Guoluo Prefecture*, February.

Li Wen, 2007, "Caterpillar Fungus Becomes a Main Source of Income for Tibetan Farmers and Herders", *Xinhua Net (Tibet Channel)*, May 17, 2007, http://www.gov.cn/jrzg/2007-05/17/content_617577.htm, downloaded on November 23, 2012.

Liu Zhaohong, Li Yuling, 2006, "Distribution of Cordyceps Sinensis Resources in Yushu Prefecture", *Pasture Resources*, 133(12), 34–36.

Mou Jingliang, Zhu Huiyin, 2005, "Legal Analysis on Cordyceps Sinensis Collection", *Fang Yuan Fa Zhi*, 13, 3.

People's Daily, 2007, "Expensive Cordyceps Sinensis Increases Local Incomes But Worsens Plateau Ecology", May 18, 2007, http://health.people.com.cn/GB/14740/22121/5747553.html, downloaded on November 23, 2012.

Qinghai News Network, 2007, "Rampant Harvesting Damages 100,000 mu of Pasture Mountain", May 23, 2007, http://qh.news.163.com/07/0523/08/3F5QM48I005800B0.html#, downloaded on November 23, 2012.

Qinghai Provincial Government, 2004, *Interim Regulations on the Management of Cordyceps Sinensis Collection in Qinghai Province*, November.

Sohu Health Channel, 2007, "Good and Bad News in the Import/Export of China's TCM Goods", August 8, 2007, http://health.sohu.com/20070808/n251483466.shtml, downloaded on November 23, 2012.

Tibetan Autonomous Region Government, 2006, *Interim Regulations on the Management of Cordyceps Sinensis Collection in the Tibetan Autonomous Region*, April.

Wen Yiwei, 2007, "Scientists Believe Caterpillar Fungus is Under A Man-Made Disaster", Xinhua.com.cn, July 26, 2007, http://www.ce.cn/cysc/cysczh/200707/26/t20070726_12322589.shtml, downloaded 23 November, 2012.

Wen Yiwei, Yang Shoude, Jiang Chenrong, 2004, "Expensive Caterpillar Fungus Brings 100,000 Harvesters, Threatening 'Three-River Source'", CCTV, August 16, 2004, http://www.cctv.com/news/china/20040816/102171.shtml, downloaded on November 23, 2012.

Xie Zongwan, Yu Youqin, 1996, *National Compendium of Chinese Herbal Medicine*, Beijing: People's Health Press.

Yu Qian, 2003, "Kingdom of Cordyceps Sinensis", *Tibetan Literature*, October, 124–132.

Zhang Jinghua, 2007, "Rational Thinking on Cordyceps Sinensis Mania", *Guangming Daily*, January 31, 2007, http://www.gmw.cn/content/2007-01/31/content_543758.htm, downloaded on November 23, 2012.

CHAPTER 6

Impoverishment Risks Caused by the Ecological Resettlement Project

JIN Chengwu

Abstract

Having conducted field research on the ecological resettlement of Tibetan villages in Qinghai, this chapter found that ecological re-settlers face significant risks of impoverishment in host communities, as they can no longer work and live in ways that they are used to, and once they join these host communities their earning capacity is in fact worsened. The risks of impoverishing this group of people can in fact undermine efforts to protect the land. Moreover, such approaches may pose new challenges to poverty alleviation work in Tibetan areas, and thus merit further attention. On the basis of our findings, this author recommends that in addition to financial compensation to populations displaced by the ecological resettlement project, investing in the human resources of these populations (i.e. both adults and children) is extremely important for ecological re-settlers to improve their earning capacity in the host communities and to integrate into their new urban environment.

Keywords: Ecological Resettlement Project; Impoverishment Risks; Tibetan Areas.

The author would like to thank Prof Jiang Zhongyi, Prof Li Shi, Prof Meng Xianfan and other scholars for their valuable comments and advice on this chapter.

I Background of the Research Project

From early to mid July 2007, the Research Team of the Chinese Academy of Social Sciences (CASS), of which the author is a member, conducted a comprehensive survey on the work and life of local Tibetan farmers and herders in Maqin County and Dari County of the Guoluo Tibetan Autonomous Prefecture, and Yushu County and Chengduo County of the Yushu Tibetan Autonomous Prefecture; all found in Qinghai. The main theme of this survey was poverty alleviation and development for Tibetan farmers and herders found in alpine areas and at the sources of large rivers.

Poverty in China derives from multiple causes.[1] The risks of impoverishment, caused by ecological resettlement projects, are a special type of poverty-inducing factor in the Tibetan areas of Qinghai Province, which is a key focus of this survey. During the process of resettlement from their original pastures to host communities, some ecological re-settlers face significant risks of impoverishment in their new host communities (relative to original inhabitants of the host communities), although it is not necessarily the case that they have now been impoverished to the extent that they are on the poverty line. This is because they can no longer work and live in ways that they are used to and their earning capacity in these new communities is in fact worsened. This chapter aims to discuss the risks of impoverishment associated with the ecological resettlement project.

This survey includes the sources and upstream areas of China's three major rivers: the Yangtze River, the Yellow River and the Lancang River. The areas are high in altitude, and have a harsh climate, complex terrains, frequent natural disasters and a vulnerable ecological system. For instance, Guoluo Prefecture has an average altitude of over 4,200 meters, with annual precipitation of 400 millimeters to 700 millimeters, as well as an annual mean temperature of −4 °C. Over the course of the year, there is no

---

[1] According to Sen (1999), poverty can be understood as the deprivation of capabilities, while low income only has instrumental significance. However, considering the important relationship between income and capabilities, especially the relationship between changes in income and changes in the capabilities of ecological re-settlers, this chapter approaches poverty mainly from the perspective of income.

period in which the area is frost free and the atmospheric oxygen content is only 60% of that found at sea level. The Prefecture has a total population of 153,600 (including 119,400 herders), of whom 90.95% are Tibetan. Of the 30 autonomous prefectures in China, Guoluo Prefecture has the highest altitude, the worst climatic conditions, and the harshest natural environment; it is the most backward in terms of socioeconomic development, and has the highest proportion of people who are ethnically Tibetan.[2]

Apparently, compared with other poverty-affected regions in China, improving poverty alleviation and tackling development in these areas is a particularly challenging task. While it is important to concentrate on the goal of improving the earning capacity and living standards for all ethnic groups (the majority still being Tibetan), we must not lose sight of the powerful external impact of various human activities in this region. The river basins of the Yangtze River, Yellow River and Lancang River (the "Three Rivers") cover in total 2.76 million square kilometers in China, or more than 28.7% of China's land area, covering 23 Chinese provinces (autonomous regions or municipalities) and five other countries.[3] It would be a terrible decision to try and secure economic growth at the expense of damage to the vulnerable local eco-systems. This is because the improvement of living standards would not only be unsustainable, it would also have a catastrophic impact on the territories downstream (be it territories in other parts of China or in other countries).

---

[2] Guoluo Prefecture Government (2007).

[3] According to the *2004 Communiqué on Water Resources in the Yangtze River Basin and Rivers in the Southwest* (http://www.cws.net.cn/cwsnet/gazette/changjiang/2004/1.html, downloaded on September 10, 2007), Yangtze River Basin covers an area of 1.8 million square kilometers, crossing 19 provinces, autonomous regions and municipalities. According to the *2005 Communiqué on Water Resources of the Yellow River* (http://www.yellowriver.gov.cn/other/hhgb/2005.htm, downloaded on September 10, 2007), the Yellow River basin has an area of 795,000 square kilometers, crossing nine provinces and municipalities. According to the Yunnan Channel on Xinhua.com (http://www.yn.xinhuanet.com/topic/2005-06/29/content_4536173.htm, downloaded on September 10, 2007), Lancang River has a basin area of 164,800 square kilometers in China, crossing only three provinces (autonomous regions) and six countries (known as Mekong once it leaves China's borders).

Over the past few decades, large-scale degradation and desertification have occurred in the pastures of the Three-River Source. This has happened in part because of the natural climate, but some of the change is also a result of human activity.

Glaciers, snow mountains, lakes and wetlands have been retreating and have even dried up in some cases. Wildlife habitats have been damaged, bio-diversity reduced, the eco-environment has been degraded, and the capacity to conserve water has been diminished for many areas. These phenomena have seriously affected the eco-security of the Three Rivers' basins and even other parts of China, threatening local economic sustainability.[4] Within the Three-River Source, 125,000 square kilometers of pasture lands have been severely degraded. This area accounts for 58% of the region's usable pasture lands. Moreover, there are 28,000 kilometers of seriously degraded black soil, which accounts for 15% of all arable pasture lands. Fairly severe soil erosion (defined as above medium severity) has affected 96,200 square kilometers of land, which accounts for 26.5% of the total land area in this region. Around 15%–20% of all species (both plants and animals) in this area are under threat. This is 5% higher than the world average.[5] The importance of protecting the eco-environment in the Three-River Source is self-evident.

In order to protect the local environment and raise living standards, starting in 2003, Qinghai Province has carried out the "Three-River Source Ecological Resettlement Project". One of its key goals is to return grazing land to pasture land and restore its former ecological makeup. Ecological re-settlers from Maduo County of the Guoluo Prefecture and Changmahe Township of the Maqin County have been resettled in Heyuan New Village and Qinyuan New Village in the Maqin County, Guoluo Prefecture (the two villages this survey focuses on). According to the plans laid out for each of these villages, Heyuan New Village will receive "permanent re-settlers", who no longer hold a contract over the land from which they have migrated from and will not be returning there. In Qinyuan New Village, they will receive "temporary re-settlers", who still have some rights over the land they left and may still return to those

---

[4] Refer to the report by the Qinghai Provincial Government (2007).
[5] Cui (2007).

lands at a later date. Both of the new resettlement villages are located in the suburbs, several kilometers away from the Maqin county seat. The houses and courtyards have been built through state funding and are available to the re-settlers free of charge.

The necessity of setting up an ecological resettlement project is undeniable, especially given the need to restore and protect the vulnerable eco-environment in the Three-River Source area, where the ecological conditions continue to worsen. However, we should note that ecological re-settlers of this project used to live in the remote and high-altitude upstream regions of the Yellow River, and that most of them are Tibetan in terms of their ethnicity and have had little contact with people from outside of their communities. Additionally, their daily work and their lives revolve around animal husbandry and gathering. Once the re-settlers had begun their new life in their new homes, they had to change their ways of working and living. However, many of them were not able to adapt to their new socioeconomic environment, either in the short term or long term. Not only did they lack the experience and skills of other trades beyond husbandry, they were also not able to learn and master new skills that were necessary for a successful life in their new environment, because of their own shortcomings. Thus, they found it very hard to make a living, and were very vulnerable to the risks of becoming impoverished in these new host communities. In addition, such risks also resulted in other socioeconomic problems which require a greater degree of understanding.

Taking the above analysis into consideration, this chapter focuses on examining the risks of impoverishment associated with the ecological resettlement project in the surveyed region. It investigates the changes in the lives of the settlers once they have moved to their new host communities and the socioeconomic effects of the resettlement projects, as well as attempts to identify possible improvements to resettlement policies, which are compatible with the resettlement project.

II Livelihood Changes Facing Ecological Re-settlers

Resettlement is an inevitable outcome of social development and also presents socioeconomic problems that need to be addressed by all countries as they develop. In general, resettlement falls into two categories: voluntary resettlement and involuntary resettlement. It is apparent that the re-settlers of the Three-River Source ecological resettlement project are involuntary re-settlers. Hu Jing has made a number of detailed research pieces summarizing involuntary resettlement.[6] Her summaries include the following types of research: (1) Research on the involuntary resettlement of peoples from an economic point of view; (2) Analysis of the institutional background of resettlement in terms of project planning and the decision-making mechanisms in place, as well as a discussion on how to improve the resettlement systems in relation to specific resettlement projects; (3) Research on the resettlement of involuntary migrants; (4) Research on the compensation associated with involuntary resettlement. This part of her research includes a cost-benefit analysis of resettlement, evaluation of the losses incurred as a result of resettlement, the methods and standards of compensation for re-settlers, and understanding the benefits these re-settlers receive from various projects. These studies have provided a useful reference point for this chapter.

The World Bank's website states: "*Involuntary displacement can be caused by environmental degradation, natural disasters, conflicts or development projects. It is associated with loss of housing, shelter, income, land, livelihoods, assets, resources and services, among other things.*"[7] According to research done by the World Bank, resettlement projects may have a series of impacts on re-settlers, such as the destruction of their system of production, a loss of work-related income sources, a weakened rural organizational structure and social relationship networks, the scattering of whole families, a loss of distinctive local cultures, as well as an end to traditional social structures and a breakdown of mutual assistance networks.[8]

We have found from our survey that the ecological resettlement project has also brought about some similar consequences. However, it also has a unique impact on the livelihood of re-settlers, given the distinct

---

[6]Refer to Hu (2007).

[7]The World Bank (2011).

[8]Cernea, Michael M, 1996, *Resettlement and Development*, Nanjing: Hehai University Press. Referenced from Shi *et al.* (2009).

natural and social environment of surveyed region. We will use the following cases to show the changes that took place after the implementation of the resettlement project.

Case 1 Family A of the Heyuan New Village

The four members of Family A are all of Tibetan ethnicity. Mr. A was born in December 1955 and his wife (from his second marriage) was born in February 1975. They have a son who was born in May 1979 and a daughter who was born in March 1998. Family A resettled from the Requ Animal Husbandry Cooperative in the Huanghe Township (Maduo County, Guoluo Prefecture), into Heyuan New Village (Dawu Town, Maqin County). According to the plans associated with the resettlement project, Heyuan New Village receives permanent re-settlers, i.e. re-settlers that do not have the option to return to their homes, as it has been decided that the eco-environment in their original lands needs to be protected over the long run. The government had already built resettlement housing for all re-settlers, before Family A moved to the Heyuan New Village. The allocation of this housing was determined by the government, according to the order of registration of all the households. In the words of Mr. A, "Whichever house you have been allocated, you have to accept it. You have no right to choose." In addition, the first 20 households to resettle into the new village were given the additional incentive of getting housing with warm sheds.

For the three years prior to being resettled, Mr. A was a driver for Maduo County Hospital. He was a temporary staff, and his salary was 225 yuan per month. Some time later, he became a temporary driver for the Maduo County State Tax Bureau, earning a monthly salary of 390 yuan (with a daily allowance of 10.5 yuan for travel to and from Xining City, the capital of Qinghai Province). According to Mr. A, he was forced to leave the State Tax Bureau due to a new policy that prohibits government departments from hiring temporary staff like him. In order to make a living, he found a job as an automechanic in Maduo County. He learned how to drive by himself many years ago, and when he started driving, he drove government cars for the most part. In 2005, before his family was resettled, he bought a second-hand minibus which cost him 4,000 yuan and then, in 2006, he sold it for 3,000 yuan. After selling the old minibus, he bought a new minibus for 34,000 yuan. His rationale was simple: After his family was resettled, he wanted to ensure he could earn some income through driving.

Before they were resettled, Family A raised between 40 and 50 cattle and about 150 to 160 sheep. Grazing was their main source of income. After the resettlement, the family could no longer graze cattle on their original lands, as the policy forbade such action. Unfortunately, the new village did not offer them any additional pasture lands either. So, their only option was to sell their cattle and sheep. In order to maintain livelihood in the new village, Family A opened a grocery store in their house. They used the minibus to transport passengers in the vicinity of Maqin County (for which they charged two yuan per passenger). As Mr. A puts it, "Now, as I grow older and sicker, I am no longer fit to dig caterpillar fungus and no one is willing to hire me. In order for me to make money, my only option is to open this store and be a self-employed driver." Because the new village already has two or three grocery stores, and the customers are mainly re-settlers, his business is not flourishing.

At the end of April or early May each year, the Maduo County Animal Husbandry Bureau dispenses 8,000 yuan to each re-settler to cover the costs of resettlement. So far this fee has been given out for two years (2005 and 2006). But Mr. A is not clear about how long they will continue to provide these funds. He heard that it will be dispensed for five to ten years at most.

While talking about the changes to their livelihood after resettlement to the new village, Mr. A and his wife both sighed, summing up their new predicament with this statement: "Everything is so expensive now, and what used to be free now costs us money." Mr. A only attended the first year of elementary school and his wife received no schooling whatsoever. The whole family used to live a nomadic life, living off animal husbandry; they cannot speak much Putonghua (Chinese). After moving to the new village, they no longer live off animal husbandry and now live at a fixed residence, but it is hard for them to find a job that can give them their original level of income.

In addition to providing a short-trip transport service via their minibus, the couple undertook miscellaneous work occasionally at the prefecture's textiles plant. Some of these jobs in the prefecture involve cleaning, while others involve driving cars or tractors. They commented at the time, "We do as much work as our strength permits." However, these temporary jobs only bring them a low and unstable source of income. They have never undertaken the task of collecting caterpillar fungus, and are not skilled at it. If they did decide that collecting caterpillar fungus would be a good source of income, they would need to pay a fee of several thousand yuan to the owner of the pasture land (the fee can be as much as five to six thousand and at least two or three thousand yuan, with the final figure decided through face-to-face negotiations with the land owner). As complete strangers to the area, they have no real opportunity to make money from collecting caterpillar fungus.

Their son studied at the law schools in Maduo County and Xining City, and passed the higher education self-study examinations for an associate degree. He currently teaches Chinese and Tibetan languages at the vocational school and the elementary school of Heihe Township, Maduo County. His monthly salary is 500 yuan and he receives an additional 1,000 yuan from his family. Although this is a temporary teaching post, it took him more than a year to find it and he has been teaching for over a month now. As a result of studying for years, he now suffers from myopia. Even though he managed to obtain a diploma, he is unable to do any manual work, such as digging for caterpillar fungus or grazing animals. Their daughter is now in her second year of elementary school and also needs money. In 2006, the mother had to have an appendicitis operation at the prefecture hospital. This cost around seven to eight thousand yuan, taking into account various expenses.

In the past, the family did not need to pay for any by-products of animal husbandry such as beef, cow leather, cow hair, cow dung, milk, mutton, sheepskin, and wool. But now they need to spend money on buying these goods as they no longer raise cattle and sheep themselves. "Prices are increasing too fast in the city," Mr. A said with a sigh. He explained that now pork, beef and mutton all cost around 24 yuan per kg, but it used to be less than 18 yuan per kg; butter now costs 24 yuan per kg, milk 6 yuan per kg, coal 0.6 yuan per kg, and cow dung 10 yuan per bag (a bag of dung can burn for two to three days). With the rise in the price of meat, it is now the case that the family lives mainly on rice and wheat, rather than meat, as they did before. In addition, food and clothing are much more expensive in the city, so the family feels that the resettlement fee of 8,000 yuan per year is insufficient. Mr. A remarks, "I'm afraid of urbanites talking about the rising salaries, because once there is talk, everything becomes more expensive, even before salaries actually rise." With little increase in the amount of money they earn each year, the whole family is very sensitive to price changes. They currently owe over 20,000 yuan, of which 30% is borrowed from private individuals, and the rest is a loan from a credit cooperative.

Almost all of the re-settlers in Heyuan New Village used to lead nomadic lives, so it is often the case that they are now "unfamiliar with the neighbors", even though they might have moved here from the same township.

In 2005, Family A participated in the new rural cooperative medical system in the Maduo County, and received a medical certificate. However, they were "a little unclear about how to use this certificate" and "participated in the system simply because all the others did". After moving to the new village, Family A encountered a rather acute problem. Since their hukou is still of Maduo County and the availability of the medical care is tied to participants' hukou, there will be some "cross-regional transaction costs" associated with reimbursement by the system. In the words of Mr. A himself, "The reimbursement I receive in Maduo County is not worth the cost of travel."

Although Couple A did not clarify exactly how much they earn and spend over the course of a year, it is apparent from what they said that it is not easy for them to lead an urban life. When the couple thought about the future, they were at a loss.

(Interview in Heyuan New Village on the morning of July 4, 2007)

Case 2 Family B in the Qinyuan New Village

All the four members of Family B are of Tibetan ethnicity. Mr. B was born in 1961 and his wife was born in 1968. His first son was born in 1992, followed by their second in 1995. In August 2003, their whole family moved from Xuema Village in the Changmahe Township (Maqin County, Guoluo Prefecture), to Qinyuan New Village. According to the resettlement project plan, Qinyuan New Village is for temporary re-settlers. If the eco-environment in their hometowns recovered significantly, the re-settlers could move back to their original residences. Meanwhile, not all the herders in their original residences have moved out. Seven herding households remained there and were allowed to graze their animals on the land. The rationale behind such an arrangement is to prevent herders from other regions from grazing on the pastures contracted by the herders, who have been displaced by the resettlement project. Following the arrangement, the family of Mr. B's brother was allowed to stay on the land, and before moving out, Mr. B gave all his cattle (more than 100 cattle and 600 sheep) to his brother to graze. In addition, Mr. B left his eldest son to assist his brother with the grazing of their herd as his brother has no children. The agreement between Mr. B and his brother is simple: Every year, the eldest son brings home some meat, milk, butter, dung, skin and fur, and moreover, if Family B returns to their original village, his brother will return all of his cattle and sheep to Mr. B.

As in the previous case, re-settlers in the new village also have free housing provided by the government. According to the resettlement policy, a household that has the pasture use permit in their original residence will be granted a house of 62 square meters with a courtyard of 250 square meters, and it is also entitled to an annual resettlement allowance of 6,000 yuan. In contrast, a household that has no pasture use permit will be granted a house of 43 square meters with a courtyard of 250 square meters, with an annual resettlement allowance of 3,000 yuan.

Mr. B's eldest son received no schooling and does not live at home with his family because he spends his time tending to B's

brother's animals. The second eldest son has received no schooling so far, but is preparing to attend elementary school this
September. When he was asked why his children received no
schooling, Mr. B said quite frankly, "They would end up as hooligans
if they did not study hard at school. In addition, it's difficult to find
jobs even if they do go to school, and besides, if they did go to
school, they would forget how to tend to the animals."

Like other re-settlers, Family B had a small income and encountered a number of difficulties after moving to the new village. In
1999, before his family was resettled, Mr. B opened a grocery store
in his original residence. In 2000, he bought a minibus with over
20,000 yuan to transport goods from Dawu Town, Maqin County to
the grocery store. After resettlement, however, Family B no longer
raises cattle or sheep and Mr. B continues to run a grocery store in
the new village, while doing some short-distance passenger transport. For both the running of his grocery store and the usage of his
minibus to earn extra money by taking passengers back and forth,
Mr. B lacks a number of important permits. He explains this by
saying, "It's because the fees are too high for the licences." Because
Mr. B lacks the correct permits, he does not dare to use his minibus
to transport passengers as often as he used to.

Meat, milk and dung are all expensive in the city. Luckily, Mr. B's
eldest son can regularly bring some back home (especially over
festivals). Reflecting on the changes to his life after resettlement,
Mr. B said that desertification was a serious problem on his pasture
lands. The environment and the climate were bad, but many herders had to stay because all they knew was cattle herding. They still
find it hard to adjust to life in the new village and if possible, they
would choose to go back.

(Interview in Qinyuan New Village on the morning of July 6, 2007)

Case 3 Two Tibetan Youngsters at the Prefecture Government
Hotel

One night, I met two Tibetan youngsters at the guardhouse of the
hostel where I was staying. I found their life stories extremely

interesting. One of them is called C and serves as security guard of the hotel; the other is called D, who is a dancer in a private troupe. They are cousins.

There are six members in C's family. In addition to his wife, the family includes his parents, his daughter and his son. Mr. C was born in 1984, his wife was born in 1983, his daughter in 2006, and his son in 2007. The whole family have been displaced by the ecological resettlement project, and moved to the Heyuan New Village. Currently, their main source of income comes from digging caterpillar fungus in the pasture lands, but this requires a "pasture fee" which has to be paid to a local pasture contractor on an annual basis. In 2006, his family earned 4,000 yuan from digging caterpillar fungus. In 2005, Mr. C got married and had children just after his graduation from the junior middle school. He speaks good Putonghua (Chinese) and wears a pair of glasses, which are in sharp contrast to his security guard uniform. Mr. C said that at first he also collected caterpillar fungus, but later on he gave up because he had developed myopia due to studying. This prevented him from seeing the caterpillar fungus clearly, making it harder to collect. He found other jobs instead. In August 2006 he got this security guard job through the security brigade. The reason that he was able to get this job was that he had studied till junior middle school and could speak Putonghua fluently. The security brigade assigned him to duty at this hotel. His monthly salary is 600 yuan, but the brigade deducts 100 yuan per month. Due to ill health, his parents stay at home most of the time. His wife's job is digging caterpillar fungus, and she also does miscellaneous jobs in the prefecture, earning between 400 and 600 yuan per month. When talking about the future, Mr. C said that he had not thought about it a great deal. When describing the changes that have occurred since he moved to the new village, Mr. C remarks, "I eat less meat and cannot use dung or drink yogurt as much as before. I spend more and earn less. I earn (annually) about 20,000 yuan less than I did before the resettlement."

Mr. D is Mr. C's cousin and younger than Mr. C by one year. His mother is Mr. C's aunt. Their family has also resettled in Heyuan

New Village. As they are of similar age, they often dine and chat together. Mr. D attended five years of elementary school. Besides his parents, he has two sisters and two brothers, who are all in school. In March 2006, he was hired by a troupe, and he sings and dances for them. Now every month, he earns a base salary of 400 yuan at the troupe, and his actual income is from 1,000 yuan to 4,000 yuan depending on the number of his performances and the amount he gets per performance. His troupe has tournaments around neighboring counties and charges 5 yuan per ticket. The furthest the troupe has been to are large cities such as Shanghai, where he was able to earn as much as 400 yuan per performance. Compared with Mr. C, Mr. D looks more fashionable in terms of clothing and hairstyle, more handsome and brimming with a youthful vitality. Like Family C, Mr. D's parents' income depended on collecting caterpillar fungus and other family members would help. In 2007, the family made a net income of 7,900 yuan. Before working for the troupe, Mr. D had a cleaning job in the prefecture, but his income was meager. Their family had 80 cattle and 200 sheep. Before moving to the new village, these cattle were all sold to local Hui people (an ethnic minority in China).

(Interview at the prefecture government hostel on the evening of
July 5, 2007)

It can be seen from the above cases and other studies that the Tibetan re-settlers (including local Tibetan aboriginals) are all motivated to seek happiness for themselves and their families, on the basis of their situation and external environment. Moreover, the Tibetans have few choices when they are faced with resettlement. We must closely look into the various interconnected changes that affect the ecological re-settlers when they move into their host communities.

1. *Changes to everyday life*

It is worth noting that these changes are linked to the changes in the re-settlers' income and expenditure after their resettlement.

Before resettlement, herders wore traditional ethnic clothing that suited both their nomadic work and life. After resettlement, the re-settlers were increasingly found to wear Chinese Han style modern clothing. This clothing is cheaper than their traditional dress, more varied in style, and more suitable for urban life. In the above cases, all the male interviewees wore Han-style clothing, while the women still wore their ethnic clothing. In addition, the interviewees' homes had Han style interior decoration and furnishing. This indicated a strong sense of "Tibet-Han integration".

Before their resettlement, the diet of the herders lacked variety, dominated by beef and mutton. They were completely self-sufficient when it came to food. Conversely, after resettlement, the herders were no longer able to keep their animals as before so meat could only be bought at the market. It is important to note that meat is more expensive in the cities. Without experiencing a corresponding increase in their incomes, the re-settlers had to lessen the amount of meat in their diet.

Before their resettlement, the herders had led a nomadic life. After resettlement, they had to settle down and familiarize themselves with the new way of living and the rules associated with living in a sedentary community. For instance, herders often used motor vehicles (motorcycles and cars in most cases) for travel. In the vast majority of cases these vehicles were unlicensed, and usually either abandoned or second hand. The herders were used to driving in the countryside, where there were few restrictions. After resettlement, however, re-settlers had to face stricter driving rules, so unlicensed cars, and those that should be scrapped, were not permitted to be driven on the urban roads. Unable to pay these new fees, the re-settlers were unwilling to apply for a license plate, and thus, chose not to drive a car. As a result, they faced greater travel restrictions than before.

Before resettlement, herders spent little time watching TV. This was, in part, because their TVs were not portable, and more importantly, a stable source of power was hard to secure. After resettlement, they no longer spent time looking after animals and thus, had more spare time to watch TV. In these host communities, TV sets can be conveniently installed and access to power is much more stable. TV plays a significant catalytic role in transforming the work and life of Tibetan re-settlers, enabling them to learn much more about life outside of their communities.

2. Changes in sources of income

It should be noted that for many Tibetan ecological re-settlers, relocation means a reduction in their earning capacity as some of their previous methods of obtaining income are no longer available to them and it is harder for them to develop new sources of income.

Before resettlement, the main source of income for the herders was animal husbandry. Moreover, by-products (e.g. meat, milk, fur, skin and dung of yaks) could be either used by the herders themselves, or sold for cash. Many re-settlers may well have gathered caterpillar fungus on their contracted pastures, in order to earn a sizeable and stable cash income. After resettlement, because they no longer have the rights to the original pastures, they are unable to graze their cattle or sheep, or collect caterpillar fungus, as they did before.

The counties studied in this chapter are major caterpillar fungus growing areas (the fungus, a precious medicine, mainly grows on alpine pastures at an altitude of 3,500–4,500 meters in the Qinghai–Tibet Plateau). However, as discussed previously, the contract rights to the pastures are, for the most part, owned by local Tibetans. Due to the high unit price of caterpillar fungus (40,000–160,000 *yuan* per kg depending on quality), the gathering of this precious medicine in the pastures is monopolized by local Tibetan pasture contractors. Without the permission of those contractors or the village committees, non-locals are prohibited from gathering caterpillar fungus there. During the high season, for those people who are not from the local area and want to gather the caterpillar fungus, they have to pay a "resource royalty" that is quite high to those contractors or the village committees (the per capita seasonal resource royalty ranges from 1,000 *yuan* to 4,000 *yuan*, depending on the quality of the caterpillar fungus). Non-locals are generally not permitted to dig caterpillar fungus during the peak harvest period. Put simply, the local population has erected a number of barriers to prevent non-locals from digging for caterpillar fungus.

For aboriginal Tibetans in host communities, collecting caterpillar fungus has become an important source of income and in some cases, even their sole source of income. Although gathering the fungus is hard work, it is only seasonal (i.e. usually only in the months of May and June) and because unit prices are high, this activity is only short-term, but extremely profitable. Generally speaking, if a family has sufficient labor resources and the contracted pasture lands are abundant with caterpillar fungus, it will take only two months to make a level of cash income that is high enough to support the family for the whole year. However, for ecological re-settlers, not only have they lost the opportunity to harvest caterpillar fungus in the pasture lands from where they came from, but there are many restrictions which prevent them from gathering caterpillar fungus in the lands they have moved to. These restrictions prevent them from earning a reasonable profit in their new host communities.

The resettlement project generally required that compensation of 6,000 *yuan* be provided annually to each resettled household that owned the contract rights to land, and 3,000 *yuan* to those that did not, regardless of the number of people in each household. This compensation is an important source of revenue for most re-settlers. But generally speaking, it is difficult for re-settlers to maintain their past dietary habits and life-styles with this fixed level of compensation because of the increasing prices of most commodities in urban areas where they have moved to. For many herders, a significant part of their income in the past was not in the form of money. It was accessible directly from the animals they kept at home (e.g. meat, fur). But now, almost everything costs money. In particular, they find it hard to afford meat; and now even dung has to be bought. In addition, it is unclear how long this compensation will be provided for. Once the government stops handing out compensation to the re-settlers sometime in the future, re-settlers will have to fend for themselves. Due to resettlement, many herders have lost previous sources of income and are forced to look for non-farming jobs in urban areas.

We must pay great attention to these transitions. It is worth noting that before the implementation of the ecological resettlement project, the secondary and tertiary industries in host communities had already been monopolized by migrant populations from outside the province or prefecture (i.e mainly those who are either from the Han or Hui ethnic groups). The migrant populations overcame all kinds of difficulties to make a living in the alpine and oxygen-deficient regions, and are therefore elites in the small business areas they engage in. These migrant populations have succeeded in the market, and are courageous, enduring, and experienced in doing business (see Case 4). Their striking difference from

the re-settlers is that the latter are Tibetans who are used to a more traditional way of life, speak a different language, and for the most part, have
little or no experience of work that is not farming related. It is difficult
for the Tibetan re-settlers to compete with the migrant populations when
it comes to activity in the non-agricultural sector, so many Tibetan re-
settlers cannot find good jobs and earn a stable income, regardless of how
hard they try.

Case 3 reminds us that although some ecological re-settlers can secure
a stable income by digging for caterpillar fungus in the host communities,
these re-settlers have to meet a basic condition in order for them to do
so, i.e. their families must have sufficient labor to dig for the caterpillar
fungus. In reality (as Case 3 shows), the more labor a family has, the more
capable it is to earn other sources of income.

It is fair to say that those re-settlers who have been interviewed are not
living below the poverty line, but they are very vulnerable to impoverishment as their original earning capacity has been greatly reduced. Without
improvements to their earning potential, it is hard to say what will happen to their work and life in the future. During the interviews, all the
re-settlers expressed different degrees of concern with respect to their
future livelihood. They generally felt that for the most part, even if there
are opportunities to get work, they are either not up to the job, or they
are not viewed as an attractive candidate by the recruiters. It is the
author's considered view, that running a grocery store is what most
re-settlers choose to do (in the non-farming sector) and it is what they
are capable of. But in order to do this, the re-settlers need start-up funds,
which only those from relatively rich backgrounds have. The family in
Case 1 opened up a grocery store. The couple are fairly intelligent and
speak a bit of Putonghua Chinese (though it is fair to say, fairly limited).
They started a grocery store just after resettling in their new house, but so
far there has not been a lot of business. Thus, they are worried about what
the future might bring. There are not many re-settlers in the new village
who are in a better situation than they are, and even for people like them,
making a living is not easy.

Comparing traditional animal husbandry and gathering with non-
farming related work, there is a clear difference. The latter is more

susceptible to changes in the market. Thus, workers that operate in the non-farming sector need to be adaptable to the ever-changing market place, rather than relying on one skill (i.e. farming). Evidence suggests that this is too demanding for most Tibetan ecological re-settlers.

Currently, the local government also provides some job opportunities for the re-settlers, which tend to be in three areas: the county blanket plant, urban environmental sanitation and security services. However, these job opportunities are limited in number and insufficient to cover the needs of the large number of re-settlers. As most of the re-settlers used to engage in rather conventional primary sector work, there are very few who are sufficiently educated to meet the tougher criteria for the new urban jobs.

From the interviews with re-settlers, discussing the above-mentioned problems and difficulties of making a living, the author became aware that some re-settlers have already planned or are planning for some of their family members to secretly return to their original homes to continue herding. This undoubtedly undermines the goal of protecting the environment, and thus the whole rationale for the ecological resettlement project. This is an important trend that deserves our attention.

Case 4 Non-Local Business Owners

In the four county seats (towns where the county government is located) that the author has been to, it is apparent that almost all of the shops, eateries and places to hang out are run by non-locals. Although almost all shop tablets have both Tibetan and Chinese (there is usually a line of Tibetan above the Chinese) that includes the shop's name and what it sells, walking into the shops, it became apparent that very few of the shopkeepers were native Tibetans. In Dari County, shops that sell clothes (i.e. wholesale and retail, Tibetan or Han Chinese apparel), are almost entirely run by non-locals. Looking at the issue from a geographical perspective, most of these people are from Qinghai Province, Gansu Province, Sichuan Province, Chongqing Municipality, Hunan Province and Jiangxi Province; and most of them are either ethnically Han or Hui.

In trying to understand this common "phenomenon", the author and colleagues had the following questions:

(1) Why are there so few Tibetan shopkeepers in the areas visited?
(2) In the high altitude areas where the transport infrastructure is underdeveloped and the climatic conditions are harsh, why did the non-locals decide to start businesses here? In particular, analyzing those who have come from Hunan and Jiangxi, who would have had to travel thousands of miles, and encountered countless hardships, why did they choose this particular place, rather than somewhere else?
(3) The stores are small on the whole and are fairly homogenous. So, how are they able to make them profitable, and thus earn enough to stay in this area?
(4) If starting a small business is so profitable, why have many native Tibetans not done the same? According to comments made by the local inhabitants, it has been the case, for many years, that there are not many Tibetan shopkeepers.
(5) It is true that some Tibetans are "itinerant traders", and trade across a number of regions, like many of the non-local business people. Some of them should have some business acumen, so why have they chosen this life instead of setting up their own store?

With these questions in mind, the author and colleagues went to a number of stores run by non-locals. The first store made clothing. It is a well-known fact that many of these stores not only sell clothes but also make bespoke pieces of clothing, in line with the needs of their customers. Many such stores are specialized, making and selling Tibetan garments. Obviously, Tibetans are their main clients. Although the tailors can skillfully make Tibetan outfits, many of them are not Tibetans. At a fur clothing store in Maqin County, the author was able to ascertain why this is the case.

Author: "Where are you from?"

Shopkeeper (female, replying while continuing to sew a piece of fur clothing): "Hunan Province."

Author (somewhat surprised): "That's far. Why did you come to this alpine and remote area?"

Shopkeeper (calm and replying without raising her head): "We saw the map and knew it is cold here, so we came here to sell fur coats."

Author (still quite bewildered): "Is it easy to do business here?"

Shopkeeper (replying without hesitation): "Local Tibetans can dig caterpillar fungus in May and June and make a lot of money, so they can afford to buy from us."

Author (beginning to understand their rationale): "I'm assuming you were not aware of this place at the very beginning, were you?"

Shopkeeper: "We were introduced to it by our relatives."

Author: "Your relatives? Where are they now?"

Shopkeeper (thinking that we might not have understood what she was talking about, she gave a fuller explanation): "Our relatives are in Xining and when we were at home, they told us that there is a lot of business here, so we decided to make the journey from our hometown. We are traveling all over the country, and willing to work wherever it is possible to make money. The Tibetans make money when they dig caterpillar fungus. They like our coats, but they cannot make them, so they come to us."

Author (questioning further): "Why are local Tibetans unwilling to go into business like you have?"

Shopkeeper (smiling): "How can the locals do business? It's a small place and everyone knows everybody else, so it is hard to bargain. Plus, they don't have the relevant skills to make these coats."

Author (naively doubtful): "Is it not possible for the locals to learn?"

Shopkeeper (with another smile): "They make a hell lot of money digging caterpillar fungus, so why should they bother?"

This simple conversation seems to have answered the author's doubts.

There is an important situation that needs to be pointed out concerning non-locals doing business in this area. These stores are superficially independent, and appear to be open to competition, but in fact, many have developed a form of alliance with other shopkeepers. Many shopkeepers are related to each other, or are friends and fellow villagers. In many cases, these people swarmed to the area opening up a lot of shops at once, and it was often the case that the stores were apparent competitors to one another. It appears that these stores are not simply in competition with each other, but quite the opposite. They help each other, reallocate inventories, and cooperate when it comes to issues around supply, sales and pricing. The non-locals have formed stable social relationships, which make them feel stronger and more secure.

The counties analyzed in this chapter are all very large geographically, but sparsely populated. In each county, only a few thousand locals have local hukou, a great proportion of whom is government staff. The local population is small and the members have been living closely together for some time. As the statement from the shopkeeper referenced above shows, many local Tibetans know each other, and this is indeed a disadvantage when it comes to bargaining (especially considering the influence of their traditional culture). Some capable Tibetans are more willing to do business outside their hometown, and this is why very few local Tibetans run their own stores and instead choose to be itinerant traders.

While local Tibetans are able to earn a decent income through gathering caterpillar fungus, the non-local and non-Tibetan population can provide daily necessities and make a reasonable amount of profit as well, thus forming a special division of labor. It must be admitted that the division of labor and how the two populations professionally interact are important: Local Tibetans monopolize the gathering of caterpillar fungus, so that their skills of gathering caterpillar fungus and maintaining the pastoral lands are utilized and improved; on the other hand, non-local populations have developed an effective system for supplying goods to the local market.

(Interview in Maqin County on the afternoon of July 5, 2007)

III Conclusions and Policy Discussions

We have drawn the following conclusions from the analysis cited above, with respect to the consequences (i.e. potential impoverishment) arising from the ecological resettlement project:

1. The ecological resettlement project brings few positive changes to the situations of those who are the poorest, and indeed is likely to trap more people into poverty. Facing a new natural environment and new market conditions, ecological re-settlers must face multiple changes to their work and life. During the transition, it is often the case that those who cannot adapt to their new environment find themselves poverty-stricken. Under the constraint of their personal experience (i.e. it is difficult for them to apply the skills and knowledge, which they developed over many years of leading a nomadic life, to a completely new environment), it is very difficult and even impossible for certain groups of people to improve their livelihoods and adapt.

2. Ecological re-settlers and existing residents of host communities are in competition for local resources, and the former are usually quite vulnerable. It takes time for both to integrate. Moreover, most business activities in central urban areas (e.g., the urban areas in the county seat) are dominated by non-locals, and it is hard for locals to compete with them. Thus, the local population mainly engage in tertiary industry activities, which are scattered across the townships and villages. Local Tibetan residents mainly engage in animal husbandry and gathering (caterpillar fungus), while most other industries are dominated by non-locals or other ethnic groups. Due to limited skills, language and experience, it is hard for ecological re-settlers to improve their livelihoods. Many ecological re-settlers have attempted to gain employment, but were unsuccessful.

3. Some ecological re-settlers returned to their original habitats, and once again turned to raising cattle and sheep in order to make a living. This has reduced the effectiveness of the environmental protection that was intended to come about as a result of the policy.

Without security and enhancement of ecological re-settlers' income capability and living standards, there might well be severe consequences with respect to economic development, social stability and national unity in the host communities. These impacts must be taken seriously. The government should continue to assist ecological re-settlers, who have made great personal sacrifices for the protection of the eco-environment. Efforts to assist ecological re-settlers will pay off, in terms of development and stability, in the future. According to our survey and the above-mentioned analysis, this chapter identifies the following policy recommendations:

1. Ecological resettlement projects may consider resettlement to more prosperous areas or areas with more opportunities to earn a decent level of income, rather than to poor regions with underdeveloped transport infrastructure, as is the case now. The two new resettlement villages in our survey are both located several kilometers from the central urban areas of Maqin County. Maqin County is geographically remote (both in Guoluo Prefecture and in Qinghai Province), sparsely populated, small in terms of its urban land mass and economically underdeveloped. The new resettlement villages are on the outskirts of Maqin county seat. From the above points, it is possible to conclude that the ecological re-settlers will have to lead an urban life, but their disadvantage is inherent. Although Qinghai Province is large, sparsely populated, alpine and remote in China, there are many small villages along central highways, many of which are economically developed. It appears that these regions have more opportunities and should be considered as potential host communities for future ecological resettlement projects. This should mean that the re-settlers will not be marginalized from the outset.
2. In addition to cash compensation to individual households, public facilities should be constructed and public services provided in resettlement areas for the re-settlers, free of charge. This should help foster a sense of belonging and identity for ecological re-settlers and a spirit of social responsibility. Urban resettlement entails adequate infrastructure and urban management, including security, healthcare, education and firefighting. These activities will not only increase the

overall quality of life for re-settlers, but change their original perceptions of work and life as well, facilitating their integration into urban life. Basic education and public healthcare services will increase the quality of the ecological re-settler's human capital at a fundamental level and empower them to fight the risks associated with poverty.

3. Poverty alleviation policies should identify specific target groups, rather than be indiscriminately applied. It is unnecessary for poverty alleviation work to pursue "universal" effects. Rather, targeted policies should be developed in light of the status of specific groups in market competition, so that the limited poverty relief funds can be brought into greater play, maximizing their effectiveness. Despite common characteristics, there may be different causes of impoverishment for poor people. Poverty relief policies should thus be developed and implemented in light of those specific causes, rather than be indiscriminately applied to all the different groups of poor people.

4. Resources should be mobilized for effective human resource investment, especially free language training and the development of other skills for the ecological re-settlers. The training should focus on the improvement of individual skills and competencies, in light of market demand, so as to avoid a futility of effort. Human resource investment should be carried out for people of different age groups and cultural backgrounds. For younger groups, training may focus on basic skills such as language, arithmetic and computer skills, with a focus on teaching them how to self-learn. For the middle-aged and older groups, the priority should be on the skills that are most needed in the market.

5. It is not advisable to simply copy policies that have been implemented to address the issue of poverty in other areas of the country, without fully understanding the situation on the ground. It is important to note that not all poor families have the same market-competing potential and that they face different external environments. On the other hand, successful pilot schemes are sometimes indeed being replicated privately (at least among those in neighboring regions) before the government's promotion. In other words, the public are ahead of the government when it comes to implementing effective ideas. Thus, the government may choose to do a grass-roots survey, before rolling out successful practices to other areas. This would give them

an opportunity to see what results have been achieved as a result of these actions. At the very least, the government should avoid rolling out practices or policies that have been privately proven to be successful in one place, but unsuccessful in another place.

6. For the first generation of re-settlers, if the results of poverty alleviation policies are insignificant due to the personal inadequacies of individuals in question, the priority should be to develop the competencies — particularly market competitiveness — of the second-generation of re-settlers. There should be greater investment in basic education, training, infrastructure, and basic healthcare services. Proactive efforts must be made in order to avoid the intergenerational transmission of "resettlement-induced poverty".

Bibliography

Cernea, Michael M, 1996, *Resettlement and Development*, Nanjing: Hehai University Press.

Cui Jing, 2007, "CPPCC Members on the Protection and Development of Source Areas of the Yangtze River, Yellow River and Lancang River", *Xinhua News*, August 12, 2007, http://env.people.com.cn/GB/6102543.html, downloaded on September 10, 2007.

Guoluo Prefecture Government, 2007, "A Survey of Guoluo", August 13, 2007, http://www.golog.gov.cn/html/59/5713.html, downloaded on September 10, 2007.

Hu Jing, 2007, "Summaries on the Research of Involuntary Resettlement", *Hubei University of Economics Journal* (Humanities and Social Sciences Edition), 4(7), 28–29.

Qinghai Provincial Government, 2007, "Provincial Leaders on the Ecological Protection in the Three-River Source", July 17, 2007, http://www.qh.gov.cn/html/381/20070717163344.html, downloaded on September 10, 2007.

Sen, Amartya, 1999, "Poverty as Capability Deprivation", In *Development as Freedom*, Oxford: Oxford University Press. pp. 87–110.

Shi Zhilei, Yang Yunyan, Cheng Guangshuai, 2009, "Involuntary Resettlement, Resettlement Patterns and Capacity Loss", *South China Population*, 02.

The World Bank, 2011, "Involuntary Resettlement", http://go.worldbank.org/MRNITY6XN0, downloaded on September 10, 2007.

CHAPTER 7

Preventing Intergenerational Poverty Transmission with Antenatal Care

Zhu Ling

Abstract

Antenatal care can help children from poor families get a good start to their lives and thus avoid the transmission of intergenerational poverty. Therefore, this chapter argues that focusing on the provision of antenatal care for children from poor families is the right place to start if your objective is to reduce poverty. The Chinese government has launched a program which aims to reduce maternal mortality and tetanus in newborns. This program plays a similar role to that of antenatal care. However, women living in pastoral areas in Yushu and Guoluo (the two Tibetan Autonomous Prefectures in Qinghai Province) do not sufficiently use antenatal care. Based on information collected through fieldwork, this chapter will try to find out the reasons behind this pattern of behavior, as well as understand the policy implications of this phenomenon.

Keywords: Poverty Reduction; Antenatal Care; Tibetan Women and Children.

Based on evidence gathered from fieldwork in Yushu and Guoluo, this chapter discusses how to reduce intergenerational poverty transmission by improving maternal healthcare. This issue has arisen because of the following: Governments and the general public in the developing world (including China) are increasingly conscious of the importance of the

125

nutrition, health and education of children living in poverty. They regard investing in human capital as an important way to reduce the transmission of intergenerational poverty.[1] However, for children from poor families, who already suffer from congenitally stunted growth, interventions at the postnatal stage may have some effect, but these measures will not be as effective as they could be. This is because the children's defects cannot be corrected at this stage. In order to ensure that children can get a good start to their lives, both the mother and the fetus need to be properly cared for. By the same token, poverty relief efforts must start at the moment of the fetus's conception, i.e. the moments when life is formed, and not later. Specifically, poverty relief actions should begin from "antenatal care".

Previous studies on the reproductive health of farming and herding women in Tibetan settlements were either from a medical perspective, such as the distribution of gynecological diseases; or how the division of labor affected women's social status from an anthropological and sociological perspective. There have been very few debates on the threat of poverty-related gynecological diseases to the reproductive health of farming and herding women in Tibetan settlements. Discourse is equally sparse on the relationship between the reproductive health of these women and familial poverty, in particular how their reproductive health relates to intergenerational poverty transmission.[2]

Hence, this chapter focuses on young and middle-aged married women from rural households in the aforementioned Tibetan areas. It identifies their needs for maternal health services, the barriers in place that prevent them from accessing such services, as well as what can be done to remove these barriers. In order to answer these questions, between 2006 and 2007, the author conducted fieldwork in the Tibetan Plateau, interviewing the following institutes and individuals: the women's federation, health bureau, family planning commission, hospitals, maternal and child health hospital and disease control center, all at the county level. After the initial set of interviews, the author went on to meet employees at township health centers, private clinics and pharmacies. Finally, in

---

[1] Adato and Hoddinott (2007).
[2] Wang *et al.* (2008); Zhagyai and Lu (1998).

the third set of interviews, the author met village health workers and housewives from farming and herding households who were less than 50 years old. In addition, the author also analyzed work reports from county governments and pieces of briefing from the work bureaus and disease control centers. Most information about the areas that have been studied is gathered from these interviews and other document-based evidence. Other types of material used in this chapter falls into three broad categories: reports and conference documents issued by the WHO and China's Ministry of Health, Tibetan surveys by well-known sociologists and geologists published in the 1940s and fieldwork reports on health service provision in Tibetan areas, as well as oral histories by Tibetan women since the 1950s.

This chapter will introduce the WHO's philosophy on antenatal care, as well as case studies from relevant countries. Using the information collected from the fieldwork, it will then go on to explain the causes behind the sub-optimal use of maternal health services in the Tibetan Plateau. Finally, having identified the problems with reproductive healthcare, this chapter will then suggest various policy options to resolve them.

I Antenatal Healthcare Services

The WHO defines antenatal care as a series of services including education, counseling, screening, treatment and monitoring to promote the well-being of the mother, fetus and newborns over the course of a woman's pregnancy, conception and childbirth.[3] In order to ensure that every pregnant woman has access to antenatal care, European countries have made antenatal care free of charge and have provided formal medical training for midwives at a grass-roots level and have extended antenatal care networks to the communities that are closest to women. As indicated by existing medical evidence in these countries, maternal and child health can be substantially improved by early identification of the potential risks through antenatal care, nutritional supplements or medical treatment, aimed at the specific needs of pregnant women and fetuses. In addition, education and counseling services for both providers

---

[3] WHO Europe Health Evidence Network (2005a).

and users are also effective.[4] Due to limited financial resources, developing countries are only able to set up a routine antenatal care service package and establish a corresponding organizational system. This system is set up in accordance with the kinds of epidemics found locally, the prioritized health objectives, the available resources, as well as the preferences of those who benefit from these services. The WHO has specifically designed a number of simple and practical service models for their reference.

There are two main trains of thought around China's approach to maternal health. The first is the concept "bear and rear better children". The second is to look after the health of both the mother and fetus. Chinese urban households, especially those that are not poor, are now openly requesting maternal health service packages, which are offered by the Ministry of Health. This group of people sees the package of services as a priority area for household expenditure. Moreover, many urban health service providers are competing with each other in order to obtain the license to offer these services. However, in poor rural areas, the quality of service provided and accessibility of the aforementioned services is far inferior to those found in urban areas. It has been found that some of the women in poor areas have suffered from stunted growth during childhood. Others are suffering from malnutrition. Many lack even basic awareness of the importance of health, as well as the capacity to pay. Unfortunately, poor families can only use the services offered by these institutions as a last resort. Thus, the good health of the mother and the child in these households cannot be guaranteed. Consequently, maternal and neonatal mortality rates are both higher in rural areas than in urban areas. It is quite possibly because of this reason that the Ministry of Health did not set high standards of maternal and infant health in poor areas, and instead, set a target to reduce the maternal mortality rate and eliminate neonatal tetanus. In 2000, the Ministry launched a program of systematic maternal health management (i.e. the provision of a maternal health service package) in order to meet this goal.[5] Under the program, women should receive an examination early in her pregnancy, at least

---

[4] Banta (2003).
[5] Ministry of Health (2005).

five more antenatal examinations, sterilized midwifery and a postpartum visit during the pregnancy, within 28 days of delivery of the child.

II Reasons for the Low Utilization of Maternal Health Services for Poor Women

Both the Yushu and Guoluo (Golog) areas in Qinghai Province are covered by the program to reduce maternal mortality and eliminate neonatal tetanus. Although this program has effectively improved the local maternal and child healthcare service facilities, the services are still not used sufficiently by the women who live in pastoral areas. According to statistics issued by the Maqin County Health Bureau,[6] in 2006 only 49% of pregnant women used the maternal health service package. Through observations, the author believes that even this very conservative figure may well be an overestimate. The government seat of Guoluo Prefecture found in Maqin County is an area where the local populace enjoys relatively superior healthcare services compared to those in neighboring counties. However, the herdsmen's settlements are dispersed and the grass-roots healthcare service networks are weak. Moreover, the monitoring of the population and the quality of statistical data is also far from ideal. One example highlighting the poor quality of statistical data is that the report indices only include percentages, rather than absolute numbers. During a period of time in which the author undertook fieldwork in Maqin, Dari, Yushu and Chengduo Counties, original statistics from the gynecology census or maternal health services could not be obtained despite numerous attempts. However, whether the reports were accurate or not, the figures do indicate one trend: A considerable number of pregnant and lying-in women have not used whole-course maternal health services. This begs the question, why is this the case? This is a key question that the author attempted to answer on numerous occasions during the course of the fieldwork.

In terms of service provision, several problems need to be solved with respect to how the healthcare networks are organized, the incentive structures and managing the quality of service provided.

---

[6] Maqin County Health and Family Planning Bureau (2006, p. 7).

First, it became apparent that maternal health networks are not extended to the villages and the places where these services are provided are far from the households. Although most administrative villages have health workers, it is difficult for them to provide education, counseling and regular visits (in line with the mothers' needs), because of the imbalanced gender ratio and the lack of people with the correct qualifications. The Dari County in the Guoluo Prefecture provides a perfect case in point. There are no women among the 33 health workers in the county. According to local regulations, village health workers are responsible for a number of different things including the immunization of children, reporting on epidemics, publicizing family planning, as well as the routine task of looking after the general health of the villagers. For providing these services, each healthcare worker can expect to be rewarded between 1,200–1,400 *yuan* from the county each year. Although this is obviously not a large sum of money, it does provide a stable cash income for the herdsmen (which is important as they are often found in poor pastoral areas). It is often the case that women are not able to take advantage of these opportunities. There are two key factors underlying this fact. The first is the poor level of literacy among women, and the second is that they have little say in village affairs. Moreover, the powerful influence of local customs and their own psychology means that unless they find themselves in dangerous situations, pregnant and lying-in women are unwilling to accept healthcare provided by men of the same village who are not their husbands because of their own moral outlook. Furthermore, the education system in pastoral areas is fairly backward. The more remote villages are, the less professionally trained health workers are available and the more difficult it is for their knowledge and skills to meet the demands of the local population. It has been noted that even the wives of the health workers themselves did not fully utilize the systematic maternal management services during pregnancy and childbirth (see Case 1).

Case 1 The Way a Health Worker Chose Maternal Health Services for His Wife

Zhenqin Township No. 2 Village is located 100 kilometers from Chengduo County (Yushu Prefecture). The author visited a woman in the village who had given birth a little less than four months ago. Her name is Zhuo Ma (pseudonym) and her husband Zha Xi (pseudonym) is a health worker in the village. Zha Xi (31 years old) had not received any formal schooling, however in a school in Nangqian County, he had undertaken the study of Tibetan medicine for around four months. This experience resulted in him knowing a lot more about antenatal inspection than the other villagers. Before the birth of their third daughter (Zhuo Ma already had a daughter before she married Zha Xi), Zha Xi brought his wife for an inspection at the maternal and child health center in the county town. They decided on where to have the baby delivered on the basis of the inspection results. Zhuo Ma concluded, given that they lived a long way away from the county seat, and they lacked financial resources, that she would not go to hospital unless it was a difficult labor. When she gave birth to her first daughter, both of them realized that the fetus was in the incorrect position and thus they decided to have the baby delivered in the prefecture hospital. Their second and third child were delivered in tents that they had made at home with the help of an old woman hired from a nearby village. During his wife's delivery, Zha Xi once performed a "medical disinfection" for his wife, but he was unable to do anything for her pain in the lower back area. Whenever the pain became unbearable, she would see a doctor in the county town, because she believed that the township health center's medical facilities were inferior.

(Based on the record of an interview conducted on July 16, 2007)

Second, among maternal health networks, township health centers failed to effectively fulfill their function as a hub. Pastoral areas are sparsely populated and transport infrastructure is poor, making it difficult for the herdsmen, who are dispersed around the area, to travel. In terms of distance, it is often the case that it is about 20 kilometers from the herdsmen's temporary winter shelters (located in the village committee site) to the township health centers. In some cases this distance can be as far as 50 kilometers. Moreover, in most cases, the summer pastures are at least 40 kilometers from the health centers. Back when China still had the "people's commune", the doctors found in the health centers were either from the villages or acted as "horseback doctors" to the dispersed populace. They were familiar with their patients' ailments and were generally trusted by them. Nowadays, most of the younger generation of doctors are from well-to-do families in a county seat or have settled down in a county town. They usually receive patients at the health centers and will go back to the county towns whenever possible. They rarely interact socially with the herdsmen. Compared to the village health workers, township health centers are not nearly as close to the villagers. Additionally, if one compares the county hospital to the township health centers, the latter possesses far inferior technology. It is also the case that private and monastery clinics are their competitors. It is therefore quite understandable that the herdsmen do not tend to visit the township health centers, given that the service is quite ordinary.

When a field visit was made to the health center in Xialaxiu Township in Yushu County, it was observed that around seven or eight members of staff were sweeping the courtyard. The author talked with them for about 40 minutes, but there was no sign of any patients. It is noticeable that at around the same time, Longxi Monastery Clinic, which is only 100 meters away from the health center, saw more than 20 patients in a crowded diagnosis room. According to an old Party Secretary at Team (village) No. 2 of the Jianshe Township, Dari County (the village had kept the name from the time of the people's commune), when villagers do go to see a local doctor in their township, more than half of them go to see Duo Ji (pseudonym); a Tibetan doctor at his private clinic. Monastery doctors, the Tibetan doctor Duo Ji and the other staff that work in private clinics are of the opinion that they are not responsible for child immunization or gynecology. Apparently, this is where the township health centers come in. However, the most acute problem is a lack of an incentive system to encourage these centers to proactively serve the herdsmen. The existence of this gap can be shown by the implementation of a stand-by system. The day the author visited Xiewu Town in the Chengduo County happened to be a Sunday. The author was informed that the total number of the employees in the health center is currently 14. However, when the author called for help in the courtyard of the health center, no one answered. In comparison, even during their lunch break, the clinic of an individual doctor Cai Rang (pseudonym) still had a male and female employee on rotational duty during that time.

Third, the capacity of county-level gynecological services is so inadequate that the health service institutions lack even the capability to respond to medical emergencies. In the 1960s and 1970s, despite very simple premises and facilities, the health institutions in Guoluo and Yushu had a good reputation among the local herdsmen because medical colleges in Beijing, Xi'an and Qinghai sent graduates to work there. Between 1984 and 1985, the Chinese government reduced controls over the mobility of technical and medical staff, and therefore for the most part, these doctors went to large cities and coastal regions in the southeast of China. In the words of a former President of the People's Hospital in Dari County, "*The technology and skills of the county hospitals suddenly dropped to the level of a township health center, and the damage caused by this change has still not been repaired.*" It is the author's view that this problem also applies to Chengduo County. There are 47,000 people residing in Chengduo County. The maternal division of the county hospital undertakes various functions under the banner of family planning, maternal health and gynecology, but is staffed with only one doctor, assisted by nurses who are only trained in midwifery. This doctor is of Han ethnicity and graduated in 1996 from the Yushu Prefecture Health School before undertaking a year's training at the maternal division of the No. 2 Hospital in the Qinghai Province. It is not easy for one doctor to have to undertake such a heavy workload. Over the course of a survey conducted at the hospital, the author met a young couple of herders who had traveled over 50 kilometers for advice relating to birth control measures. However, the gynecological doctor did not speak Tibetan, so the author had to find someone in the corridor next to the doctor's examination room to act as a translator, in order for this young couple to understand the doctor's advice.

The situation the author encountered in the maternal service division of Chengduo's county hospital is not common in Tibetan areas. However, in most places where there *are* county-level maternal health professionals, medical competence is weakened by the segmentation of medical institutions. For instance, Maqin County has a total population of only 40,000 and Dari County has no more than 23,000 residents, but the government departments and public service institutions are modeled on a system aimed at far larger counties. An example is the separation between the county hospital's maternal division and health center for maternal and child services. After the separation, both sides only had between four to five staff. The team, already understaffed, had lost its economies of scale (see Case 2). Although the provincial government assigned a family planning service vehicle and a medical service vehicle to each county, each township is only able to receive one mobile service a year. However, these counties are still less capable of providing a mobile response in line with the needs of pregnant and lying-in women. The young and middle-aged herding women the author interviewed still rely on their family to move them to prefecture and county hospitals when they are feeling unwell.

Case 2 Main Service Items and Prices in the Maternal Division of Maqin County Hospital

The county seat of Maqin is Dawu Town, which is the location of the headquarters of Guoluo Prefecture's and Maqin County's government and public service institutions. The county hospital employs a total of 38 doctors, nurses and other staff. Four staff members, aged between 29 and 39, are found in the maternal division. Prior to 2003, the women and children's health center in Maqin County shared 12 members of their medical team with the maternal division of the county hospital. After the outbreak of SARS in 2003, the women and children's health center and quarantine center were combined into a disease control center. As a result, the county hospital's maternal division was understaffed, and it took three to four years for them to train new staff. The author interviewed two gynecological doctors: Deji and Deyang (pseudonyms), who were both graduates from the Guoluo Health School in 1996, and used to work in township health centers. After transferring to the county hospital, both of them were assigned to the No. 2 Hospital of Qinghai Province and Red Cross Hospital for a further six months of training. Their division mainly works in the field of family planning service, midwifery and the treatment of gynecological diseases. They frequently receive patients suffering from adnexal or pelvic inflammation and cervicitis. They can do type-B ultrasonic scans but cannot do the laboratory tests. With respect to antenatal examinations, they are able to see whether a fetus's position is normal and they charge 25 yuan for each examination. Another examination they are able to undertake is to listen to the fetus's heart. This examination costs five yuan each time. In terms of additional tasks, the ligation of oviduct plus anaesthesia costs a total of 200 yuan, in-hospital delivery costs 200 yuan while natural labor and a sickbed costs 15 yuan per day. When the mother experiences a difficult labor, they will often transfer her to a prefecture hospital.

           (Based on records of interviews conducted on July 3, 2007)

The reasons for the limited demand for maternal health services found in herding communities can be summarized as follows: First, most family members lack even basic knowledge and information about the importance of maternal health, particularly how preventive medicines can be a useful component of antenatal care. Moreover, it has been found to be the case that pregnant women will not see a doctor unless they sense that there might be dangers or difficulties during conception, thus they miss the ideal time for medical intervention. Take for example Yang Zong (pseudonym, 39 years old) who lives near the Manzhang Township Health Center in Dari County. She has given birth to five children, but did not even receive a single basic antenatal examination. Unfortunately, her fourth child was only found to have a hearing impairment after birth. Now, sadly, this ten-year-old boy is both deaf and dumb.

Second, because of the way health services are provided, herders must leave their homes five to six times in order to receive maternal health services at health centers or hospitals. Each time they visit these health centers or hospitals it takes at least half a day of their time, if not more. If there are no elderly members in the family, herders will need to hire someone to take care of their cattle and attend to other housework. For many herders, who are scattered across the area, the opportunity cost of accessing maternal health services is just too high.

Third, the financial resources of these poor herding families are very limited. As far as antenatal examinations are concerned, even if the services are free of charge, the transport costs associated with utilizing these services act as a deterrent. When it comes to making a decision as to whether to deliver the child in a hospital, even with the reimbursement of funds from the new cooperative medical fund and the program of reducing maternal mortality rates and eliminating neonatal tetanus, the small additional expenses not covered under the program will still play a significant part in the decision-making of poor families (see Case 1). Yin Cuo (pseudonym, 27 years old) from the Budong Village, Manzhang Township in Dari County, explained to the author the true costs of her hospital delivery. Yin Cuo's home is more than 50 kilometers away from the township health center and 105 kilometers away from the county seat in Jimai Town. Her third child was born at the county hospital two years ago. Her family spent in total more than 1,000 *yuan* on the delivery, but only received 500 *yuan* worth of compensation from the cooperative medical fund. In comparison, in the program aimed at reducing the maternal mortality rate and eliminating neonatal tetanus carried out in Dari County in 2006, 30 poor women received 2,500 *yuan* in compensation, for medical expenses accrued as a result of having their children delivered in a hospital. On average, that meant less than 84 *yuan* per person. Assuming their expenses are of a similar nature to Yin Cuo's, they would still have to pay more than 400 *yuan* out of their own pockets. This is equivalent to more than half of the local poverty line (defined as a per capita net annual income of 800 *yuan*). However, the per capita cash income of ordinary herding families in the survey areas is below this standard.

III Conclusions and Policy Options

Appropriate antenatal care refers to the health services that are medically proven to be necessary for maintaining the health of pregnant and lying-in women, their fetuses and newborns. Ensuring that pregnant women from poor families as well as their fetuses receive timely access to such services helps the individuals born in these families to acquire a healthy start in life. It also means that efforts aimed at alleviating poverty can be moved forward to the early stages in life. Hence, ensuring everyone has access to appropriate antenatal care is consistent with the social objective of eradicating poverty. In the era of economic globalization, once children from herding families grow up, they are supposed to compete with their urban counterparts from the same country and even from Europe and America.

Reducing the disparities in antenatal care among individuals will help reduce inborn health inequalities. It will also help to reduce the gap between individuals at the beginning of their lives. In this sense, ensuring access to antenatal care for everyone is also consistent with the principle of social justice. For this reason, appropriate antenatal care can be regarded as a merit good. Its benefits to individuals are consistent with social expectations. In other words, the social value contained in consumption of such goods and services does not hinge upon the desires and preferences of the consumers themselves.[7] Therefore, it is necessary for the government to take action and implement appropriate antenatal care in a similar way to how it delivered compulsory education. Based on this understanding, it is considered that the government needs to take the following interventions in order to address the problems existing in maternal health services in pastoral areas similar to those found in Guoluo and Yushu.

First, the government needs to include fetal health in maternal health programs in poor areas. It needs to work to reduce the mortality rate of mothers and eliminate neonatal tetanus, so that everyone can gain a healthy start in life. But, it is important to note that health programs with this objective tend to stress the importance of survival rather than the quality of life.

Before modern medicine became prevalent in the Tibetan Plateau, the reproductive process of Tibetan herders had been free from artificial intervention and was characterized by a high birth and mortality rate. Although surviving newborns are usually healthy, having such a pattern of births can seriously damage the women's, children's as well as the family's welfare. Today's reproductive health interventions have achieved the

---

[7]For the definition on merit goods, please refer to Johnson (1994).

outcome of a reduced maternal and infant mortality rate. However, among surviving infants, it is not uncommon to see defects or various "underdevelopments" as a result of midwifery. These children will not only face higher household economic vulnerabilities due to higher risks of disease but will also often fall into the poverty trap once they have grown into adults.

This problem should not be left to self-correction, or to concepts in line with "natural selection". Instead, the health of the fetus should be protected through high quality antenatal care. For instance, during epidemics in the Tibetan Plateau, women who wish to give birth should be screened for communicable diseases so as to prevent intergenerational transmission of sexual diseases, tuberculosis, hepatitis and other diseases. Pregnant women should also take folic acid supplements to prevent developmental defects of the neural tube, and take iodine supplements to prevent congenital dementia. Pregnant women suffering from anemia should take iron supplements to prevent their fetus from being born underweight or even from dying.[8]

Second, the government should provide free maternal healthcare for farming and herding women in poor areas, through fiscal procurement of a standardized maternal health service package, and subsidize additional transport and healthcare services for high-risk pregnant women from poor families. The significance of this measure is that it will not only eliminate the financial barriers to service access for herders, but also ensure appropriate antenatal care for every life as well as improve the quality of life for the Chinese nation as a whole.

Third, efforts should be taken to make maternal healthcare a priority in the poverty alleviation program, increase the opportunities for effective gynecological staff to attend further training and hire non-local experts to hold training sessions locally. In the lower altitude Tibetan areas in Qinghai and its neighboring provinces, gynecological technology is far better than that found in the prefectures of Guoluo and Yushu. This makes it necessary to hire doctors from these more advanced areas to deliver training. Not only will it be less difficult for trainers from other Tibetan areas to adapt to the high-altitude environment found in the

---

[8] WHO Europe Health Evidence Network (2005b).

prefectures of Guoluo and Yushu, their health service experiences will also be more closely in line with those found in Guoluo and Yushu.

In fact, some local herders suffering from diseases have already developed the habit of seeking medical attention in neighboring Tibetan areas. The author interviewed a herder named Sang Cuo (pseudonym) in Dongqinggou Township, Maqin County. In 2003 she was found to be suffering from tuberculosis of the lumbar spine and underwent an operation at the Ma'erkang Hospital in the capital of Sichuan Aba Prefecture. The reason she chose to seek treatment there is that she heard a Tibetan-speaking lay Buddhist saying that the medical facilities there are of a high quality and the doctors can speak Tibetan.

The fourth policy that should be pursued is to establish a service incentive mechanism at township level. Pastoral areas are sparsely populated and the village-level health service facilities are on the whole very poor. The most effective way to implement systematic maternal health management is to strengthen the system where the township health center sends medical staff to treat patients at their homes. This requires not only the dedication of the medical staff, but strict management implementation as well. For instance, the county health bureaus can issue maternal health whole-course service cards. The medical staff can then claim service remuneration and a transport (fuel) subsidy after service recipients sign the cards. The level of remuneration will be set in line with whether they have met their objectives.

Systems like this have already been in place in Chun'an County, a poor area in Zhejiang, in the form of a "community doctor responsibility system". Over recent years, this system has also been trialed in Lufeng County in Yunnan, a pilot county for a new cooperative medical system. The Amity Foundation (a private Christian group in China) implemented a program for treatment and prevention of women's diseases in Zhuoni County, a Tibetan-inhabited area in Gansu.[9] A similar management model has achieved great results. It is fair to say that if an incentive structure and hard control mechanisms are not in place at public health institutions, it will be hard for the poor pregnant and lying-in women to obtain the benefit of maternal services, regardless of how

---

[9]CASS Task Force (2007, p. 9).

much the government decides to increase expenditure on the service provision.

The fifth approach, at the county level, is that gynecological health service professionals should be reconsolidated to provide the integrated services of family planning and antenatal care. County and township-level health institutions should be made more complementary to each other and aim to enhance network service functions. Priority should be given to interventions for pregnant and lying-in women, as well as fetuses and newborns. China should further develop its mobile response capabilities in county-level maternal health institutions in poor areas. In this respect, the China Foundation for Poverty Alleviation has gained practical experience through the implementation of a maternal and child safety program in the mountainous areas found in Lijiang County, Yunnan.[10]

Finally, they should train more female village health workers in order to ensure the supply of health services that suit both Tibetan culture and customs. For the development of health professionals in Tibetan areas, China should not only stress gender equality, but also include their proficiency in Tibetan when evaluating the performance of medical staff. Otherwise, they will fall short on their promise to deliver good health services to the herders found in that area.

Bibliography

Adato, Michelle and John Hoddinott, 2007, "Conditional Cash Transfer Programs: A "Magic Bullet" for Reducing Poverty?", 2020 Focus Brief on the World's Poor and Hungry People, Washington, DC: IFPRI. http://www.ifpri.org/2020Chinaconference/pdf/beijingbrief_adato.pdf, downloaded on December 20, 2007.

Banta, David, 2003, "What is the Efficacy/Effectiveness of Antenatal Care and the Financial and Organizational Implications?", Copenhagen, WHO Regional Office for Europe (Health Evidence Network Report), http://www.euro.who.int/Document/E82996.pdf, downloaded on January 1, 2008.

CASS Task Force, 2007, "Socioeconomic Survey in Farming and Pasturing Areas of Gansu Province", Selected Works of Economic Leaflets, 04, 1–32.

---

[10]Zhu (2005, p. 159–162).

Johnson, Paul M., 1994 "A Glossary of Political Economy Terms", www.auburn. edu/~johnspm/gloss/merit_good, downloaded on January 15, 2008.

Maqin County Health and Family Planning Bureau, 2006, *Maqin County Health Work Summary for 2006 and Work Plan for 2007*, Document No. 87, November 28, 2006.

Ministry of Health, 2005, "Circular on Ensuring Implementation of the Program to Reduce Maternal Mortality and Eliminate Neonatal Tetanus, Document No. 9 (2005)", www.law-lib.com/law/law_view.asp?id=88744, downloaded on January 3, 2008.

Wang Zhiyuan, Ma Wannian, Nao Jiaman, Gazang Zhuoma, 2008, "Survey and Analysis on the Productive Health of 1,132 Tibetan Women in Plateau Pasture Areas", *Health Vocational Education*, 08, 129–130.

WHO Europe Health Evidence Network, 2005a, "What Is the Effectiveness of Antenatal Care?", http://www.euro.who.int/HEN/Syntheses/antenatal-supp/20051219_11, downloaded on January 1, 2008.

WHO Europe Health Evidence Network, 2005b, "What is the Effectiveness of Antenatal Care? Lifestyle Considerations", www.euro.who.int/HEN/Syntheses/antenatalsupp/20051219_6, downloaded on December 28, 2007.

Zhagyai, Lu Mei, 1998, *Tibetan Herdsmen: Survey Report on No. 5 Village in Yuqag Township of Amdo County in Northern Tibet*, Beijing: China Intercontinental Press.

Zhu Ling, 2005, *Following the Footsteps of Development*, Jinan: Shandong People's Press.

CHAPTER 8

Research on Compulsory Education in the Tibetan Regions of Qinghai and Yunnan Provinces

WEI Zhong

Abstract

China has launched an all-out campaign to eradicate "basic and semi-illiteracy", and achieve "basic universal access to compulsory education" (two basics). In Diqing Prefecture found in the Yunnan Province and Yushu and Guoluo Prefectures in Qinghai, where we undertook our survey, this task has become a major priority for the local government and has been carried out through a short-term campaign. School infrastructure has been improved greatly, but similar progress has not been made with regards to the competence of the teachers. Due to disparate levels of cultural exchange and economic development between the Tibetan regions of Yunnan and Qinghai, there are great differences in the attitude of local residents towards sending their children to school. Hence, the difficulty of promoting compulsory education also varies between the two provinces. In addition, the promotion of compulsory education has, to some extent, crowded out private schools and other forms of assistance. This chapter also describes some success stories and undertakes a brief analysis of the relationship between private and government-funded education. In conclusion, this chapter makes a number of policy recommendations focused on the promotion of compulsory education in Tibetan regions.

Keywords: Compulsory Education; Tibetan Regions; Government.

China has launched an all-out campaign to promote universal access to compulsory education in its Tibetan regions. But this is a challenging task given the low levels of access to compulsory education in Tibetan regions. In light of local realities, the local provincial government and educational authorities in China's Tibetan regions proposed the objectives of "universal access to at least six years of compulsory education", and "universal access to nine years of compulsory education" respectively. The responsibility of delivering this task falls to the local Party Secretary, though the county education bureaus are competent authorities that jointly work with other government authorities to promote universal access to compulsory education.

This ongoing campaign has received a lot of attention from researchers focused on the Tibetan regions. Some research conducted on the outcomes on basic education in Tibetan regions has already been published (e.g. *Dilemmas and Options of Educational Modernization for Ethnic Minorities in Qinghai*). In addition, Li Shurui[1], Mei Duanzhi, Zhang Heping,[2] Nian Cili,[3] Wang Zhenling and Ding Shengdong[4] have also conducted research on the topic of compulsory education in China's Tibetan regions. A member of our research project, Professor Lu Aiguo, also wrote some research reports on this issue.[5] Additionally, Professor Ma Rong, an expert on the education of ethnic minorities in China's western regions, also conducted some research on recent trends in bilingual education in China's western region.[6] However, most of these research efforts are made by educational administrators, scholars of educational management, or sociologists. Very few research papers have been written from an economic perspective. Hence, this chapter will deal with the issue from an economic perspective, looking at compulsory education in Tibetan regions, using an analytical framework based on supply and demand. Our survey includes the Tibetan regions of Qinghai and Yunnan Provinces.

---

[1] Li (2007).
[2] Mei and Zhang (2006).
[3] Nian (2005).
[4] Wang and Ding (2007).
[5] Lu (2002).
[6] Ma and Guo (2009).

I The Government's Role in Promoting Compulsory Education

According to the official objective, the campaign to improve student enrollment and educational quality in Tibetan regions aims to eradicate "basic and semi-illiteracy", and "achieve basic universal access to compulsory education" (known as the "two basics" in China's official vernacular). The Chinese government refers to this campaign as both arduous and far too shortsighted. As a result, after a large and hasty campaign was made to promote universal access to six years of compulsory education, no effort was made to consolidate its results, and shortly after, another campaign was launched to promote universal access to nine years of education. Needless to say, the effectiveness of the second campaign was not helped by the weak foundation provided by the previous work.

During these campaigns, the government and educational authorities have attached unprecedented attention to education. The magnitude of incentives and inputs is remarkable. In this section, we describe specific government actions and evaluate their effectiveness.

1. School infrastructure substantially improved due to a large increase in funding for compulsory education

We were most impressed by the quality of school infrastructure during our survey in Tibetan regions. Almost every county in our survey had many schools under construction. We were curious about why the construction of schools was deemed such a priority in this campaign. With this question in mind, we interviewed the directors of many schools and education bureaus and found that the promotion of compulsory education is regarded by schools as a rare opportunity for them to get funding from the government. Once the "two basics" campaign is over, it may take them an indefinite period of time to get funding for renovation and refurbishment.

2. County Party Secretary established an ad hoc department to encourage school attendance

Like other regions, compulsory education is extremely important to the local government in the Tibetan regions of Qinghai and Yunnan. There is a system of "one ballot veto" for compulsory education, which means that the central government attaches a huge amount of importance to the success of compulsory education. If the local government performs badly in this area of policy, it does not matter how well they perform in other areas, they will still be judged very harshly. Most regions have established a "two basics" steering committee led by the county's Party Secretary and involving directors from bureaus who are responsible for relevant functions. This steering committee is coordinated by the director of the education bureau. At the level of township and town (which is below the county level), there is also a similar system. Moreover, townships and towns have sent work groups to rural households to encourage school attendance. In this respect, Tibetan regions found in Qinghai and Yunnan do not differ much from other regions.

However, the Tibetan regions of Qinghai and Yunnan also have certain unique traits when it comes to the fight to promote compulsory education. Moreover, supervision has been greatly enhanced to prevent false attendance. In the past, the local authorities only had to fill in enrollment quotas, but now supervision is in place to ensure real-name attendance, making it more difficult to avoid attending. The following case is a story from the Jianshe Township of the Dari County.

Case 1 *Faking Attendance*

Mr. Suo Zha is opposed to sending his children to school, because if they attend school it means a lost opportunity for them to learn the skills needed to be an effective pastoral farmer. Moreover, he believes they are currently at the perfect age to pick up these skills. His eldest son has become a monk and his second son is pasturing at home. His second son should have gone to school three years ago, but he did not send his son there. At that time, false attendance was very common despite the fact that it was forbidden by the county authorities. The county authorities turned a blind eye to it and only gave a school attendance quota, which was set against the village's local population. As long as the number of children enrolled met the required target, no one would care whether the positions were filled by the intended children or not. The quotas in his village required at least three children and at most nine children to attend school. Among the nine children who attended the school, only five were from his village, with the other four being hired from other villages just to meet the quota (i.e. false attendance).

In the past few years, people in Mr. Suo Zha's village hired children from the Tehetu region, which is a nearby region with little supervision on compulsory education. According to the quotas, Mr. Suo Zha should have sent his nine-year-old son to school three years ago, but he spent RMB 4,000 *yuan* to hire a replacement, and it is said that it can cost as much as RMB 7,000–8,000 *yuan* to hire a replacement. He thinks that as long as someone goes to school, the requirement is met. Now, all school-age children are required to attend school, but because these families have already paid high prices to hire replacements in the past, they are very reluctant to send their children to school.

3. A source of funding guaranteed as many county governments raised debt to support compulsory education

As the "two basics" policy has begun to take effect on the enrollment rate in schools, it can be seen that there has been substantial improvements in the enrollment rate for school-age children in the Tibetan regions of Qinghai and Yunnan. Specifically, the demand for compulsory education has surged. The other side of the story is supply. Because most schools were designed and constructed with the expectation of less than full attendance, this sudden increase in enrollment has intensified the shortage of classrooms and dormitories.[7] Hence, mass construction has become an urgent priority. In the surveyed regions, we saw that many schools are under construction.

Construction requires a great amount of funding. Although China's compulsory education funding prioritizes the western regions of China — particularly Tibetan regions — there is still a tremendous

---

[7] Tibetan households are dispersed, and therefore many students need to live in a school dormitory. New students are mostly from more remote regions and thus need to stay in the dormitory all the more, intensifying the shortage.

shortage. In order to meet the objectives set under the policy, the "two basics", many county authorities in China's Tibetan regions make up for the shortage of funds through debt raised from financial institutions. This financing effort is essential if they are to deal with the pressure created by the "two basics" program. But it should be noted that county governments may not be able to repay the loans, and the local people's congress seem to be uninterested in whether and how the debts can and will be repaid. The leaders in local government completely ignore the views of the people's congress when it comes to the issue of raising funds through debt.

4. Free schooling and allowances have increased the enrollment rate

In recent years, the Chinese government has issued a policy to cancel tuition fees, provide free textbooks, and subsidize boarding for students, in order to promote rural compulsory education. This policy has been in effect since 2001, and in terms of the breakdown, China's central government finance provides free textbooks and funding and the local government is responsible for the cancellation of miscellaneous fees and boarding allowances. By 2007, students from poor families in China's rural areas have all benefited from this policy.

This policy has been effective in other parts of western China, where most farmers are willing to send children to school, but the dropout rate is particularly high for children from poor families. Free schooling, free textbooks and allowances have given certain incentives to those in dire need. The situation is somewhat different in Tibetan regions, because in this case, the inhabitants have formed a unique way of life over generations. In Tibetan regions, children start working at an early age. At the age of five or six years, they are expected to engage in work on the pastures. This conventional way of life for the inhabitants contradicts sharply with the principles of compulsory education. In addition, religion holds a lot of sway in Tibetan regions, particularly in Guoluo and Yushu Prefectures, which are found in Qinghai. The average household has a traditional practice of sending their sons to the monastery. This is also incompatible with the principles of compulsory education. It is not possible to change these practices purely through offering free education. This policy may well have some effect in Tibetan regions, but the effect is much smaller compared with other parts of western China. It has only increased the enrollment rate in Tibetan regions to a limited extent.

5. Supervision on compulsory education focuses on enrollment rate

The campaign to promote compulsory education has received close supervision. In the surveyed counties, we could often see banners bearing words like *"We welcome officials to inspect our county's efforts to promote the 'two basics'."* Obviously, inspection is frequent and helps urge lower-level authorities to meet the requirements set from above. But, this kind of inspection only occurs over a short space of time. In addition, the inspection is focused on the enrollment rate and school infrastructure; it does not cover the quality of education.

II Farming and Herding Households' Responses to the Compulsory Education Campaign

Different regions had different responses to the campaign which promoted compulsory education. Some regions still resist this idea and hold on to a more traditional way of life. However, in other places, the enrollment rate is on the rise. The former situation is common for the Yushu and Guoluo areas found in Qinghai Province, while the latter is seen in the Shangri-La region in Yunnan Province.

Why do Tibetans have such diverse views on compulsory education, despite sharing the same ethnic and religious background? We summarize our analysis into four main factors below.

1. Employment prospects

Employment prospects are vastly different for the Tibetan regions of Yunnan as compared to Qinghai. When looking at the prospect of employment, according to economic principles, the accumulation of human capital is extremely important. Different attitudes towards compulsory education are the result of such an economic choice.

Following many years of advertising, the Diqing region in Yunnan has now become a famous tourist destination. Thus, the local Tibetans have increasingly been brought in touch with people from the outside. There is a tremendous demand for labor in the prosperous catering and services industries. Educated local Tibetans who can speak decent Mandarin are able to find non-agricultural jobs, which are well-paid and therefore make education and training much more attractive to the locals.

Take for example the Bita Sea, which is a tourist destination in Diqing Prefecture. This very scenic destination originally had around a hundred employees, but this number has now reached a thousand. The Diqing Prefecture Government announced a policy which prioritized local people who applied for job positions. However, they were unable to find sufficient numbers of qualified staff. For example, a local tourist car company needed five to ten drivers, but only two of the applicants were sufficiently qualified. Similarly, an urban cleaning company needed contract workers with at least a junior middle school level of education. Therefore, in Diqing Prefecture there are many job opportunities for those who are relatively well-educated. It should be noted that such job prospects are not available in Yushu and Guoluo.

2. Traditional ways of working impede the spread of compulsory education

Farmers and herders in Yushu and Guoluo Prefectures resist measures to educate their children. It is also true that before tourism developed in Diqing, the school enrollment rate was also very low. This is because in Diqing, Yushu and Guoluo Prefectures, farming and herding requires few skills, but farming and herding skills must be acquired at an early age. Attending school means giving up such early-age training and therefore dampens local enthusiasm towards compulsory education.

As described above, in Diqing Prefecture, tourism provided job opportunities for educated locals and therefore promoted educational development. In Yushu and Guoluo Prefectures, however, education may not lead

to clear employment prospects. There is a popular saying that the educated youth cannot graze as well as his dad and nor can he farm as well as
his brother's wife. Due to the lack of job opportunities, some youngsters
are indeed unemployed after graduation. This situation has enhanced the
prejudice of local farmers and herders against compulsory education.

3. Conflict between monasteries and compulsory education

According to Tibetan customs, families should send their young children
to monasteries and nunneries. Traditionally, Tibetan Buddhism also
requires monasteries to receive monks at a very early age, so as to learn
the scriptures and get used to life in a monastery. This tradition is now in
conflict with today's compulsory education. The influence of this tradition in Diqing is fairly weak, as the area is more socially and economically
developed. But the conflict is apparent in Yushu and Guoluo Prefectures
in Qinghai, where religion is far more influential.

Given the conflict between compulsory education and religious customs, the local authorities in Yushu and Guoluo Prefectures in Qinghai
have taken open and pragmatic policy measures: All school-age children
must receive compulsory education according to the *Law of Compulsory
Education*. However, taking into account the custom that once a layman
becomes a monk, they are unable to return to normal society, the local
authorities have allowed child monks to study at schools wearing their
religious clothing.

4. Dilemma of a bilingual education: Mandarin
   is not of much use locally and Tibetan is not useful
   in the outside world

A bilingual education is commonly applied to China's ethnic minorities.
In Tibetan regions, this system refers to the use of both Mandarin and
Tibetan. But in fact, except for a few counties and schools, courses are
taught in only one language. In most cases, in rural primary schools, les-
sons are taught only in Tibetan. Yet in most counties, most schools teach
only in Mandarin. Tibetan is still taught in a few schools, such as county
ethnic middle schools.

Having a bilingual education should promote inter-ethnic communi-cation and ethnic culture, but in fact it actually increases the burden on students. The bilingual education in itself is not the problem. For instance, a bilingual education is quite common in India, and is applied to good effect. However, in China's Tibetan regions, a bilingual education is applied in a single language environment. Moreover, there are prob-lems in the interconnection between courses taught in both languages. Children of farmers and herders attend primary school in the local village or township, where courses are taught in Tibetan. After junior middle school, there are no Tibetan language versions of physics, math, chemis-try, etc. Due to the change in language, it is very difficult for the Tibetan students to catch up. More importantly, for children of farmers and herd-ers, there will not be many opportunities for them to use Mandarin locally; yet if they continue to learn in Tibetan, communication with non-Tibetans will be difficult and not many books are written in Tibetan.

In Diqing Prefecture, which is on the border of Tibetan settlements, tourism and close contact with non-Tibetans has greatly improved the locals' Mandarin skills. Conversely, their Tibetan is arguably not as good. In Yushu and Guoluo Prefectures, which are core Tibetan regions, local Tibetans mainly speak Tibetan because there are not many people who are native Mandarin speakers. Hence, both regions have weaknesses when it comes to the application of a bilingual Tibetan and Mandarin education. Table 1 provides a comparison of compulsory education between the Tibetan regions in Yunnan and the situation in Yushu and Guoluo Prefectures.

As a result of promoting compulsory education, the public schools in the Tibetan regions of Yunnan and Qinghai underwent some change. First, there was a period of intensive construction of new schools, which led to a substantial increase in enrollment. In addition, schools also upgraded their facilities such as computers, musical instruments and sports facilities. The schools in Tibetan regions had greatly improved their infrastructure. However, under the special campaign on compulsory education, there is not a great deal of improvement in the quality of teaching. Some students attended school earlier than others and student performance is also uneven. Becoming a teacher is seen as a very desirable job, second only to becoming a civil servant. But given that the job is

Table 1:   Comparison between Tibetan Regions of Yunnan, Yushu and Guoluo.

	Tibetan regions of Yunnan	Yushu and Guoluo Prefectures
Before the campaign on compulsory education	The condition of school facilities is very poor. Students are unenthusiastic.	Roughly the same. Low enrollment, opposition from parents.
Current status	Improved school infrastructure. Increased equipment input. Students are more enthusiastic.	Renovated school infrastructure. Increased equipment input. Enrollment has increased but enthusiasm is still low.
Cultural exchange	Close to Mandarin-speaking regions, making it easier to learn Mandarin.	One of the core Tibetan-speaking regions with little contact with Mandarin-speaking people. It is difficult and not very useful to learn Mandarin.
Employment prospects	Tourism has increased the number of jobs but participation requires a higher level of education.	Future jobs are in farming and herding, and the knowledge acquired from school is not of much use.
Religious influence	Religious influence is not strong and its impact on compulsory education is limited.	Religious influence is strong and contradicts with compulsory education.

seen as an "iron rice bowl", there is a real shortage of competent teachers. In addition, there are tremendous gaps in the pay grades between employee teachers and contractual teachers, giving rise to friction between ethnic groups.

III The Private Sector and Compulsory Education

The private sector in China's Tibetan regions has always played an important role. With regards to education, private schools and public schools have coexisted for many years. The private sector has played a two-fold role in both founding schools and financing education. While private schools are not welcomed by the educational authorities, donations are well received, at least among many local educational authorities. Under the large-scale campaign of the "two basics", the local government in China's Tibetan regions have once again faced the question of how to balance the relationship between compulsory education and private education.

1. Advantages and drawbacks of private education

In addition to public schools, there are also some private schools in China's Tibetan regions, including those found in the areas we surveyed in Qinghai and Yunnan. What role do private schools play in supplementing the education provided by public schools?

(A) Private schools are not encouraged because of political considerations

Private education is subject to certain restrictions in China's Tibetan regions. In fact, many private schools do not have the approval of the educational authorities, i.e. these schools are illegal. In fact, the local educational authorities are not in a position to approve some private schools because their curriculum is not "standardized" and it is not entirely clear what is taught in these schools.

(B) Conflict between the curriculum in private schools and that found in compulsory education texts

In addition, private schools often have a different curriculum to that found in compulsory education. Thus, it can be the case that students may not meet the curriculum requirements after a certain number of years of schooling. Furthermore, some educational authorities believe that compulsory education is the government's responsibility. For instance, the vice director of a county's Educational Bureau said, *"Tibetan schools run by the public and tulku (living Buddha) should also be included in the national educational system. Compulsory education should be run by the government."* He also added that some schools did not offer courses in line with the curriculum.

(C) *Negative attitudes of the educational authorities and the private sector makes private education unstable*

Another difficulty of private education is stability. Unlike other parts of China, where schools are founded by people from the educational system, most private schools in China's Tibetan regions are run by the *tulku* and local residents, who lack educational experience and may not have a proper understanding of how to deliver contemporary education. Local educational authorities therefore oppose private education for this reason.

(D) *Potential for private education: Capital, teachers, educational resource distribution, and vocational education*

Funding for private education is not very stable. Unlike other parts of China, most of the private schools in Tibetan regions are non-profit and their financing comes from various donations. Thus, their funding stream can be described as being "unstable". I am aware of at least one private school that has encountered financial problems. The constant turnover of teaching staff is another drawback of private education, particularly in Tibetan regions. The teaching faculty includes far too many volunteers and long-term teaching staff are almost non-existent.

But private education also has its advantages. For example, it can help improve the distribution of educational resources and has made a number of steps forward in vocational education. Amidst the efforts to promote compulsory education in Tibetan regions, the consolidation of village primary schools has become a major step towards improving the quality of teaching, while at the same time this measure has also created a new problem. Due to the fact that most households are dispersed over a wide geographical area, many young children have to walk long distances to go to school. This factor greatly dampens their enthusiasm for schooling. If such schools are allowed to open in the more remote areas, private schools will help to increase the enrollment rate among Tibetan children. In addition, private education in China's Tibetan regions is mostly related to vocational education. Most private schools offer subjects such as painting, traditional Tibetan handicraft making, conventional apparel making, etc. Offering practical training suits the local needs and is an approach that public schools could learn from. A very good example of such a school can be found in the Guoluo Prefecture in Qinghai. The school is called the Jigme Gyaltsen Welfare School.

Case 2 Jigme Gyaltsen Welfare School

There is a famous monk named Jigme Gyaltsen in the Luozhou Prefecture in Qinghai. Born to a family that worked on the land, Jigme Gyaltsen was an extremely good student in his early years and then went on to study Buddhism at Ta'er Temple and China Buddhism College. After graduating, he moved to a local monastery and managed to open a private school. The school has grown quickly, and there are now more than 600 students.

A particularly impressive feature of Jigme Gyaltsen's school is the combination of a Tibetan monastery education and contemporary basic education. His approach is to teach Tibetan grammar to all of the students in the first semester, so that they will learn to read. Once they are able to read, they can then increase their vocabulary through reading. Once the students are fairly proficient when it comes to reading, they will be able to undertake various courses in the language. Another improvement is the introduction of debate. Debates are held in the monastery, and arguments are often focused on the Buddhist scriptures. The process of debating is very useful, in that it increases the understanding of the students on the subject matter.

These teaching methods have greatly increased efficiency. There has also been an improvement in college entrance examinations. Every year there are students who pass the exam and successfully enroll in a college. Members of the provincial political consultative conference inspected the school and recognized its innovative teaching methods.

2. Potential for private donations

In addition to private education, there are also others that provide donations in the Tibetan regions. These donations are given by either private or semi-official entities. Most of the donations are proactive in nature and play an important role in the development of education locally. In addition, the educational authorities are far more tolerant of private donations, when compared to private education. Private educational donations are welcomed by the government and educational authorities alike.

Currently, donations come from four main sources.

(A) Semi-official donations such as the Hope Project

In China's Tibetan regions, there are many semi-official educational investments and donations. These donations are in addition to public spending on education. In the Tibetan regions in Qinghai and Yunnan, there are a lot of Hope Project schools. Such schools are funded by central and local government donations as well as donations from large and medium-sized enterprises. These donations are semi-official. Official foundations such as the Hope Project also provide a certain degree of assistance on a one-to-one level.

(B) Donations from the international community

Similar to official sources of assistance, in China's Tibetan regions, international non-governmental organizations (NGOs) also provide donations to improve school infrastructure.

(C) Donations from overseas Tibetans

Such donations are also invested in the construction and renovation of schools. This activity provides some proof of the surge in demand for classrooms, following the increase in the number of Tibetan students.

(D) *Educational donations from domestic NGOs*

Donations from local NGOs are different from donations received from other sources. NGOs have limited financial resources and are unable to invest in the construction of schools. On the other hand, NGOs are familiar with the needs of those who live in the Tibetan regions, and can therefore deliver the much needed assistance. A typical example of this kind of assistance can be found in Chengduo County, Yushu Prefecture, Qinghai Province.

Case 3 *Gesanghua, a Private Educational Assistance Organization*

This story starts in a similar manner as other examples of private educational assistance. In 2005, a volunteer named Hong Bo in Keke Xili founded a private educational assistance organization called "Gesanghua" together with two or three friends. This organization faced a number of difficulties at the outset as it failed to gain the cooperation of selected regions. At this time, Gesanghua's manager Ms. Hong Bo established contact with Chengduo County. Moreover, the president of Chengduo First Middle School, Mr. Zhiming Longzhu, made direct contact with Ms. Hong Bo and they agreed that they should work together. Shortly after some one-to-one assistance was delivered, there was a major snow disaster in Chengduo County, and Mr. Zhiming Longzhu sent a request for assistance to Gesanghua. Having received the request, Gesanghua swiftly delivered some disaster relief materials, transporting them from Xining to Chengduo. It took less than three days for the goods to be delivered to Chengduo County. This example of assistance strengthened the mutual trust between Chengduo County and Gesanghua. Currently, Gesanghua has expanded its assistance from one-to-one assistance, to the supply of winter clothes, stationery, sports goods, books, etc. In addition, Gesanghua developed a Tibetan Teacher Training Plan. The concept behind the plan is to send teachers from China's eastern region to train local teachers in Chengduo County. Some local teachers in Chengduo are also selected to take part in long-term training activities in China's eastern region (lasting about a semester). Having built up a great deal of trust, the Gesanghua educational assistance organization has overcome its registration difficulties, a common problem for NGOs located in Chengduo.

From this case we can see that Gesanghua and Chengduo built mutual trust through providing assistance in times of difficulties, and subsequent activities enhanced their ties further. One aspect of this case needs to be highlighted. The Gesanghua educational assistance organization built an effective relationship with Chengduo's educational authorities, and took on an acceptable role in compulsory education. In doing so it ensured that its activities aimed at helping the area are mutual and long-term. For instance, Gesanghua identified an appropriate way to assist the local area pertaining to the realities on the ground and sensibly chose not to set up an independent school. This was a good idea, given the stance of Chengduo's County Educational Bureau, which welcomed Gesanghua's educational assistance and made the latter's work easier when it came to late-stage supervision. This case provides a good example of how private educational donations can work.

IV Educational Assistance Options in Tibetan Regions

A great success attributable to increased access to compulsory education is the improvement and renovation of the schools found in Tibetan regions. School buildings and classrooms have been greatly improved, and so have the desks, canteens and dormitories. With improved infrastructure, however, the lack of competency of the teaching staff stands out. Therefore, sending teachers to Tibetan regions is the most important way to provide educational assistance and there are three different ways this assistance is provided: official education volunteers, private education volunteers and teacher exchange and training programs. In the following section, we will discuss each of the three options.

1. *Official education volunteers*

In general, official educational assistance refers to the educational assistance activities in China's western region organized by the central committee of the Communist Youth League. These activities are nationwide and serve two purposes. The first is to improve the competency level of teaching staff found in the western regions. The second is to ease the problem of unemployment among China's college graduates. This activity became extremely popular. But according to what we have seen in Tibetan regions, this type of educational assistance failed to deliver on its primary target. A school president commented, *"The volunteers became a burden. First, they cannot even take care of themselves. Second, they are more ambitious than capable, and are unable to teach effectively, so we did not dare to accept them. Third, the underlying intention behind educational assistance is good, but the volunteers have their own selfish motivations and lack the spirit of sacrifice and dedication."*

The reasons are simple: The volunteers came to the remote regions not because they wanted to help raise the quality of local education, but because of certain incentives that promise better job opportunities in future. Second, most of the volunteers are those who failed to land jobs after graduation and thus it is reasonable to surmise that they must have certain weaknesses. In addition, the needs of the local populace were not considered; the subjects as well as the underlying knowledge that some volunteers acquired during their studies are of little use to local people.

2. *Private education volunteers*

There are also many volunteers in private schools found in Yushu and Guoluo Prefectures in Yunnan and Qinghai. Most of these volunteers are from private organizations. Unlike official volunteers, private volunteers are enthusiastic and have good intentions. But their involvement has not been particularly successful either. On one hand, the local conditions are too harsh for them, and on the other, there is no binding contract between the volunteers and employers, so the volunteers can leave at any time and for any reason. This instability is the biggest headache for employers.

There are official volunteers who manage to endure the hardships and perform well and there are private volunteers who work at local schools for a long period of time. But generally speaking, the enthusiasm of the former is in doubt and the willingness of the latter to stay for a long time is also somewhat dubious. For the most part, volunteers can only teach less important subjects. In general, the efforts of sending volunteer teachers to these schools has been far from successful and the key lesson learned is that the right teachers should be selected to assist Tibetan schools according to the situational context.

3. Teacher exchanges and training

Local educational authorities are preoccupied with the imperative task of increasing enrollment and have little time to address the problem of incompetent teachers. The educational system has (or at least claims it has) opportunities for teacher training. However, it is very difficult to find examples of where these opportunities have been delivered. Nevertheless, even with training, it is not difficult to imagine what the result would be, given the lack of good local teachers to deliver the training.

A shortage of teacher exchanges and training opportunities requires volunteer teachers to fill the gap. Sending teachers from other regions to Tibetan regions for short-term training courses and offering opportunities to send local teachers on exchange tours with teachers from other provinces and regions seem to be viable options. In the previous section, we described some activities by the private organization Gesanghua in the Tibetan regions in Qinghai which have been well received.

V Conclusions and Policy Recommendations

This chapter summarizes the conclusions from our research and policy recommendations concerning the promotion of compulsory education in the Tibetan regions in Yunnan and Qinghai.

1. Despite various problems, the work to promote compulsory education in the Tibetan regions in Qinghai and Yunnan can certainly be described as somewhat hasty, but, on the other hand, it has been generally successful. This work has substantially increased the enrollment rate for school-age children, and will further increase the competence of local residents in future, providing good human resources for the socioeconomic development of China's Tibetan regions.

2. Promotion of compulsory education and the inflow of capital have greatly enhanced school infrastructure and increased the enthusiasm of children to attend school. The infrastructure provides a good foundation for the further development of education in the Tibetan regions in Yunnan and Qinghai.

3. Current work on promoting compulsory education is undertaken through "campaigns", which seems to give good results in the short term but cannot provide job prospects for the students; worst, it seems to be financially unstable. The former will cause reductions in the rate of enrollment once the campaign is over. The latter will lead to financial difficulties for the local government. Therefore, vocational education should be carried out to improve job prospects. Given limited local finances and the low rate of central funding for compulsory education, China should permit the establishment of private schools or private donations under the framework of compulsory education.

4. Unfortunately, the competency of teachers in the Tibetan regions in Yunnan and Qinghai is not up to the standard required to properly promote universal access to compulsory education. Therefore, it is imperative to provide human resources to support education in Tibetan regions. However, it is still the case that volunteers in official and private education have failed to achieve the expected results. Hence, a new approach should be considered to increase the training for teachers, not only by inviting teachers from other areas but also by sending Tibetan teachers to take part in exchanges and training programs in the more developed parts of China.

Bibliography

Chen Wei, 2007, "Effective Ways to Achieve Balanced Development of Compulsory Education in Tibetan Regions of Qinghai Province", *Journal of Qinghai Institute of Nationalities* (Social Sciences Page), 33(3), 113–115.

Li Chenling, 2005, *Dilemma and Options for the Modernization of Ethnic Education in Qinghai Province*, Beijing: Nationality Press.

Li Shurui, 2007, "Traditional Monastery Education Philosophies and Mistakes of Modern Education in Tibetan Regions", *Journal of Qinghai Normal University* (Philosophy and Social Sciences Page), 01, 126–129.

Lu Aiguo, 2002, "Questions of Educational Development", In *Development Path Options for Late Developed Regions: Case Studies of Tibetan Regions of Yunnan Province*, Wang Luolin and Zhu Ling (Eds.), Beijing: Economic Management Press, pp. 125–155.

Ma Rong and Guo Zhigang, 2009, *Development of Education for Ethnic Minorities in China's Western Region*, Beijing: Nationality Press.

Mei Duanzhi, Zhang Heping, 2006, "Research on the Uniqueness of Human Resources Development in Ethnic Regions of South Qinghai Province", *Journal of Qinghai Institute of Nationalities* (Social Sciences Page), 32(4), 59–63.

Nian Cili, 2005, "Creating a Modern System of Ethnic Education in Light of Characteristics of Tibetan Regions", *Journal of Northwest University of Nationalities* (Philosophy and Social Sciences Page), 02, 57–61.

Wang Zhenling, Ding Shengdong, 2007, "Background, Status and Countermeasures of Elementary Education in Tibetan Regions of Qinghai Province", *Ethnic Education Research*, 18(1), 66–72.

CHAPTER 9

Effects of Radio and TV on the Cultural Lives of Farmers and Herdsmen

ZHOU Ji

Abstract

Based on field surveys[1] conducted in the rural Tibetan-inhabited regions of Gansu, Qinghai and Yunnan Provinces, this chapter has found that radio and television (TV) — compared to other forms of media — currently play an indispensable role in promoting Party and state policies, influencing public opinion among farmers and herdsmen, expanding the channels they can use to access information and knowledge, enhancing their ability to participate in market activities, as well as improving their material living standards and cultural life. This chapter also found that the cultural life of farmers and herdsmen has been enriched and improved remarkably, thanks to the popularization of radio and TV in the remote regions in the west. This is reflected in the comprehensive implementation of state projects such as the "Tibet–Xinjiang Project for Radio and TV Coverage" and the "Extend Radio and TV Coverage to Every Village Project". Meanwhile, the accompanying new demands and problems require special attention from relevant government departments.

Keywords: Radio; TV; Cultural Lives; Farmers and Herdsmen.

---

[1] The field surveys in this chapter were completed in 2007. The data and cases quoted here all refer to the statistical results and the situation prior to and in 2007.

As a form of mass media that has penetrated into every aspect of daily life, radio and TV are characterized by their vividness, timeliness and their universality compared with other forms of media, including newspapers, magazines, audio-visual products and the internet. These factors explain why they have a comparative advantage in disseminating information quickly, influencing public opinion, influencing trends in the consumption of entertainment, enriching cultural life and improving one's quality of life. As part of an effort to extend such advantages to the vast rural areas and the remote regions in western China, starting in 1998, the Chinese government has carried out a nationwide project to "extend radio and TV coverage to every village". The first round of this large-scale project (that involved many regions) was initiated in 1998 and was finally completed in 2005. The latest round was initiated in 2006. The stated goal was to introduce radio and TV into all villages with over 20 households and access to electricity by 2010.[2] A survey conducted in Haiyan County in Zhejiang, entitled "The Cultural Needs of Farmers", showed that watching TV is the primary means of entertainment for 94% of the farmers in the region.[3] If it is true that so many farmers are influenced by TV in the economically developed regions in the eastern areas of China, does this still hold in the less economically developed regions in the west? What about those areas in the west that are largely inhabited by Tibetans? Despite having looked at a range of sources, we found very few studies on this topic. In this chapter, the author provides a general discussion of the role of radio and TV in the daily cultural lives of farmers and herdsmen, as well as an analysis of some of the existing problems related to this topic. This chapter was written after visiting the counties of Zhuoni and Xiahe (which are both under the jurisdiction of southern Gansu Tibetan Autonomous Prefecture), the county of Shangri-La (which is under the jurisdiction of the Diqing Tibetan Autonomous Prefecture of Yunnan), the counties of Maqin and Dari (which are under the jurisdiction of the Guoluo Tibetan

---

[2] Refer to the General Office of the State Council's statement in 2006: "Notification on Improving the Introduction of Broadcast Television to Every Village in the New Period".

[3] http://zjnews.zjol.com.cn, downloaded on December 26, 2007.

Autonomous Prefecture of Qinghai), and finally the counties of Yushu and Chengduo (which are under the jurisdiction of Yushu Tibetan Autonomous Prefecture).

I The Status Quo in Agricultural and Pastoral Areas

Currently, due to various factors, the standard of cultural life in the above-mentioned agricultural or pastoral areas which the author visited cannot be compared with the areas where the county government or the prefecture is located. In the agricultural and pastoral areas, they have far poorer access to the radio and TV. Standards also differ greatly between those farmers and herdsmen who live near cities and towns, and those who live far away. Today, radio and TV programs are no longer inaccessible to the latter. In particular, for families who enjoy comprehensive comparative advantages, radio and TV have become so integrated into their daily cultural lives that they cannot do without them.

1. Radio and TV: A primary part of the daily cultural life for many farmers and herdsmen

Over the course of doing their work and conducting their lives more generally, farmers and herdsmen in Tibetan regions in western China have not only created material wealth which they rely on to cover their living expenses, but have also developed a cultural life around ethnic customs and plateau features, such as horse racing, dancing, singing and watching Tibetan dramas. Over time, the content of their cultural lives keeps diversifying and developing. However, it is important to bear in mind that the traditional cultural activities in Tibetan regions are held, for the most part, during ethnic festivals. For the most part (i.e. excluding festivals), many farmers and herdsmen find it hard to participate in these traditional cultural activities, due to multiple restrictions in terms of both time and other practical considerations.

After the nationwide liberation, while promoting the development of the ethnic regional economy, the Party and the government have also invested large amounts of human and material resources in the construction of local cultural facilities, such as cinemas, libraries, museums, as well

as central and provincial people's radio stations which feature radio programs in Tibetan. While these modern cultural facilities have greatly
enriched the cultural lives of those who live in these ethnic regions, only
a small percentage of the population has access to these public services
given that the provision of these services is mainly concentrated where
the local government is located, be that at the prefecture, county, village
or town level. Apart from that, Tibetan-inhabited regions are characterized by a vast land mass but relatively small population, poor transport
infrastructure, and high mountains and deep valleys. Thus, it is extremely
difficult for a large number of farmers and herdsmen, who live far away
from cities and towns, to experience modern cultural life.

With the implementation of reform and opening up and the western
China development strategy, remote ethnic regions have witnessed
remarkable progress in social and economic development, accompanied
by a noticeable improvement in the material living standards of farmers
and herdsmen. Moreover, the construction of local radio stations, TV
stations as well as the broadcast of Tibetan-speaking TV programs, have
satisfied the cultural needs of farmers and herdsmen to some extent. This
is especially the case after the implementation of projects such as the
"Tibet–Xinjiang Project for Radio and TV Coverage" and "Extend Radio
and TV Coverage to Every Village"; the cultural life of farmers and herdsmen in remote western regions has been enriched on a larger scale and
to a far greater extent. Nowadays, in addition to participating in various
traditional cultural events during festivals and holidays each year; listen-
ing to the radio and watching TV have become an indispensable part of
the daily life of farmers and herdsmen, particularly so for the latter.

Case 1 Mr Gan's TV Habits

Mr. A Gan is a member of Wunong Cooperative in Nishi Village. The
village is found in Jiantang in the Shangri-La County (Diqing Tibetan
Autonomous Prefecture, Yunnan). In 1987, he spent nearly 1,000
yuan on a 14-inch black and white television and his family became
the first household in the cooperative to own a television set.

In 2002, Mr. Gan exchanged his black and white TV for a
25-inch color one, which cost him about 2,000 yuan. In addition, he

spent 800 yuan on a satellite TV receiver (which is commonly referred to as a "sky wok"). By replacing the old television set and upgrading the receiver, Mr. Gan greatly improved both his television and the picture quality of the programs he viewed.

Ever since the family bought the television, Mr. Gan and his family members have spent most of their free time — especially the evenings — watching TV. However, Mr. Gan and his family still have regrets. Specifically, they are as yet unable to watch the local news in the same way as they are able to see satellite TV programs.

2. Radio and TV: Primary means for farmers and herdsmen to access various information and knowledge

A noticeable difference between a modern open society and those societies that are less open lies in how fast information and knowledge can spread and how easily accessible they are. In a modern open society, a variety of information can spread quickly through various channels. Moreover, from this vast source of information and knowledge, individuals can pick and choose what they want to consume based on their personal needs or preferences. As time passes, their outlook will become broader and their thought processes increasingly vivid. Undoubtedly, such subtle influences would tremendously assist overall social and economic development. In contrast, societies that are less open (i.e. a semi-closed society) are characterized by the slow flow of information, an imbalanced spread of knowledge, as well as limited channels of communication between its people and the outside world. Such a closed structure undoubtedly impedes the rapid development of the social economy in the long term.

Over the years, for the farmers and herdsmen found in the remote plateau regions, their connections to the outside world have been affected and restricted to varying degrees. To varying degrees, they have lived in a "semi-closed environment" for quite some time stemming from a lack of manpower, poor transport infrastructure, the lack of transportation and poor climatic conditions. For example, in the inland parts of China, a letter or magazine can be delivered very quickly. However, in the western Tibetan regions, especially in remote areas far from towns and cities, it takes at least a month or in some cases even longer for local farmers and herdsmen to receive such things. Because of these difficulties, regulations or policies made by the local government cannot be distributed to a scattered population in a short time.

Since the reform and opening up, remote regions found in the west of China have witnessed noticeable improvements in various aspects of their infrastructure. However, there is still a big gap between these regions and the inland regions. For example, there are no post offices in some villages and towns. Frankly speaking, in order to eliminate the differences between these two types of areas, there will need to be an extended effort over a long period of time. In this sense, modern media, such as TV and radio, can play an indispensable role by considerably compensating the development lag in these remote regions, and thus breaking down the conditions that have lead to these areas being "closed" or "semi-closed".

Case 2 Mr. Zha — A TV Fan

Mr. A Zha, a member of the No. 1 Cooperative in Xiewu Village of Xiewu Town in Chengduo County (Yushu Prefecture, Qinghai), is a fan of television. In 2000, he bought a 1,600 yuan 25-inch Changhong color television, and spent an extra 1,400 yuan on a receiver which he boasted was the best you could buy at the time; it still functions well to this day. His family was one of the first households to own a television. In 2004, he bought a new 29-inch Gaoluhua color TV which cost him 1,700 yuan. Every morning he gets up at 6 a.m. and if there is no work that needs to be urgently done, he will turn on the TV and watch the morning news programs. In the evenings, he usually watches TV before he goes to sleep. His favorite TV program is the news on CCTV, though historical dramas come in a close second. We were informed by Mr. Zha that since there is no post office in town, it is impossible for him to find a place nearby to subscribe to a newspaper or magazine. Despite the fact that Xiewu is quite close to the prefecture government, he still has to trek a distance of 47 kilometers over the mountains in order to get there. Xiewu is even further away from the county government, which is roughly 80 kilometers away. Although the post offices in the county and prefecture offer subscription services, they are unable to deliver to Xiewu because of the distances involved. There is also a "cultural station" in town, but he has never been there for the simple reason that when the station is open during the day, he is at work, and when he is free in the evenings, the station would have already closed for the day. Therefore, watching TV is his only means of accessing various kinds of information and knowledge.

Mr. A Zha also mentioned that through watching TV, he has heard a lot about significant national news and has learned about the colorful world that exists outside of his immediate area. Nevertheless, it is a great pity that he does not have access to some of the TV programs he wants to watch, such as CCTV Channels 3, 5, 6 and 8. It is also unfortunate that he is not able to view the Yushu Prefecture's local news programs and programs made by Chengduo TV stations. It would be a significant improvement if he were able to watch cable TV programs like those in the town of Jiegu[4] and the county. Even if he had to pay a monthly fee for the service, as urban residents do, it would be very worthwhile.

3. *Radio and TV: A significant influence over farmers' and herdsmen's daily lives*

The younger generation of farmers and herdsmen who live in western Tibetan regions have a passion for life, are enthusiastic and generous, have a thirst for knowledge and dream of a better future. Faced with a harsh reality, they are not in the least bit satisfied with the status quo and work hard to pursue their goals bravely. Due to an unyielding optimism (an attitude they bring into their daily lives), they try by every means available to improve their standard of life and living conditions, regardless of any price they have to pay. In the context of a market economy, the farmers and herdsmen have heard of and in some cases have even seen an ever-changing and infinitely fascinating world outside. It is thus unsurprising that the younger generation has a deep longing and wish to pursue a modern life.

---

[4] This is the location of Yushu Tibetan Autonomous Prefecture Government in Qinghai.

In modern times, the popularization of radio and TV in the remote regions in the west has, in a quite abstract sense, shortened the distance between these regions and the inland regions. As a result, the locals who have lived in these western regions for many generations no longer feel that the outside world is very far away. It is true that their economic development lags far behind the inland regions. However, this fact does not stop these regions from adopting the faster-paced and more varied lifestyles like those found in the inland regions. At the places where the author and other members of the research group visited, most of the Tibetan elementary or middle school students we met could speak standard Mandarin. When asked why they spoke Mandarin to such a high standard, they all gave pretty much the same answer: All stressed the important impact of both the TV and radio.

Case 3 The Influence of TV

At the clean and tidy home of Ms. Zhuo, a villager from Dangqian in eastern Qinggou of the Maqin County (Guoluo Prefecture, Qinghai), we saw a slim lady wearing a black skin-tight jacket, a pair of double-belted jeans (which even in inland areas is fairly rare), a necklace made with red and turquoise corals and a pair of black high-heeled shoes. The way she was dressed made her look like a young and modern lady. Seeing such a smart and fashionable outfit in this remote plateau village, located far away from the bustling cities, the author could not help but wonder why she was dressed so fashionably. Ms. Zhuo answered the author's query in a light and proud voice, "I learned from watching TV." To be honest, it was quite hard to believe, even with the verification of a village office, that she was already 45 years old and a mother of three children.

4. Many households in rural areas with access to electricity own TVs

One of the ways one can measure the economic and social development level of a region is the amount of property an individual or a household owns and by looking at the proportion of expenditure allocated to different items within the family budget. Regardless of the place in question or the period of time, survival is the first and foremost priority for any family. It is only when a family has enough to eat and sufficient clothes to protect them from the weather that they will consider spending money on other things. After all, in comparatively poor and remote regions, buying a TV can still be considered a fairly sizeable purchase for most households. In addition, individual or household expenditure is determined by a number of different factors. It is often the case that it increases gradually, with purchases moving from a lower to higher standard over time. Excessive consumption, facilitated by the borrowing of money, is not a common practice in rural areas. It is common practice and a widely accepted concept for farmers and herdsmen to live within their means.

While conducting the surveys, the author caught sight of many satellite TV antennae in the yards and on the roofs of houses in villages with access to electricity. Indeed, they could be found almost everywhere the author looked. In Diqing Prefecture for example, there are over 60,000 rural households prefecture-wide, and more than 40,000 of these households own TVs of various brands and sizes.[5] In some of the new migrant villages found in Guoluo Prefecture in Qinghai, every single household owns a television.[6] Even in Yushu County of Yushu Prefecture, which is found in the hinterland of the Qinghai–Tibet Plateau, the percentage of households that owns a television has been found to be as high as 92%.[7]

Moreover, in regions with no access to electricity, a few farmers and herdsmen who are relatively well-off have tried to watch TV by purchasing small gasoline generators or solar power storage batteries. Some villages in eastern Qinggou of the Maqin County in Guoluo Prefecture have no access to electricity whatsoever. When the seasons change from summer to winter and vice versa, you can often see some of the herdsmen driving

---

[5] Refer to the print version of the "Report on the Undertaking of Broadcast Television in the Diqing Tibetan Autonomous Prefecture of Yunnan", 2007.
[6] Most of the TV sets in rural households of new migrant villages where the author visited are gifts from relevant departments of the central and provincial governments.
[7] Refer to the mimeograph version of the "Report on the Management of Broadcast Television and the Cultural Industry in Yushu County", 2007.

herds of cattle and sheep and walking along the pastures, while carrying power-generating equipment, televisions and receiving antennae.

5. *TVs preferred over radio*

Back in the early days of the reform and opening up policy, radio was treasured by the farmers and herdsmen and seen as a luxury good. Despite the poor audio quality, the radio still attracted a lot of listeners because it was the only tool bridging the gap between them and the outside world. However, because of the improvements to living standards, as a result of the reform and opening up policy, a radio is no longer seen as a particularly valuable item. TV sets, which over the years have changed from black-and-white to colored, and from small to larger sets, have now entered the households of ordinary people.

According to the results of our survey, most of the farming and herding households in southern Gansu, Guoluo and Yushu, also own the following, in addition to their TV sets: a VCD player, DVD player, and a HiFi. Additionally, most farmers and herders no longer own basic radios. Instead, they own radios that also have twin cassette recorders. Farmers and herdsmen, regardless of their sex or age, whether they are illiterate or literate, all watch TV or DVDs during the long winter. Only in purely pastoral regions does radio remain as the only means of entertainment and source of information for herdsmen who are confined by a lack of electricity and signal coverage.

Inadequate or poor broadcasting television signal coverage is common in the regions that were surveyed. Despite significant improvements after the implementation of the "Tibet–Xinjiang Project for Radio and TV Coverage" and the "Extend Radio and TV Coverage to Every Village" projects, the quality of reception still varies by region, and is not just dependent on geographical location but also on the quality of the equipment used. Based on a survey conducted in 2006, Table 1 shows the TV and radio coverage in different regions.

After years of development, those who live in the prefecture or county government areas are fortunate to receive full TV and radio signal coverage. However, looking at the village level statistics, particularly those villages that are in remote areas, it is not yet possible to obtain detailed information on the percentages of TV and radio signal coverage.

Table 1: TV and Radio Coverage by Region.

Regions	Radio coverage rate (%)	TV coverage rate (%)
Zhuoni County	68	60[8]
Shangri-La County	90	90[9]
Maqin County	85	65[10]
Yushu County	67.5	92[11]
Villages with access to electricity		
Diqing Prefecture	81	89[12]
Guoluo Prefecture	71.42	61.52[13]

II Problems and Analysis

Looking at the factual evidence, it suggests that the popularization of television and radio and the implementation of the "Tibet–Xinjiang Project for Radio and TV Coverage" and the "Extend Radio and TV Coverage to Every Village Project", have significantly enriched the spiritual and cultural lives of farmers and herdsmen in the remote regions found in the west. It should be noted however, that due to their actual situation, the remote regions in the west lack the facilities and activities commonly found in the inland regions, which had made TV and radio an important part of their cultural lives. With further implementation of these projects, more and more farmers and herdsmen have access to high quality radio and TV programs. After meeting their basic requirements in terms of their spiritual and cultural lives, new requirements emerged. Moreover, due to equipment and technical difficulties in the initial

---

[8] Data taken from the interview with the head of Bureau of Radio and Television of Zhuoni County.

[9] Refer to the print copy of the "2006 Work Summary and 2007 Work Outline of Bureau of Radio and Television of Shangri-La County".

[10] Refer to the "Work Report of the Culture, Sports and Tourism Bureau of Maqin County", 2007.

[11] Refer to the "Work Report of the Culture, Radio and Television of Yushu County", 2007.

[12] Refer to the Bureau of Radio and Television of Diqing Prefecture's report, "Village by Village Project for Radio and TV Access in Diqing Prefecture", 2007.

[13] Refer to the Bureau of Radio and Television of Guoluo Prefecture's report, "Socio-economic Research at Tibetan-Inhabited Regions", p. 12, 2007.

stage of the "Extend Radio and TV Coverage to Every Village Project",
some new problems gradually emerged.

1. First, farmers and herdsmen lack access to local news and CCTV Channels 3, 5, 6 and 8. A clear difference emerged between rural and city areas, in terms of the types of programs available.

With the increase in social and economic development, the remote prefectures and counties in the western regions of Tibet have already built
local TV and radio stations. Local news and policy regulations are already
broadcasted on local radio and TV programs; these are used to inform
farmers and herdsmen about the policies of the central government, as
well as the arrangements, measures and objectives of the local government. In short, although they are currently unable to access these programs, all the interviewees in remote areas expressed interest in watching
them. There was a kind of intimacy and a sense of identity towards the
things and people around them.

In addition, farmers and herdsmen have high expectations with
respect to TV and radio programs. They want to watch a variety of art
and sports programs, films, and TV series. However, CCTV Channels 3,
5, 6 and 8 are encoded and only available to cable TV subscribers. Sadly,
getting access to the coverage of these channels is unrealistic to farming
households in the sparsely populated regions in the west.

2. Second, after the first round of the "Extend Radio and TV Coverage to Every Village Project", inadequate maintenance and funding led to a reduction in local TV programs.

The "Extend Radio and TV Coverage to Every Village Project" began in
1999.[14] The life span of most TV and radio transmissions and receiving
equipment is normally five to six years. However, the special climate in the
plateau and mountainous regions accelerates the damage to the outdoor

---

[14] www.xinhuanet.com, downloaded on March 6, 2007.

equipment and spare parts. In order to keep the TVs and radios functioning normally, timely maintenance would be required. However, due to a shortage of technicians, poor transportation, and a lack of maintenance funding and spare parts in the regions affected, the farmers' and herdsmens' access to quality TV and radio programs was restricted.

3. Third, quite a few farmers have installed satellite TV receivers.

At the moment, the coverage rate of the "Extend Radio and TV Coverage to Every Village Project" is quite low in western regions. According to incomplete statistics from the Bureau of Broadcasting and Television of Diqing Prefecture, by the end of 2006, there were a total of 38,178 satellite TV receivers in Diqing Prefecture, among which 645 were provided by the project. This meant that there was a coverage rate of less than 20%.[15] Secondly, due to the technical reasons in the early stages of the project, users had limited access to broadcasting and TV programs. In some cases, individuals only had access to a single program. Therefore, the implementation of the project fell somewhat below the needs of the farmers and herdsmen.

According to government regulations, individuals are not permitted to install satellite TV receivers. However, due to their interest in enriching their spiritual and cultural lives, the rich farmers and herdsmen preferred to install the receiver themselves. Thus, they chose to pay out of their own pockets rather than wait for the government's assistance. Despite the varying quality of the receivers, they have met the farmers' needs for the most part.

4. Fourth, language barriers and an unstable power supply in some areas resulted in TV sets not being used or sold to others.

It is reported that there are only two provincial-level TV stations in Qinghai and Tibet that use a satellite to broadcast programs in Tibetan. Any other Tibetan language programs broadcasted at the prefecture or county level TV stations are only available to cable TV subscribers. The

---

[15]Refer to the Bureau of Broadcasting and Television of Diqing Prefecture's management data of satellite TV users in Diqing Prefecture.

announcer on the Tibetan TV station speaks Baiba (a Tibetan dialect), while the announcer on the Qinghai TV station speaks Anduo (another Tibetan dialect). The Tibetan language also includes the Kangba dialect. Each dialect has its own audience, and the farmers and herdsmen from different regions can only understand their own dialect.

An even more acute problem is that the power supply in some of the remote areas is often cut off, only to come back after some time. For example, solar power plants were built in some areas but have been left unused due to lack of funding and spare parts. Similarly, power infrastructure in some areas has been damaged by floods or landslides. These factors led to a lower utilization rate of TVs in some households. Moreover, due to language barriers and an inadequate power supply, some households even decided to sell their TV sets, which had been given to them by the central government.

III Countermeasures and Suggestions

It is undeniable that among all the different kinds of cultural services provided to farmers and herdsmen in the remote regions in the west, the provision of TV and radio programs, as a policy, is the most popular. In particular, TV has its unique advantages. Concerned departments should adjust their thinking and methodologies to avoid similar problems.

1. *First, they should adopt wireless digital transmission technology, consolidate achievements in the "Extend Radio and TV Coverage to Every Village Project", and ensure that everyone can tune in to the same programs.*

By constructing a wireless digital transmission network, the farmers and herdsmen can have access to more than 40 high quality TV programs including the encoded CCTV 3, 5, 6 and 8 channels as well as local TV and radio programs. In one fell swoop this would completely solve the problems of low coverage rates and low quality TV programs in agricultural and pastoral areas. If some form of cooperation agreement can be reached with China Mobile, then the agricultural and pastoral areas covered by a mobile signal can also have access to wireless digital broadcasting programs through the mobile network. Moreover, the wireless digital transmission mode requires little investment, the effects of the technology can be seen quickly and it is very easy to man-age. Additionally, using this technology, it is possible to have wider and far more reliable coverage. According to estimates from the Bureau of Broadcasting and Television of Diqing Prefecture, investment in this technology, either in terms of initial input or maintenance cost, will be less than 10%[16] of the cost of a cable TV network.

Instead of technical issues, it is the institutional mechanism of TV broadcasting that is the main obstacle to meeting the growing need of farmers and herdsmen with respect to watching TV. The most direct problem relates to the fees. Using the above method, it will be very hard to collect cable fees. Moreover, those urban households who have already installed cable TV will lose out. Despite the small proportion of house-holds that fall into this category, without receiving such fees, the burden of maintaining a cable TV network will be all the greater. Therefore, government departments who are able to exert influence on this matter should reform the system of collecting TV subscriptions. On the one hand, they should increase targeted investment which will address the problem at hand so as to not waste their efforts. On the other, they need to formulate some new rules and management practices that differ from those found in other areas. The population in remote western areas is relatively small, therefore, with China's growing national economic strength, it is possible to pay for their cable TV fees using other sources of money.

2. *Second, there is a need to strengthen coordination of broadcasting and TV development in agricultural and pastoral areas.*

With a growing amount of concern about the situation in the remote regions in the west, there is a corresponding increase in the number of activities aimed at assisting this region. However, for the most part, these

---

[16]Refer to the Bureau of Broadcasting and Television of Diqing Prefecture's report, "Feasibility Analysis of the Demand on Digital Radio and TV", 2007.

activities lack consistency and thus fail to achieve their expected results. For example, TV sets and antennae were donated to farmers and herds-men but funds for maintenance personnel were not allocated. Therefore, similar considerations should be included in the "Extend Radio and TV Coverage to Every Village Project". Technicians and special funds should be provided to ensure that adequate services are provided to the sparsely distributed farmers and herdsmen.

3. Third, there should be a register of households who have had a satellite TV receiver installed.

The privately installed satellite TV receivers reflected the farmers' and herdsmen's eagerness to improve their spiritual and cultural lives. The frequency of such acts also reflects the inadequate public services provided by the government. These households should be included in the "Extend Radio and TV Coverage to Every Village Project", so as to provide services to them in the future should they need additional spare parts or their appliances repaired.

CHAPTER 10

Private and Social Aid in the Eastern Tibetan Regions

WEI Zhong

Abstract

In the Tibetan regions, there are already some systems in place to help the poor and support the elderly in local villages and tribes. And with the rural social security system in the process of being implemented across the country, social aid has begun to take on an even more important role there. In the eastern Tibetan regions, where we conducted this survey, we found some changes to the pension insurance scheme and the social aid system for the aged and the poor. Yet, the new social insurance scheme and social aid mechanism inevitably face some problems. It is these problems that this chapter sets out to elaborate on.

Keywords: Social Support; Social Aid; The Elderly; The Poor.

I The Elderly in Tibet and the Government's Assistance Mechanism

According to the 2010 census, about 10% of the population in the Tibetan Autonomous Region could be classified as elderly. This high-lights the trend that the Tibetan populace is ageing. Although the figure is lower than the national average, it is significantly higher than it was in 2010, when the comparable figure was just 8%. So, it is apparent that we should pay more attention to the aging population in the Tibetan regions and offer them proper aid and assistance.

In the Tibetan regions, there are two main types of social aid offered to the elderly: the "five guarantees" system and the new rural pension scheme. The latter is only recently being implemented, but the government has already encountered problems expanding the scheme's geographical coverage. Since people above 60 years old are entitled to a RMB 50 *yuan* pension every month, it turned out that more than 10% of the population in Gongjue County, Jiangda County (both in the Changdu District, Tibet) and Dege County in Sichuan are enjoying the benefits associated with having a pension, which is higher than the percentage of the aging population in the Tibetan Autonomous Region.

1. *The "five guarantees" system*

The Tibetan regions, including the Changdu District and Ganzi Autonomous Prefecture, have adopted, in essence, the same "five guarantees" system. This system offers a certain amount of money to those elderly who are living alone and lack familial or other forms of help, as is the case elsewhere in China. In Changdu District, about 4,000 people each receive RMB 2,200 *yuan* per year from the system. The situation in the Ganzi Autonomous Prefecture is similar.

The "five guarantees" system was initiated in the 1950s and has never been suspended. This shows that this system is quite mature and comprehensive. After 2000, the Ministry of Civil Affairs called for progressively realizing the policy of the "five guarantees" across the whole nation. The eastern Tibetan regions, where we surveyed, are also working towards implementing this policy.

However, this plan encountered some problems when it came to implementation. There is no appropriate environment to support this social aid system and even the construction of nursing homes is behind schedule. For instance, the Gongjue County and Jiangda County both have nursing homes under construction, but as yet, those homes do not meet the requirements that would enable them to be opened. In contrast, Dege County, which is not in great financial shape, has rather surprisingly constructed a nursing home and put it into service.

Case 1 Mani Gange Nursing Home

Mani Gange, a town in Dege County, is at the junction of two major transport routes. This town has a government-run nursing home, which was built in 2008, and now run by one full time staff and one temporary employee. There are nine old people living in this nursing home. When we visited, it was undergoing renovation, even though there were some elderly people still living there. One objective of the renovation was to build prayer wheels so that the inhabitants did not need to go to a temple.

These elderly people, for the most part, are from two nearby villages. They are also relatively well looked after. If they get ill, the nursing home gets the health center in town to pick them up, and all of their medical fees are covered by the government. Despite this, the elderly have more faith in Tibetan medicine for curing their illnesses and would rather spend their own money consulting traditional Tibetan doctors.

The doctors from the township health center come to the nursing home three times a month to check on the physical well-being of the elderly in the nursing home. If the doctors find one of them to be gravely ill, they will call for an ambulance. But local people are still somewhat suspicious and may well refuse to go. The prefecture government once sent some medical experts to check on their health. The staff working in the nursing home tried to get the seniors to see the doctors, but most were unwilling to do so. Because Kanding Town was so far away, they said that they were afraid of getting carsick and dying on the road.

Mani Gange Nursing Home is the only government-run nursing home in the three counties that we surveyed. We also found out that there was another government-run nursing home in Dege County, which is located in the county. The conditions found in the Mani Gange Nursing Home were not fantastic, but certainly better than the houses where the elderly used to live. Each resident has his or her own room. However, they do not get a great deal of furniture to go with it. Moreover, because of their different backgrounds, the residents seldom communicate with one another, thus diminishing the benefit of living together.

Case 2 The People in the Nursing Home

Quduo is 76 years old and is from Xuegou Village, which is three to four miles away from Mani Gange.

His parents died when he was little and he has lived with his elder sister ever since. After his sister got married, he started to live alone. He never married and had no children.

When the household responsibility system was first implemented in Tibet, Quduo was assigned seven cattle and some land. But due to poor management, the cattle died over a short space of time. He did have his own house, but it was accidently burned down about 20 years ago. Since then, he has been on the go, trying to find work where he can. Sometimes he would live in a Lama temple and sometimes in his employer's house. He lived his next 20 years working as a seasonal laborer. He did a variety of things including doing chores, cutting wood, digging for caterpillar fungus and fritillary. After he got old, he took on the job of guarding houses when their owners went out digging for the fungus.

Before he came to the nursing home, he gave all his land to his sister. Another nursing home, set up by the living Buddha, once asked him to spend his last years there, but he rejected their proposal. He thought that it was too far away from home and he would feel lonely, without any friends or relatives living there.

Since last year, his monthly income was 200 RMB.

It is interesting to note that Quduo was previously a rural resident, but since he moved to the nursing home he has of course become an urban resident. This change took away his rural pension, which amounted to 50 yuan per month. He complained, stating that he had never worked in a town, but it was no use and he was still changed to an urban resident. His benefits, obtained from minimum living standard system, were also cut. He went to the village Party Secretary, hoping to get his benefits back, but he did not see the secretary. Instead, he was told by a clerical assistant that he has become an urban resident because he now lives in a town.

Quduo is quite old now and has some health problems. For instance, there was something wrong with his lungs and he went to a hospital to have it looked at. He received medication intra-venously and stayed in the hospital for nine days. After his nine days in hospital the problem with his lungs has disappeared. In addition, his blood pressure was a little high and his diet was far from ideal. The second issue is largely attributable to the fact that he lives on a plateau. The health center gave him some anti-hyper-tensive drugs, and Doctor Yang, the director of the health center, regularly went to the nursing home to give him a checkup.

In addition to all of his other problems, he also has arthritis. However, he would rather go far uptown to see a traditional Tibetan doctor than go to the health center. Interestingly, Tibetan medicine turned out to be very effective. In the past, he needed a walking stick to get around, but now, when he goes to see his Tibetan doc-tor, he can walk there. For these kinds of illnesses, he still trusts the Tibetan doctors more.

Even though they live together in the nursing home, the residents do not talk to each other a great deal. According to comments made by the staff and the residents, they usually stay in their own rooms and only ask to go outside if they are bored. Another reason for the limited communication between these elderly people is that most of them have poor hearing. However, every few days, they will inform the hospital that they want to take some leave to see their relatives. They only need to make a phone call before coming back.

However, some people do not like the feeling of being restricted or restrained, so they go without asking the staff if they can leave and do not tell the staff where they are going.

Although the financial situation in Ganzi Autonomous Prefecture is not great, the construction of its nursing homes is as good as those found in other Tibetan regions in Yunnan and Qinghai. In contrast, the con-struction of nursing homes in Changdu District is lagging behind some-what. The two counties both have nursing homes under construction, but neither has realized the initial objective of the elderly living together. From the two cases, we can easily find that progressing towards such an objective largely depends on the willingness of the local government, not their financial power.

2. New rural pension scheme

Although still a pilot scheme elsewhere, the new rural pension scheme has been fully implemented in Tibet. Farmers and herdsmen who are over 60 in Tibet are now enjoying pensions provided by the scheme. The system provides a monthly pension of RMB 50 *yuan* to anyone over the age of 60. It is also being implemented in Dege County of the Ganzi Autonomous Prefecture in Sichuan, which is separated from Changdu by just a river.

The scheme has met some obstacles in its implementation: low public awareness, low participation rates and, above all, the problems associated with the local household registration system.

From previous surveys in the Tibetan regions, we found that the household registration system was not fully carried out there. Many Tibetans have not gone to a local police station to register since birth. And because a great number of them do not have a "*hukou*" (registered permanent residence), they are unable to get an identity card. Thus, the local authorities have far from complete information on the local populace.

The pension scheme, a major part of a modern social welfare system, requires a series of supporting modern institutions. But the Tibetan regions lag behind others in terms of social and institutional development. This has left their modern institutions far from perfect and has resulted in a number of problems for the new rural pension scheme. The pension scheme requires individuals to hold an ID card number, which is used to verify their identity. Unfortunately, the farmers and herdsmen in Tibet do not have an ID card. In addition, because of the imperfect household registration system and the incomplete ID card system, the local authorities do not know the exact number of elderly people in the local populace. This makes implementing the policy particularly arduous.

There are many residents with no identity cards in the Gongjue County and Jiangda County. In the past, the farmers and herdsmen had little need for identity cards as for the most part they did not travel far from home and only interacted with those people they knew. Only those who left the area to look for work or those who wanted to travel to Lhasa to pay their respects to the Buddha would apply for an identity card.

Ordinary people in Tibet do not have such cards and many do not even have a household registration certificate. In order to provide pension insurance to the Tibetans, the local police force undertook a number of activities, in conjunction with the department for civil affairs. They sent staff to rural areas to handle ID card applications and extended working hours in the relevant county agency so that they could increase the number of applications processed. It turned out that the two counties had far more people over the age of 60 than they had expected.

In Gongjue County, a significant number of urban residents do not have ID cards and have only just begun to apply for one. This means that the rural pension scheme in Gongjue may well have made very little headway. The situation in Jiangda County is slightly better. There is a large number of people between the ages of 45 and 59 who are eager to join the new rural pension scheme. But in general, the lack of ID cards and an incomplete and imperfect household registration system still prevent the implementation of an efficient rural pension scheme.

Case 3 Gongjue's Dilemma

In July 2010, Gongjue conducted a pilot trial of the rural pension scheme. The government also launched a campaign to promote the scheme among its rural residents, informing them of the insurance premium standard, eligibility for the pension and how pensions can be inherited. Villages were asked to report the number of people over the age of 60 by June 2010. In October of the same year, once this information was obtained, they launched pilot schemes across the county.

However, the experiences associated with this process do not bode well for the scheme. There are two principal problems. First, some people do not feel a sense of urgency when it comes to participating in this scheme. In essence, they are just waiting for government support. Second, there are some problems with the household registration system. Some people do not have a residence booklet, others lack an ID card. Moreover, some elderly willing to participate in the scheme cannot join the system because of restrictions imposed by the household registration system and the ID card system, especially so for those who are over 60.

People in Gongjue have an adequate income compared to those in other poor regions. This is because most families are able to sell caterpillar fungus. Therefore, they are able to afford the RMB 100 yuan annual premium. However, because of their outdated perception that the government is untrustworthy, the participation rate is low.

The local police network is also somewhat backward. Police stations in the villages and the county do not have an internet connection, which meant that the county police authorities had to send people to villages to handle ID card applications. Due to the incomplete household registration system, there were also some controversies surrounding age identification. According to the statistics from the County Statistics Bureau, Gongjue should have a population of around 40,000. However, the 2010 census showed that it only has about 38,000 people. Thus, because of the inadequacies of the household registration system, the number of people who are over 60 years old in Gongjue has reached 4,527, which accounts for 12% of the total county population.

The network construction of the new rural pension scheme is another problem. Local villages do not have an internet connection, which makes it imposible to manage pension insurance over the internet.

In the past, ID cards and the household registration booklet had no practical use to local residents, and only those who needed to go to Lhasa would apply for the household registration booklet and ID card in a police station. Now, they are closely connected to one's benefits, and therefore, getting hold of both of these documents has become a top priority for the locals. Every day, there is a long queue of people applying for the household registration document, ID card, and even a certificate of disability (it is required for receiving medical aid and a minimum standard of living allowance).

In contrast, Jiangda and Dege County are doing much better in terms of participation rates than Gongjue County, although both are slightly lower than the national average. According to our survey, the relatively low levels of participation may have been caused by the following reasons.

First, the low life expectancy diminishes the possibility of getting a pension. The low life expectancy in Tibet is mainly due to slow economic development, its climate and the thin air. The local residents do not have much of a chance of benefiting from the scheme. Ultimately, this undermines any enthusiasm they may have had for joining the system. *"I don't know if I can live that long"* is a fairly common answer to a question on this topic.

Second, the locals are not aware of the scheme's importance and do not put much faith in the government. Local farmers and herdsmen do not understand the relatively modern concept of pension insurance. They are also quite dubious about a scheme which requires payment in advance but only gives out pension many years after. In fact, this short-sighted perception shows how little they trust the government. In other words, the locals doubt that the pension scheme can retain and increase the value of their investment.

Third, long-term external aid can make people dependent on welfare. This problem is quite severe in Changdu District. In our survey of Changdu, many civil affairs officials mentioned the idea of waiting for support. Of course, such an idea is not particularly helpful, but after some careful analysis, we found that this idea is prevalent not only among ordinary farmers and herdsmen, but also among local government officials and even the Tibet Autonomous Government. Because the central government gives a lot of financial support to Tibet, it is relatively easy for them to access funding, and thus for quite some time, in terms of financial matters, Tibet has been far from self-sufficient. Under such a context, both officials and residents are prone to grow ever more dependent on government welfare.

Finally, there are a number of defects in the design of the pension scheme. The purpose of establishing a new rural pension scheme is to provide appropriate care for the elderly. That is why those over 60 can directly receive a pension without having to pay a premium. However, this has resulted in a high participation rate within the elderly population, but a low participation rate of those who have to pay the premium. Some eastern regions have taken steps to solve this problem. For example, in some areas at least one child of a parent who currently enjoys the benefit of a pension must participate in the scheme. Such measures can help to increase the participation rate, but the Tibetan regions where we con- ducted our survey have no such regulations. That is to say, currently the Tibetan regions do not fully understand the scheme and have made few innovations on how the scheme has been implemented.

In Tibet, there also exists a special welfare policy targeted at people over the age of 80, "Special Subsidy for People of Longevity". At different ages, they can get anything from 300–1,000 *yuan* every year. In Changdu District, a total of 6,601 old people are eligible for this subsidy and it costs the district government more than RMB 2 million *yuan* every year. Such a system, which differentiates those who are particularly old and those who are not, is a forward-looking policy response to an ageing population. However, it faces almost exactly the same problems as the pension insur- ance scheme, i.e. how can they ensure that those who get the subsidy are actually over 80, in a region with incomplete household registration records?

II Extremely Poor Families and Social Aid in Tibetan Regions

1. *Minimum standard of living system*

Like the new rural pension scheme, the minimum standard of living sys- tem also faces a problem in the Tibetan regions. The policy needs to be implemented in the context of an underdeveloped economy. We know that in a region with a weak and underdeveloped economy, it is difficult to determine which households are particularly poor, because the income of farmers and herdsmen is mostly comprised of non-cash assets. This issue is found in all of the Tibetan regions as well as other less developed areas.

Under this system, only households with an annual income less than RMB 800 *yuan* are entitled to receive a minimum standard of living allowance. But in practice, it is difficult to calculate family income and hence to determine which households live on less than 800 *yuan* a year. In most parts of China, including the Tibetan regions, the county govern- ments usually distribute the allowances by village. This means that each village is given a specific allocation of funds. Therefore, most villages give

Table 1:   Minimum Standard of Living in Changdu District

Type	Requirement	Annual allowance (RMB)	Percentage of all households (%)	Percentage of total population (%)
I	No source of income, inability to work, and no legal caretaker	1,070	4.6	3.5
II	Have some work capacity	772	3.2	2.3
III	Have capacity to work, but have some serious illness or family difficulties	564	5.7	6.8

the allowance to the poorest members, before giving money to others, until the allocation has been used up.

In the Tibetan regions, the villages have relatively more poor people, and many more families at or around the poverty line. This makes it more difficult to differentiate households that are entitled to a minimum living allowance and those that are not. Faced with this problem, Changdu District government designed a relatively crude policy to replace the previous practice. This new policy is called the "three standards" (see Table 1). This new approach helped to overcome the problems in calculating their incomes.

But this problem cannot be dodged in villages, especially those with many families living below the poverty line. So, in some villages, they will arrange for some people to get the allowances and for the more eligible families to share them. Moreover, in some of those villages, they even changed the minimum standard of living in light of their own conditions, and based their allowances on their own standards. Although the civil affairs authorities dislike such practices and have taken punitive measures to stop them, they are not yet eradicated. This is because the minimum standard of living system lacks an institutional design that is suited to local conditions.

In addition, there are no efficient financial services available to distribute the minimum living allowances. In Tibetan regions, it is usually the case that only towns have branches of rural credit cooperatives which are able to give out loans and allocate subsidies. However, in Changdu District, due to the underdeveloped nature of their financial services sector, the allowances used to be given to villages, and then the village committees would be responsible for giving out these allowances. But it turned out that few villages shared the allowances equally among their poor and that some of the intended recipients reported that they had not received their minimum living allowances. Thus, the current practice is that the civil affairs officials inform the recipients who then receive their allowances in town.

Case 4 The Loss of a Husband

This is a poor family with almost no furniture in their home. There are only two members in this family; Suolang, a 28 year old woman, and her three-year-old son.

Her family was once financially sound. Her husband was a mason and had a good mind for business. He made sizeable profits by carving characters into seals. However, her world turned upside down in 2008. Her husband got into a quarrel and then a brawl while drinking, which resulted in his accidental death. The perpetrator soon surrendered himself to the police and was duly punished. Suolang was compensated with RMB 6,000 yuan. But with her husband gone, the family's finances deteriorated quickly. On the one hand, she receives some government aid. On the other hand, she also needs to undertake some short-term work so as to properly support her family. In 2009, the village decided to give her a three-acre greenhouse to help her make a living. The village also sent a technician to train her. In March, 2011, the technician left; unfortunately, because Suolang is not well-educated and did not take the training seriously, she still does not know how to manage the greenhouse.

Before moving down from the mountain, the pastures around her home had caterpillar fungus. But the fungus is not of good quality and last year only enabled her to earn RMB 3,500. Such a small sum is just enough to get some food and snacks for her child.

After her husband died, her family began receiving the minimum living allowance, and would receive RMB 1,070 a year at most.

Gongjue, influenced by its historic tradition, has a reputation of locals with very fierce personalities; it also grapples with serious security problems. This resulted in a tense relationship with the neighboring county and has caused many troubles among farmers and herdsmen. The case mentioned above is just one of the many incidents. Poor public security has, to some extent, increased the cost of social aid.

2. Social aid for children from extremely poor backgrounds to enter universities

In the Tibetan Autonomous Region, there is a new social aid policy to help poor families. Under this policy, the children of poor families who go to universities outside of Tibet can apply for RMB 5,000 *yuan* aid from the district education bureau. In order to apply, they will need to submit five credentials and one paper as well as RMB 4,000 *yuan* if they are going to a community college. If they study in Tibetan colleges or universities and there is irrefutable proof provided by the local civil affairs department, they will be given 4,000 *yuan* when school starts. In Gongjue, two households received this aid two years ago; last year one household was the recipient of this assistance. All of them live in town. And because the money used for this aid is usually paid to the recipient the following March or April, the county government pays for it first. However, it is very unlikely that children from poor families will go to college. Thus, the policy did not attract a great deal of attention. Yet, the idea behind this policy is commendable and we know that a well-designed social aid system is usually made up of a series of smaller aid systems.

III Medical Aid

Like other regions, Tibetan regions have special medical aid for those families that suffer from extreme poverty. The county government uses 5% of a new rural cooperative fund to provide medical aid for residents living in pastoral areas. The system is set up so that poor households can go to the civil affairs department and apply for partial reimbursement of their medical fees, provided that they are able to show relevant certification provided by the medical authorities, a minimum standard of living certificate and a certificate of disability. The civil affairs department can then refund up to RMB 10,000 *yuan* and the county government has a limit of RMB 30,000 *yuan*. If the amount exceeds RMB 30,000 *yuan*, the refund has to be reviewed by the district government and then approved by the Department of Civil Affairs of the regional government which has a limit of RMB 60,000 *yuan*.

Among the 40,000 people in Gongjue County, 69 have received a refund from the medical aid system and the total amount they have received is RMB 192,000 *yuan*. The medical funds in Jiangda and Dege Counties also have significant surpluses. However, for those who are able to get some form of medical aid, their burden is greatly reduced.

Case 5 The Ciren Family

The Ciren family lives in Xiongba Village. Ciren and her husband are just a little bit over 40 years of age and have two sons and one daughter. The oldest son, who is 12 years old, has become a monk in a nearby temple. The younger son, a nine-year-old, is still at school. The daughter is only six years old. After moving away from her parents' family, they now just have one acre of land and only ten cattle. This is because her husband's three brothers are still living with their parents and extended family.

Ciren and her husband both had hepatitis and went to Changdu and Lhasa to see doctors, but their visits were in vain. Later, with help of traditional Tibetan medicine, her husband got better. But the medicine comes from a temple in Changdu and it is expensive. After that, her family became a recipient of the minimum living allowance and medical aid. Starting from 2010, it was possible to get a refund for money spent on Tibetan medicine. Ciren herself also needs medicine and she usually gets it from Lhasa because she has relatives there. But since her family gets their medicine from other regions, only part of the money can be refunded.

Because of their poor health, they only make around RMB 900 yuan a year from selling caterpillar fungus. However, their relatives would often offer to help, some of whom belong to the same tribe. The tribe Ciren belongs to has only 12 households in total.

Although the medical aid system cannot provide an adequate medical service and enough medicine for all of the farmers and herdsmen, it has significantly reduced their burden. At the same time, the local government needs to make some changes to the institutional structure in order to make better use of the system. There are various policy options to choose from. They could look to increase the number of people who have access to medical aid. Alternatively, they could look at moderately reducing the amount of the medical aid fund in the new rural cooperative scheme so that more funds are used to refund the medical fees of farmers and herdsmen.

IV Private Aid Targeted at the Elderly and the Extremely Poor Families

1. *Aid provided by family or relatives*

Tibetan families are usually very large. It is very rare to find what we would define as a nuclear family. Thus, it is a common phenomenon for the aged to live with their children. Among the families surveyed, most of the elderly live with their sons and a number of them live with their daughters. In these families, the elderly are taken care of by their family members.

But the situation is different for the elderly who enjoy the "five guarantees" and have no children. Since Changdu and other Tibet districts do not have enough nursing homes, most of these people are looked after by their relatives.

Case 6 The Baila Family

Baila is now 70. She lives with the family of her nephew, who takes care of her.

She was once married to a village doctor, but he passed away many years ago. She never bore a child and began to enjoy the "five guarantees" benefits, which amounts to RMB 2,200 yuan per year.

She is able to do simple daily tasks, such as boiling water and making tea. But she has a problem with her lungs. Her brother, who lives in Lhasa and is an official, had her diagnosed in a Lhasa hospital some time ago. She stayed there for two months and spent between RMB 3,000 and 5,000 yuan. However, the problem with her lungs still persisted. When she got back, she asked her relatives to get medicine from Jiangda County, which costs her about RMB 1,000 yuan per year. She also gets medicine from a Tibetan doctor, which costs her about RMB 300 yuan. Although she has participated in the new rural cooperative medical scheme, this is still a lot of money.

Because of poor health, she leased her half acre of land to other people and the lessee gives almost half of the output to her every year. She does not have cattle or sheep and because of her deterioriating health she does not dare go to the temples to pray.

Unfortunately, there are many more people like Baila in the Tibetan regions.

2. *Private or temple-run nursing homes*

There are many private or temple-run nursing homes in the Tibetan regions. This phenomenon is related to the history and cultural tradition of the Tibetans. On the one hand, when the Tibetan farmers and herdsmen get old, they are increasingly concerned about the afterlife. Moreover, out of religious piety, they tend to attach great importance to religious rites such as the wheel prayer. On the other hand, Lama temples also have the tradition of establishing nursing homes. There are a number of restrictions to doing this, however the temples have successfully avoided them by building the nursing homes outside of the temples or by having the families build houses around the temples.

For the elderly themselves, it is very convenient to live around the temples. They can access the temples with relative ease and thus have the opportunity to spin prayer wheels. Those living around the temples, especially the medium-sized and larger ones, are able to see the Tibetan doctors quite easily. The only inconvenience is that the families have to send them food from time to time.

As they grow older, the senior Tibetans, influenced by Lamaism, have different needs for the afterlife. They firmly believe in the six great divisions in the wheel of karma. If they live near or around the temples and can pray and spin a prayer wheel every day, they believe that such piety will help them achieve a better future in the afterlife.

Xiongdong Village of Gongjue has a private nursing home. Normally, when Tibetans get to a certain age, they voluntarily go the temples. This is because they are concerned that if they do not go, the quality of their afterlife experience will suffer. Obviously, if they live in a temple, it is quite convenient to spin the prayer wheel on a regular basis, and the lamas can take care of their funerals. The temples are not purpose-built nursing homes and these old people do not need to pay for the service. The only problem is that their relatives must build houses around the temple. When they become slightly disabled, their relatives are then responsible for looking after them. If there are no relatives around, the temple would send people to take care of the aged. Some big temples would also send Tibetan doctors to treat these elderly.

Two nursing homes, built by the living Buddha, are located to the east of the Dege Mountain. One can be found in A'xu and another in Cuowa. About 30 to 40 elderly live there.

3. Aid from fellow villagers

Offering assistance to fellow villagers is quite common, examples include helping others harvest in the busy season and assisting each other during times of need. In general, the Tibetan society is like a traditional community. When one family suffers from a great loss, it is more than likely that others will provide them with aid and assistance.

When we were conducting our survey in Gongjue, Ciren said her family often received help from other families. Some are from the same tribe but others were not. From this, we can infer that being in the same tribe is no longer the only basis for establishing relationships. Instead, communities begin to take on a more important role in daily life, while the tribe still has its role to play in major events.

Some poor families also get help from people outside their village. When visiting a certain village during our survey trip, we found a man helping a widowed mother. When asked, he said he had bought some food for her.

However, aid from fellow villagers basically consists of their labor and is usually offered in times of emergency. Some people may offer financial aid, but the amount they offer would not be much, because in general Tibetan families are not very well-off. So, if one runs into temporary difficulties, it is easy for them to borrow from relatives and friends; and it is also possible to get their help during busy seasons. In contrast, the possibility of poor families getting long-term aid is slim. Therefore, temporary poverty could be alleviated with village support, but those living in long-term poverty must receive assistance through the minimum standard of living system.

4. Temple aid for poor families

The temples only provide short-term aid to poor farmers and herdsmen and will ask for something in return. According to our survey, the temples may offer assistance when Tibetan farmers and herdsmen are in difficulty, but their assistance is not free. For example, in a village, the main breadwinner in a family died. This resulted in the entire family being plunged into financial difficulty. Initially, the temple provided them with some necessary means of production, such as cattle and sheep. But in return, when the cattle and sheep grew up and were put up for sale, the temple received a large share of the profits. In other instances, the family has returned some calves and lambs together with the initial allocation of cattle and sheep to the temple, though the exact scenario depends on what was agreed with the temple.

Despite this, the temples still play an active role in helping the farmers and herdsmen. While such aid can be suited to help the poor break out of poverty, political wisdom to balance the temples' role in aiding the poor and their political influence is necessary.

V **Policy Suggestions**

From our survey conducted in Tibetan regions, we found that the most serious problem in social and private aid is the mismatch between social management and modern institutions. Guided by the national economic policy, Tibet and the neighboring regions have seen rapid economic progress, but modern institutions have not been fully established there, thus the impact of having these modern institutions has been diminished. In light of this, the policy-makers of the Tibetan regions should understand which of the obstacles can be overcome.

The Tibetan regions have an advantage in that they are relatively backward and thus receive a lot of capital from the Chinese government. This lays down an economic basis for the rapid economic development of those regions. But what about the social conditions which help to form the foundation of the aforementioned development?

As such, we call upon the Tibetan government to consider the following issues when implementing the new rural pension scheme and the social aid system.

1. *Make full use of all resources at their disposal*

Our survey in the eastern Tibetan regions clearly shows that there are different forces at work in providing support and aid for the elderly: the official social aid system and the private social protection. At present, the official system cannot fully satisfy the needs of the aging population; so we need to make full use of all the available options.

2. *Design a flexible system*

We have discussed the mismatch between the social aid system and local realities. This mismatch should be resolved by making the system more flexible. But the government needs to look for answers to the following two questions: How to make the policies flexible? And how can one prevent this increased flexibility from destroying the system?

3. Implementing an advanced social welfare system necessitates stronger supporting systems

As a modern institution, the social welfare system requires a certain social and economic level of development. In this survey, we found problems in basic institutions like the household registration and ID card systems. These factors undermine the implementation of the new social welfare system. The Tibetan government should attach due attention to the construction of some necessary modern institutions for better and quicker social progress.

Bibliography

Ding Sai, 2007, "Strengthen Household Economic Security", *Working Paper of the Institute of Ethnology and Anthropology, Chinese Academy of Social Sciences.*

Hong Dayong, Fang Lijie, Qiu Xiaoqing, 2004," Dilemmas and Solutions: A Study on 'Wubao' in Post-Collective Rural China", *Journal of Renmin University of China*, 18(1), 49–56.

Lobsang Darje, Tenzin Tsundue, 2011, "Evolution of the Social Security System in Tibet", *Journal of Tibet Nationalities Institute* (Philosophy and Social Sciences Pages), 32(6), 36–40,89.

Li Xugui, 2012, "Analysis on the Current Status of the Tibetan Rural Social Aid System and Its Improvement", *Theory Research*, 23, 9–10.

Danzeng Zunzhu, Li Wenwu, 2004, "Changes of the Social Relief and Social Security System in Tibet", *Tibetan Studies*, 04, 98–101.

Wu Guoliang, Chen Ping, Xie Zongtang, 2010, "Present Social Security System, Problems and Development of the Farm and Pastoral Areas on Tibetan Plateau", *Journal of Dalian Nationalities University*, 12(4), 319–321.

CHAPTER 11

Snow Disasters and Relief Efforts: A Case Study of Tibetan Pastoral Areas in Southern Qinghai

ZHALUO

Abstract

The Tibetan pastoral area in southern Qinghai is often subjected to snow disasters which can severely damage the
income of herders' and can bring about other related hazards.
The breaking down of the relationship between snow disasters and poverty constitutes an important part of the local
poverty-alleviation strategy. Based on fieldwork conducted by
the author, this chapter examines the relief efforts of herders
and the government during and after a disaster and presents
an analysis and assessment of these efforts. Although efforts
have improved over time, the local relief mechanism still has
some defects and needs further work in order to achieve a
modicum of perfection. In order to improve this mechanism,
one needs to understand that the material losses as a result of
a snow disaster are different for pastoralists as opposed to
agriculturalists. In addition to understanding this difference,
it is important to comprehend the difference between those
who are victims of snow disasters, and those who are more
generally poverty-stricken.

Keywords: Snow Disasters; Relief Efforts; Tibetan Herders;
Public Services.

Up until now, snow disasters constitute the most common and most severe economic risk for Tibetan herders living on the Tibetan Plateau. In the snowy season (which in most areas is from late autumn to early summer the following year), pastures are so heavily covered with snow that livestock are unable to find suitable foliage. Moreover, due to the extreme cold, the animals become susceptible to sickness; thus they starve to death, die from the cold or from illness. The huge losses herders suffer in such circumstances explain the presence of a large poverty-stricken population in many pastoral areas. Therefore, any poverty-alleviation program should be targeted at countermeasures against the risks associated with snow disasters and the economic losses they create.

Countermeasures against snow disasters consist of two aspects. The first aspect is to prevent snow disasters from happening in the first place. Preventive measures should include designing an effective rule-based system for pasture use, constructing protective facilities and storing adequate relief materials.[1] When the snow disaster hits, herders are then fully prepared to cope with and avoid the economic losses and personnel casualties. The second aspect is the need for relief efforts during and after a disaster. These efforts should be undertaken in order to ensure that the victims resume their production and protect them from being plunged into long-term poverty.

This chapter focuses on relief efforts in the summer of 2007, January 2008, and the summer of 2009 respectively. The author visited numerous villages in three Tibetan Autonomous Prefectures in Qinghai (Guoluo, Yushu and Huangnan), where both severe and frequent snow disasters and their aftereffects have plagued the local population and government over the last 20 years. Based on the fieldwork conducted in these areas and the related literature, this chapter examines the mechanisms in place for local relief efforts, as well as their effectiveness, and then puts forward policy recommendations for improvement.

Normally, disaster victims, government bodies and social organizations are all involved in relief efforts. The responses of participants depend upon specific social conditions, while the effectiveness of the relief efforts depends on the rationality of those responses. A systematic examination

---

[1] For further information about prevention systems when dealing with snow disasters, see Zhaluo (2008).

of the responses and their effectiveness will help us assess the present mechanisms of relief efforts and point out how these efforts should be adjusted and improved. According to fieldwork in this area, the first actors in relief efforts are the herders themselves, with the second being the local government. On the one hand, due to the economic losses sustained and other related negative impacts, herders have to take self-help measures to prevent themselves from entering abject poverty. On the other hand, due to the fact that heavy snowfall is an uncontrollable natural phenomenon (this chapter does not cover man-made climatic interventions) and the uncertainties about the frequency of occurrence and the heaviness of the snowfall, market approaches (such as commercial insurance) are not accessible for herders to cover the risk. Thus, "public products" are introduced to the market in order to assist with prevention and relief. Much like the relief efforts employed in the wake of other natural disasters, the relief efforts associated with a snow disaster are viewed as a key responsibility of the government. Although the local government's finances were often insufficient and they often lacked the ability to influence other government departments, with the help of the central government, they can transfer materials from disaster-free areas to the affected areas. So, the government's response is critical to whether the relief efforts are successful. In addition, some organizations and individuals, driven by humanitarian principles, are involved in charitable relief efforts. However, due to scant media coverage of disasters, such charitable relief efforts are still relatively small in size and full of uncertainties. The Tibetan Buddhist monasteries sometimes assist by providing neighboring herders with daily necessities and livestock, but they are unable to provide continuous support, as they will also face their own economic hardships. Therefore, this chapter focuses mainly on the relief efforts of herders' families and that of local governments.

I Importance of Relief Efforts

In a society without a good social protection system, any risks that affect that society can lead to poverty. Snow disasters are the leading cause of poverty in the pastoral areas in the Tibetan Plateau. Between 1978 and 2008, statistics show that in Qinghai, around 24,960,000 livestock died from disasters (in most cases from snow disasters). Over this period, 500,000 heads of livestock died each year, 1,000,000 died per year for 8 years, and 2,000,000 died per year over a period of two years.[2] From 1991 to 2009, in the southern pastoral area, which the author recently visited, heavy blizzards have frequently hit and have caused huge economic losses. In the spring of 1993, four townships in the Maqin County of Guoluo experienced a snow disaster, resulting in the death of 94,225 livestock (20% of the total), leaving 110 households without livestock, 168 households with very few livestock and 219 households living below the poverty line.[3] From the winter of 1995 to the spring of 1996, 43 townships in six counties of Yushu were hit by a snow disaster which caused the death of 1,292,400 livestock (33.82% of the total) and directly affected 119,321 people. After the disaster, 8,796 people in 2,199 households had less than a head of livestock each, and 43,348 people in 7,117 households held between one to five heads. Moreover, as livestock were fed on the household's food reserves, around 5,056 households ran out of food.[4] In the spring of 2008, Dari County of Guoluo was hit by a snow disaster which caused the death of 93,359 livestock (29.09% of the total), among them, 64,092 were adults (19.97% of the total). In this particular disaster, 21,704 people in 5,387 households were affected, accounting for 98% of the local population.[5]

The statistics clearly demonstrate the detrimental impact of snow disasters on the local society and economy. Each disaster resulted in a large number of herders falling into poverty, and no other single factor has had as large an impact.[6] Apart from economic losses, snow disasters also negatively affect other areas. First, due to the poverty caused by snow disasters, herders have to live on a tight budget, which leads to malnutrition and sickness among their family members, particularly women and children. To make matters worse, in most cases, they cannot afford to see a doctor. In recent years, a new rural cooperative medical

---

[2]Geng (2008, p. 5).
[3]Maqin County Codification Committee (2005, p. 275).
[4]Geng (2008, p. 16).
[5]Civil Affairs Bureau of Dari County (2008).
[6]Of 815,339 people in the 184,216 poorest households, 394,039 were affected by disasters (48.3% of the total), larger than the total number affected by labor shortage (16,070) and sickness (211,329) (Geng, 2008, p. 32).

system has been implemented in Qinghai and other neighboring provinces that help those who do not have enough money to pay for medical expenses. However, the disaster victims cannot even afford the small residual costs that are not covered by the policy. Second, it is imperative for herders to increase their family income in order to overcome poverty, but, unfortunately, there are few options available to them. It is often the case that herders' families will turn to collecting cordyceps (a form of mushroom) and odd jobs in an effort to generate income. As a result, their children have to drop out of school and sacrifice their long-term future for short-term benefits. It can be argued that this is an important factor in determining why poverty is passed on from generation to generation. Third, herders often send their children to Tibetan Buddhist monasteries in order to cut down on family expenses. Although children can be fed and educated properly in monasteries, they are deprived of the choice to decide the direction of their own lives.

Overall, snow disasters not only contribute to the poverty of herders, but also have a negative impact on their future. It is imperative for us to improve relief efforts and bring an end to the relationship between snow disasters and poverty.

II Field Observations: Relief Efforts during Snow Disasters

Whether heavy snowfall can induce a disaster or not is a useful test of the effectiveness of the prevention system. Based on field observations, the prevention system which focuses on the construction of the "Four Sets" (i.e. houses for herders, sheds for livestock, seeds for "Quanwozi"[7] and fences for the pastures) is resistant to the impacts of low to medium-level snowfall. However, there are still two residual problems. First, the construction of the "Four Sets" is yet to be completed in some areas.[8] Second, the fodder

---

[7] "Quanwozi" is a place where herders used to set up their tents and fence off their livestock. Sheltered from wind and bathed in sunshine, it is an ideal place for planting seeds in order to make up for the shortage of fodder.

[8] See the Government of Zeku County's report in 2009. According to it, 70% of herding households in the county have not completed the construction of the "Four Sets". The percentages in Guoluo and Yushu should be much higher, because the temperature in most areas are too low to seed.

reserves in the construction of "Four Sets" are insufficient to meet the challenge of heavy snowfall. Although local governments are committed to the construction of effective prevention systems, many herders still feel vulnerable to the negative effects of snow disasters. Therefore, well organized relief efforts tackling snow disasters are viewed as the last hope to make up for the defects inherent in the prevention system. Because this system depends to some extent on the efficacy of relief efforts, luck also plays an important part. Nevertheless, effective relief efforts can reduce economic losses as well as the number of herders that fall into poverty. Relief efforts during a snow disaster can be categorized into two distinct types: herders engaging in self-help activities, and the relief efforts of the government.

1. Herders engaging in self-help

When preventive measures are not sufficient to cope with heavy snowfall and losses begin to accumulate, herders have to take self-help measures to reduce their losses. The different kinds of self-help measures they undertake are as follows:

(A) Transferring herds to disaster-free areas

This is both an effective and traditional way to reduce losses. In the tribal era before 1950s, the chief of the snow-hit tribe held the responsibility of consulting with other chiefs on the transfer of the herds. As a routine preventive measure, people living in disaster-prone areas tended to maintain good relations with the tribes (or villages) in the lowland areas. Whenever heavy snow hit, they could transfer their herds to disaster-free areas as soon as possible. In fact, they often had long-standing agreements, so that the transfer route had already been decided. For example, herders in Rirong Village, He'nan County of Huangnan, always transferred their herds to the southern lowland, Kesheng Township. However, disaster victims' use of the fertile pasture land could potentially cause a problem. In order to overcome this, the tribe affected by the disaster would either hand over a certain number of livestock or resort to other forms of compensation. In some cases the use of the land was free of charge, but this would depend on the bilateral relations between the two tribes, as well as discussions between them. In the commune period, after the founding of the People's Republic of China, the government's ability to coordinate and manage resources was particularly effective. In addition, the government endorsed the concept of providing help from all sides when one area encountered difficulties. From the 1980s to 1990s, a pasture-contracting system, which turned herders into pasture operators, was adopted. Households consulted with each other to decide on how best to use their pasture land. On the basis of evidence accumulated, it seems that the willingness of herders to receive victims of snow disasters was closely related to the number of their own livestock and whether they had room for the victims' livestock. On the other hand, leasing fees depended largely on the acreage of the land and the quality of the pastures. Therefore, the cost of such consultations soared. However, both the local governments and herders were still inclined to utilize this practice, because it was highly effective. In the 2005 blizzard, more than 70,000 livestock in 1,200 households (about 31% of the affected livestock) were transferred from the Chengduo County of Yushu to the Maduo County of Guoluo, Shiqu County of Sichuan Province and the lowland agricultural area of Yushu. This decision was arrived at after consultations between the local government and neighboring counties.[9] However, when large-scale blizzards hit, it is very difficult to transfer herds, as long-distance migration can induce even larger losses.

(B) *Slaughtering livestock to reduce the stock levels*

If the herds have not been transferred and a snow disaster is expected to worsen, some herders will opt to raise the slaughter rate of their livestock temporarily. To clarify, this means to slaughter a large number of livestock in a short time. On the one hand, they can exchange the meat and skin for cash; on the other, they are able to feed female livestock despite limited fodder reserves. However, this method is far from ideal, particularly if all herders slaughter livestock at the same time. With the oversupply of meat and skin, market prices naturally plummet. In the 2008 snow disaster, it was reported by herders in Dari that the beef price plummeted to

---

[9] Yan and Gu (2005).

4 *yuan* per kg (the price of beef usually fluctuated between 30 and 36 *yuan*).[10] Sometimes, snowfall causes damage to the transport infra-structure and thus prevents vendors from entering the affected area. Therefore, herders are unable to find proper buyers for their meat and skin. Moreover, not all the herders are willing to slaughter their livestock. Most of them tend to hope that the weather will improve and that they can manage to endure what they feel is likely to be temporary hardships. Additionally, due to the shortage of fodder reserves, herders have to feed livestock with their own food. This is the main reason why herders often run out of food during a snow disaster.

(C) *Increasing fodder reserves*

With the improvement of transportation links, businessmen from outside will transport fodder into the area and sell it to the local market. In the 2008 snow disaster, Xiadun (a 74 year old female), a Tibetan herder from the affluent Wosai Township of Dari, bought fodder from these business-men and thus solved the problem of the fodder shortage. In the pastures next to agricultural areas, for example, in Huangnan (He'nan County), the fodder trade has been growing rapidly in recent times. But in the pastures far from agricultural areas, such as Maqin and Dari, fodder trade is far less common due to the high cost of transportation.

2. *Public relief offered by local governments*

Disaster relief is one of the most important functions of government. Government bodies involved in disaster relief efforts are a part of contingency plans for snow disasters. In particular the civil affairs and livestock (agricul-ture) sectors are intimately involved in contingency planning. In accordance with their respective functions, the sector of civil affairs is responsible for the organization and coordination of disaster relief, while the sector of livestock

---

[10] Yan and Gu (2006) also reported that herders in Yushu slaughtered yaks after snow disasters and sold them at a very low price along highways. Cheap as they were (first class beef was sold at 11.8 *yuan* per kg, second and third class beef was much cheaper), it was still not easy to sell it.

(agriculture) is responsible for the prevention and alleviation of disasters.[11] In essence, the former is focused on the use of personnel, whereas the latter is focused on livestock.

According to the "2000/2001 World Development Report: Fighting against Poverty", developed countries focus more on the prevention of disasters, whereas developing countries focus on the response after the disaster, because those who are prepared and ready to react in a timely fashion can ensure that there are sufficient materials to deal with the crises and that these materials can be dispatched as soon as they are needed.[12] Field observations support this hypothesis. Given that a preventive system is not fully in place, local governments are focused on mobilizing all available resources when a disaster strikes.[13]

Case 1 Relief Efforts by the Maqin Government in 2008

In early 2008, heavy snowfall hit a large area of Guoluo, and was especially heavy in three western townships in Maqin. Lasting over 40 days with a 5 cm snow cover, the disaster affected 35 pastoral committees, 26,293 people in 7,379 households and 530,000 livestock. Once informed of the disaster, the local government reacted by immediately activating their contingency plan. The civil affairs bureau provided victims with food, blankets, clothes, tents and medicine. Efforts were very fruitful as no one died from this disaster. The agriculture and livestock bureau focused on disaster alleviation by providing victims with another

---

[11] According to the "Contingency Plan for Disaster Relief by Dari County" (for internal use only), the civil affairs sector is responsible for the release of information about disasters, appropriation and distribution of relief materials, reception and distribution of donations (home and abroad) and confirmation and collection of the disaster's impacts; the livestock sector (agriculture) is responsible for the planning and implementation of the disaster-alleviation policy, prediction and control of biohazards, meteorological disaster prevention, fodder reservation, fire prevention and pasture protection.

[12] World Bank (2001, p. 172).

[13] In the Spring Festival of 2008, Dari was stricken by a snow disaster. The local government ordered all the cadres who were spending their holidays out of the county to return before the deadline, or they would be removed from their posts. According to interviews, some cadres agreed that this order showcased the importance attached to disaster relief by the government.

550 tons of fodder, which was in addition to the 230 tons dispatched the winter before. Based on the total amount of fodder (780 tons) and the number of livestock affected (500,000 heads), there was 1.5 kg of fodder for each head of livestock. This was still insufficient, so almost 10% of the livestock died from the shortage of fodder.[14]

Case 2 Relief Efforts by Dari County in 2008

In early 2008, Dari witnessed a bout of heavy snowfall which affected 21,704 people from 5,387 households and 320,000 livestock. The disaster lasted about 70 days from 13 February to 27 April. The civil affairs bureau allocated 275,000 yuan to a relief fund (about 51 yuan per household, 12.67 yuan per capita), 210,000 kg of grain (about 39 kg per household and 10 kg per capita), 67 tents, 310 sets of padded clothes, 100 pairs of velvet underwear, 100 padded coats, 236 quilts (83 sacks altogether), 5,200 pieces of second-hand clothes, 235 pairs of cotton shoes, 4 tons of coarse coal and other relief materials which were valued at around 13,549 yuan at that time. Over the period of the disaster, fodder was distributed twice. On the first occasion, 605 tons of pellets, 90 tons of grass pellets, 40 tons of hay, 45 tons of corn and 120 tons of barley was distributed. On the second occasion, 300 tons of feed was sent, which made a total of 1,200 tons (about 3.8 kg per head). Contrast this disaster with the one that occurred in Maqin, where 93,359 livestock died from the disaster, which amounted to a death rate of 29.09% (almost a third of the total livestock).[15]

We can see from the cases above that the government bodies reacted quickly when disaster struck and they were able to mobilize many resources in order to assist with the disaster relief efforts. In the past, disasters often resulted in human casualties. For example, some people died

[14] Agriculture and Livestock Bureau of Maqin County (2008); Zhaluo, *Interviews at the Agriculture and Livestock Bureau of Maqin County*, August 21, 2009.
[15] Civil Affairs Bureau of Dari County (2008); Zhaluo, *Interviews at the Civil Affairs Bureau of Dari County*, August 24, 2009.

in the 1993 snow disaster in Maqin. However, in recent years, the guidelines around relief policies have been far more "people-oriented", stipulating strict limits to the number of human casualties. Therefore, to some extent, personal safety can be ensured after a disaster. The guidelines also dictate a "difference principle" which prioritizes the severely affected and otherwise disadvantaged households. Despite the all-out efforts by local governments, snow disasters still cause a large number of livestock deaths and huge economic losses. The reasons for this lie in the following points.

(A) *Shortage in relief materials, especially fodder reserves*

When self-help measures are insufficient or ineffective enough to deal with the impact of a blizzard (i.e. heavy snowfall and the long duration of snow cover), herders have to rely on the relief efforts of local governments. The two cases above expose the gap between the amount of fodder allocated at the time of a disaster, and the actual amount needed. Other studies have suggested that it is difficult for yaks to feed themselves when there is over 3 cm of snow cover. For sheeps, the figure is slightly higher (around 5 cm of snow cover). It has been shown that if the snow cover reaches 5 cm for a period of four to six days, the livestock begin to die.[16] In the winter, a yak usually consumes around 7–8 kg of fodder a day, whereas a sheep needs around 1–2 kg.[17] Looking at the two cases above, during the snow disasters in 2008, only 1.5 kg per head were dispatched in 3 townships in Maqin (the snow cover in this instance lasted nearly 40 days) and 3.8 kg per head were sent to Dari (the snow cover in this case lasted nearly 70 days). Thus, it is easy to see that the fodder allocated to these areas would not have been sufficient to meet their needs.

The defects in the prevention system and the shortage in relief materials highlight the financial constraints of the local government. Due to limited finances, funds for the construction of an effective prevention system had to be cut significantly, which, in turn, increased the risk of snow disasters.

---

[16] Refer to the Implementation Office (2007, p. 114).
[17] Due to the different measurements taken, the daily intake of food varies greatly across each type of livestock. See Xue (2004); Liu *et al.* (1997); Liu (1979).

Because of what can only be described as some form of cognitive malfunction, the local government officials believed that because they were unable to predict a snow disaster, there definitely would not be one. The construction fund was therefore seen as an opportunity cost (idle capital) which could be invested in other more useful areas. This analysis does not imply that there are embezzlement issues, but rather a problem of irrationality with regards to fiscal expenditure. Although the negative impact of snow disasters are widely known, the methods aimed at alleviating the effects of snow disasters are still largely reliant on relief efforts. When disaster strikes, local governments apply for relief funds and transport fodder from the outside areas, which inevitably lead to difficulties relating to fodder, such as the purchase, transportation and dispatch of fodder to the disaster victims.

(B) *Long distances between warehouses storing relief materials and the herders' production and living quarters*

Most of the warehouses storing relief materials are located on the outskirts of the townships. Those located in the pastoral areas are rather small in size. When a disaster hits, it is often the case that relief materials cannot be distributed in a timely fashion because transport infrastructure has been affected by the snow disaster (e.g. blocked passes and snow-covered highways). Hampered by a dispersed populace and inaccessible transport networks, local governments came to realize that a delay in the delivery of relief materials to affected areas greatly impacts on the effectiveness of disaster relief.[18]

(C) *Inadequate responses to the secondary disaster following a blizzard*

According to interviews, epidemics in the livestock population often break out after a snow disaster and the detrimental impact of these epidemics are on a similar level to those of snow disasters. However, local governments are not efficient in dealing with epidemics. For example, they failed to provide enough veterinarians, medicine and related training in this area.

---

[18] See Civil Affairs Bureau of Dari County (2008).

The high frequency of snow disasters and the large number of deaths of livestock underscore the defects and ineffectiveness of relief responses. However, backed by the central government, local governments still play a pivotal role in disaster relief by transferring materials from outside the affected area to the victims of snow disasters.

III Field Observations: Post-Disaster Relief Efforts

Snow disasters have a negative impact, not only on herders, but also on the operation of the wider economy. The ongoing relief efforts after a disaster, which help victims shake off the negative impacts and resume work, are beneficial both to the herders and the smooth operation of the local society and economy.

1. Self-help efforts by the herders

Livestock are both the means of production and a central vehicle by which herders make a livelihood. The high mortality rates among their livestock caused by a snow disaster deprive herders of their means of livelihood and production. The high frequency of snow disasters exposes the fragility of today's pastoralism. Due to the limitations imposed by social conditions and a lack of human capital, herders are not able to find another form of economic activity that can substitute herding. Thus, the only feasible way for them to make a living still lies in rebuilding their herd.

(A) Reinvestment in herd rebuilding

The availability of assets in order to re-invest in herd rebuilding is key to whether such attempts will be successful. Based on fieldwork, the reinvestment can be achieved through three channels: personal assets and deposits, fund-raising through social networks (social capital), or loans from banks and cooperative credit unions. In short, the ability to reinvest depends on family savings, social capital and public financial services.

Family savings include currency deposits and valuable assets. According to interviews, relatively affluent households (i.e. those who

214 Zhaluo

had abundant livestock or were running a business) are the first to recover from a disaster. They achieve this by either withdrawing funds from their bank accounts or by selling valuable jewelry. Scholars used to believe that herders purchased jewelry as a way to flaunt their wealth. In fact, it can also be viewed as a store of wealth, given the lack of a financial services sector. However, most herders have minimal savings, and certainly do not have enough to cope with snow disasters. According to relevant statistics, in 2008, 63% of herders in Dari lived below the poverty line.[19] In 2009, 40% of the population in Dangluo Township of Maqin lived with a yearly income of less than 637 *yuan* per capita.[20] According to fieldwork in Zitang Village (Zhenqin Township, Chengduo), out of 120 households, only a few were able to resume production by themselves.

Social capital refers to the ability of herders to gain access to resources through social networks.[21] However, it is often the case that their social network will include the same herders, in the same community, with the same resources. In other words, in the event of a snow disaster, it is likely that they will all require capital, and thus, none of them will be able to give any away.[22] Since all of the members in the social network face the same demand — in this case a large sum of money — their ability to help each other is reduced. What they need is a more diversified portfolio of social capital to address the shortage of financial capital in the affected area. Examples would include financial help from friends and relatives working in the government, or doing business in the city. However, some still question this assumption. According to fieldwork findings, when the social network is broader than the snow-hit area, it can play an important role in its recovery. For example, herders can lease livestock from relatives and friends from outside the area (to quote a well-known saying, "using another's chicken to lay one's own eggs"). In most cases the leasing period lasts between 3–5 years. Moreover, the fees associated with leasing the livestock depend on discussions between the

---

[19] Government of Dari County (2008).
[20] Government of the Dangluo Township in Maqin County (2009).
[21] Lin (2005, p. 28).
[22] Zhao (2007).

leaser and lessee. A common practice is for the lessee to give some of the livestock products (such as dairy products) to the leaser, while keeping the offspring of the leased livestock. It is often the case that mutual assistance between friends and relatives can lead to positive results. However, it should be noted that the lessee still faces the risk of compensation if there are any deaths among the livestock.

Public financial services refer to the special-purpose loans provided by the government and other financial services after a disaster. In theory, they can make up for the deficiency in financial capital through their social capital, however, funds are not necessarily easily accessible to herders. On the one hand, herders know little about the relief policy due to poor access to relevant information. On the other hand, other barriers are set up due to insufficient loan quotas. Most herders have to rely on their social networks in order to gain approval. As a result, the process of loan application has evolved into a complicated, secretive and impenetrable trade. However, there are some exceptions. In some communities, the practice of purchasing livestock through loans is not accepted. For example, in the Seqin Village in the Moba Township of Dari, which is located deep in the Bayan Har Mountain, herders strongly believe that the livestock bought with borrowed money (including loans) cannot survive. Therefore, many herders from these areas tend not to seek loans.

(B) *Increase in labor supply*

Confronted with few reinvestment channels, herders have found an alternative way to settle the problem: take up alternative short-term employment. However, it takes time to accumulate the money needed to rebuild the herds, because herders are poorly paid in the sectors that offer employment opportunities. According to fieldwork observations, there are various ways for herders to enter the job market, particularly when they look for work in cities. The following are some of the more popular options:

Intensive Management. Although some households are left without any livestock after a disaster, most are left with at least a few livestock. If these households lack reinvestment channels, they tend to follow the strategy of intensive management. This involves measures such as increasing the rate of reproduction, increasing the rate of survival, and decreasing the death rate among the remaining livestock. If the herders find themselves in degraded pastures, they will tend to transfer their livestock to better pastures during winter and spring. Some will decide to work for other herders. After years of hard work, they gradually gain enough capital to restore basic production conditions.

Diversify Economic Activity. Cordyceps collecting is a common undertaking for a large number of children who have to drop out of school and help their family. Indeed, collecting cordyceps has become the main source of income for herders in some areas, and in many cases the only source of family income. Some households even choose to abandon pastoralism completely and live on the income generated over the 1–2 months a year when they can collect cordyceps. Some herders may choose to be employed by those with abundant livestock. Moreover, since the implementation of the "Develop the West" strategy, disaster victims have been increasingly involved in infrastructure projects. However, they are poorly paid because they are not used to working on infrastructure projects and thus are not competitive with others who have relevant experience.

Additionally, in the areas where a household-based pasture contract system has been implemented and fencing has been placed around the pasture land, households who have little or no livestock can increase their income by leasing out their pastures. Fieldwork observations suggest that the household-based pasture contract system has not been completely carried out in some places due to various factors. Therefore, disaster victims are unable to make any profits by sharing their pastures with others or leaving them fallow.

2. Relief and support efforts by local governments

In the southern pastoral area of Qinghai, when faced with disaster victims, the first thing the local government tends to do is to provide the victims with a minimum subsistence allowance. This minimum allowance system for rural residents helps the victims to resume production through various support projects.

(A) *Minimum subsistence allowance system for rural residents*

The decision to grant the minimum subsistence allowance to any specific household is based on the mechanism of individual application followed by the community's assessment. The procedure is as follows:

Individual application → Assessment by pastoral committee (at the village level) → Verification by local government (at the township level) → Signed off by the head of local government → A report is sent to the civil affairs bureau (at the county level).

However, local governments, financed mainly through payment transfers from the central government, are unable to provide enough funds to cover all of the victims who should receive assistance, as decided by the civil affairs bureau. More importantly, many of the disaster victims are not poor enough to meet the criteria that allow them to receive benefits. In 2009, in the 3 townships of Maqin, only those with a yearly income of less than 960 *yuan* are able to apply for the minimum subsistence allowance which amounts to an additional income of 750 *yuan* per year. Moreover, the salary of those who are fortunate enough to receive these benefits are constantly monitored by a "dynamic management" system (i.e. after a period of time, those households whose salary exceeds 960 *yuan* will be excluded from the scheme). There are still loopholes in the system because of inaccurate income statistics and an ineffective monitoring mechanism. Cadres and their relatives are time and again granted the minimum subsistence allowance, which has induced a lot of criticism from herders. In short, the goal of the minimum subsistence allowance system for rural residents is to maintain a minimum living standard for those in need, and not a means for herders to accumulate capital so that they can resume production.

(B) *Poverty-alleviation projects*

One of the projects aimed at alleviating poverty, the "Improving the Entire Village Project", is a good example of where a government-funded program — selected by the herders[23]— leads to good results.

Case 3 The "Improving the Entire Village Project" in Maqin

The three western townships in Maqin are often plagued with the dual problems of pasture degradation and snow disasters. Since the implementation of the "Sanjiangyuan[24] Ecological Protection Project", most herders have now been moved to the cities. Therefore, the "Improving the Entire Village Project" has been closely combined with the ecological migration project. Here, we will examine the Xuema and Chazang pastoral committees of Changmahe Township as prime examples. There are altogether 134 households integrated into the "Improving the Entire Village Project", with each household receiving 6,500 yuan worth of funding. Based on individual selection and a collective decision-making process, the final programs supported by the program are as follows: 46 households showed an interest in purchasing transportation and completing odd jobs; 11 households were interested in starting a cooperative business (specifically, opening five small shops); 22 households were interested in building some houses which they would subsequently rent out; and 35 households were interested in pastoralism and wanted to purchase livestock with an average of four to six yaks each.[25]

---

[23] According to interviews, most herders prefer to buy livestock. However, in the area covered in the "Sanjiangyuan Ecological Protection Project", the fund for livestock accounted for no more than one third of the total for poverty-alleviation projects. Therefore, only a small number of herders were allowed to buy livestock. In Zhenqin Township of Chengduo, each household received five cows according to the "Improving the Entire Village Project".

[24] Sanjiangyuan is the area where the sources of the Yangtze River, Yellow River and Lancang River meet.

[25] See Zhaluo, *Interviews at the Agriculture and Livestock Bureau of Maqin County*, August 21, 2009.

The program described above, the "Improving the Entire Village Project", is a policy designed to help the poor more generally, and not specifically targeted at the victims of snow disasters. In Maqin, between 2002 and 2009, the program only covered 15 village (pastoral) committees with an average of two villages per year. Moreover, the government needed to ensure that all townships were covered in a balanced and fair manner. It is often the case that disaster victims are scattered across a large area. Thus, it was difficult for those who were not included in the "Improving the Entire Village Project" to get sufficient support from the government and resume their production.

(C) *The delivery of female livestock*

The delivery of female livestock to affected areas is one of the poverty-alleviation projects most closely focused on assisting victims to resume their production. Specifically, the county's bureau of agriculture and livestock purchases female livestock (be they cows or ewe) using a special-purpose fund, and sends the livestock directly to disaster victims. In 2009, in accordance with the *Purchase Plan for Livestock to Resume Production after Disaster by Dari County*, around 2,270,000 *yuan* was made available in order to purchase livestock. In a local market, the county bureau of agriculture and livestock bought 1,367 heads of one- to two-year-old cows (which were fertile and could thus give birth to calves) at an average cost of 1,660 *yuan* each. After purchasing the cows, they then dispatched them to the ten subordinate townships. Fieldwork observations showed that Wosai Township received only 115 cows which compared unfavorably to the nearly 8,000 cattle that died. Similarly, the Zhaque pastoral committee of Wosai received only 38 cows for a community of 170 households. This meant that on average each household was allocated only 0.22 of a cow.[26] Therefore, the cows that were delivered to these townships played virtually no role in the resumption of production. The inefficacy of this practice was due to a shortage of local finance.

---

[26] Agriculture and Livestock Bureau of Dari County (2009).

(D) *Resettlement projects*

In recent years, a series of projects have been carried out in the Tibetan pastoral region, such as the Sanjiangyuan Ecological Protection Project, Small Towns Project and Resettlement Projects for herders. Based on the precept that public services and welfare provision are better in the cities than it is in pastoral areas, the government encourages herders to move to the suburbs of cities as part of a resettlement process. Herders can thus enjoy public services such as schools, healthcare and better access to information. Households with little or no livestock can also be employed in substitute industries, such as parts of the low-end labor market. However, in the short term, herders still face a series of risks and difficulties. These risks and difficulties include, for example, unemployment, the gap between the urban and rural population, as well as the inability to adjust given that it is often the case that the individuals were once quite affluent herding households. In essence, during the process of urbanization, it takes a long time for the herders to adapt to the dramatic changes in their lives, both in terms of how they make their living and adjusting to life in the city more generally.

In short, both the herders and local governments undertake various actions in order to restore the herder's basic livelihood and means of production. Due to the lack of financial and human capital, most herders cannot resume production by themselves. Efforts undertaken by the local government, such as financial support and projects aimed at poverty alleviation, are not sufficient in order to ensure the resumption of production either. Based on their expectations of the difference between the herder's prospective future and their current reality, the local government strongly support resettlement projects for herders and encourage them to find alternative employment in the cities (agricultural husbandry has not been widely promoted in this area). However, rational as this policy might seem, it will still take a long time for the concept to become a reality.

IV Discussions and Recommendations

Fieldwork observations indicate that in the southern Tibetan pastoral area of Qinghai, defects exist in both the prevention system and relief efforts. Their improvement depends on linking the concept of disaster resistance with the local natural, economic, social and cultural factors. Instead of probing into all of these factors, this chapter would rather raise the following issues:

1. Recognizing the particularities of snow disasters in pastoral areas

(A) Differences between snow disasters and agricultural disasters

There is a significant difference between the impact of snow disasters and other agricultural disasters such as floods, mudslides and hailstorms. Snow disasters are far more dangerous, because in addition to threatening the fruits of the herder's labor, they also threaten their means of production (i.e. their cows, sheep or yaks). However, relief efforts during and after a snow disaster, tend to mirror those that one would expect in the case of other agricultural disasters. In the event of an agricultural disaster, in most cases it is the product of the herder's efforts that is destroyed, not their means of production. Thus, the relief efforts focus on providing products such as food and clothing. Moreover, in the case of agricultural disasters, if the herders are able to overcome the difficulties of this disaster, they can look forward to resuming their production in the next cycle. For herders, their livestock are their products, means of production and store of wealth. Therefore, relief efforts should focus on the protection and rebuilding of the means of production, i.e. livestock. Indeed, after a snow disaster, the loans and livestock provided to herders by government are similar to the seeds provided to peasants. The amount of financial capital used in a snow disaster is much higher than that used in an agricultural disaster. This is because it takes a number of years for the livestock to grow into adults. Thus, the time it takes to recover is much longer than in the case of an agricultural disaster.

(B) Distinctions between disaster relief and poverty alleviation

In a manner quite different to populations exposed to long-term abject poverty, disaster victims, who through no fault of their own, lose valuable resources in the wake of a disaster, still have the capability (labor capital) to resume basic production and life. If the relief efforts of government and the wider society can help them to overcome their losses, they can resume production by themselves. By comparison, populations who are exposed to long-term abject poverty lack both the resources and the capabilities to succeed — particularly the capability of production. It is fair to conclude that they cannot make a living, even if they have been provided with the means of production. That is the essential difference between disaster relief and poverty alleviation. Herders have frequently commented that they would rather have livestock, from which they can make a living, as opposed to government support. A key defect in the thinking around disaster relief is that the victims of disasters are in some ways the same as populations who have been subject to severe poverty over a long period of time. Moreover, efforts to integrate disaster victims into processes designed to help populations who face abject long-term poverty end up delaying the process of production resumption. Based on comparisons between the effects of long-term and short-term funding strategies, it can be concluded that short-term strategies will be more economically efficient, worthwhile and will result in better social outcomes.

2. Restructuring fiscal spending and increasing relief reserves

According to fieldwork findings, both officials and herders have pointed out that the success of disaster relief efforts depend on the availability of sufficient fodder. As stated in the previous paragraphs, although local governments deliver relief materials and fodder from areas outside of the affected region, the amount that they are able to supply never meets the demand because of a shortage in total relief reserves. It is clear from the analysis that the local government did not allocate sufficient funds to the preventive system. Here, once again, we look at the case of the village of Dari. It was estimated that during the disaster of 2008, Dari suffered a loss of 146,000,000 *yuan* (which does not include any social losses).[27] Moreover, the expenditure on fodder after the disaster totaled 2,010,000 *yuan*.[28] Therefore, it can be concluded, regardless of whether the motive is to reduce the losses associated with

---

[27] See Civil Affairs Bureau of Dari County (2008).
[28] See Agriculture and Livestock Bureau of Dari County (2008).

snow disasters, to stabilize the economy, to alleviate widespread poverty or to improve living standards, the local government needs to adjust their fiscal expenditure in order to ensure that sufficient funds are allocated to providing disaster relief and keeping material reserves.

3. *Broadening relief channels and activating a community self-help mechanism*

No doubt, the government plays an important role in disaster relief. Even in the pre-modern era, the central government or the Tibetan government took various measures to help disaster victims, such as tax reduction and exemption, as well as increasing the food supply.[29] More recently, the government has a comprehensive package of measures that not only helps to limit casualties and economic loss, but also helps the victims rebuild their means of production and livelihood, while maintaining social order. However, in the southern Tibetan pastoral areas of Qinghai, the local government, financed mainly through payment transfers, cannot effectively deal with blizzards. As a transitional and complementary methodology, the broadening of relief channels will be an effective solution, including relief efforts of social organizations like Tibetan Buddhist monasteries, and the mobilization and employment of local resources.

Case 4 Relief Efforts by Tibetan Buddhist Monasteries

Longxi Monastery, located at Xialaxiu Township, is the largest gelukpa monastery in Yushu, with more than 400 monks. According to Living Buddha Ni Zhi, it manages to sustain itself, not only by running various businesses, but also by providing public services to the neighboring herders. Apart from the opening of schools and hospitals, it has been actively involved in disaster relief efforts. On the one hand, in the disaster-free season, for a variety of reasons, local herders will often give some of their livestock to the monastery. In reality, only a small number

---

[29] Zhang *et al.* (2009, p. 310–316); Chen and Liu (2005, p. 43–84); The Historical Archives of the Tibetan Autonomous Region (1985, p. 70 and 90).

of livestock are kept in the monastery, while the rest are entrusted to the herders (who sometimes compensate the monks by providing them with dairy products, or in other cases are not required to provide anything at all). During the season where disasters are common, the livestock would be returned to the herders (who were scattered over a wide area [even in Zhiduo County] and approximately 100 kilometers away from the monastery). In the 1995 snow disaster, the monastery gave out 300,000 yuan to the neighboring villages, an average of 10,000–20,000 yuan to each of the villages, and returned thousands of livestock to the herders. On the other hand, due to the shortage of commodities after the disaster, businessmen took advantage of this opportunity and raised prices. However, the commodities found in the monastery's shops were sold at the original price. In some cases, these commodities were even sold at cost price. According to interviews, the monastery did not turn down any of the herders' demands. In the 2005 snow disaster, Living Buddha Kelsang Chilai Gyatso (who originated from Chengduo and is based in Sichuan Province) donated 100 tons of food and 6,207 pieces of clothes to the relief efforts. Of course, it is fair to assume that monasteries only account for a small proportion of the total relief efforts. As a famous proverb goes, "Poor herders lead to poor monasteries." It is true to say that the monasteries are supported by the local herders, and they depend on the growth of the local economy in order to survive.[30]

Before the 1950s, the southern Tibetan pastoral area of Qinghai was tribal in nature. Due to the absence of the government, disaster relief relied primarily on herders and the local communities. The relief concepts and traditions formed during that time should be promoted to other areas, so that others can learn from these concepts. For example, the lease of female livestock to disaster victims is an effective way to deal with disasters and is still adopted in many pastoral areas in this region. According

---

[30] Information from Zhaluo, *Interviews at Longxi Monastery*, July 12, 2007; *Interviews at the Civil Affairs Bureau of Chengduo County*, July 17, 2007.

to Shaduo, a 40 year old female Tibetan herder in Changmahe Township, in the 1987 blizzard, Changmahe received 300 sheep from the township of Lajia. The sheep were divided into five herds and sent to disaster victims (with a two-year leasing period for each household). Despite the high altitude of Changmahe, these sheep produced 15 lambs annually for Shaduo and contributed significantly to the resumption of production. The same practice exists in the Haxiu Township of Yushu, where victims often borrow female livestock from their relatives. Moreover, it does not have the negative connotations of "buying livestock with borrowed money", and thus, becomes a feasible and acceptable way for the government to transport and borrow female livestock from disaster-free areas.

Apart from the relief efforts of local governments, it is necessary to enlist wide-ranging support from a number of sources in order to survive the hardships brought about by the disaster. Media coverage should be promoted to arouse sympathy and support for the victims and a mutual aid mechanism should be set up with neighboring areas which should be distinct both in terms of their local climate and economy.

4. Establishing experimental funds for disaster relief

From the perspective of long-term sustainable development, establishing either agricultural or livestock insurance policies is an effective way to help disaster relief efforts. In the disaster-free seasons, based on the assumption of fairly high economic returns, herders and local governments can jointly invest in the establishment of relief funds or public funds. When the disaster season approaches, they can then draw down on these funds. Without this policy, and with only the support of the government, it would be difficult to resume production rapidly.

In summary, based on fieldwork in Guoluo, Yushu and Huangnan in Qinghai, defects are found to exist in the prevention system and disaster relief mechanisms. These defects increase the risk of these areas being negatively affected by disasters. Traditional pastoralism is quite vulnerable to the modern world's global climatic changes as well as local ecological degradation (a reference to frequent disasters). The question of how to best minimize the losses associated with snow disasters relies not only on more intensive relief efforts, but also on a better understanding of snow disasters and disaster relief more generally. Moreover, there needs to be a paradigm shift from the focus on the response to a snow disaster to a greater appreciation of the importance of efforts to prevent disasters through economic and particularly fiscal growth.

Bibliography

Agriculture and Livestock Bureau of Dari County, 2008, "Funding Details of Disaster Relief and Livestock Protection by Agriculture and Livestock Bureau of Dari County", April 1, 2008.

Agriculture and Livestock Bureau of Dari County, 2009, "Purchase Plan for Livestock to Resume Production after Disasters by Dari County", August 2009.

Agriculture and Livestock Bureau of Maqin County, 2008, "A Review of 2008 and Prospects for 2009 by Agriculture and Livestock Bureau of Maqin County", November 14, 2008.

Chen Hua, Liu Zhongzhi, 2005, *Disaster Relief and Poverty Alleviation: Social Efforts in the Chinese Feudal Era — 1750–1911*, Beijing: China Renmin University Press.

Civil Affairs Bureau of Dari County, 2008, "A Review of 2008 by the Civil Affairs Bureau of Dari County", October 13, 2008.

Geng Yan (Ed.), 2008, *30 Years of Civil Administration: Qinghai 1978–2008*, Beijing: China Society Press.

Government of Dari County, 2008, "A Report on Disaster Resistance and Livestock Preservation by Dari County", May 2008.

Government of the Dangluo Township in Maqin County, 2009, "A Review of 2009 by Dangluo Township", August 2009.

Government of Zeku County, 2009, "A Report on Poverty-Alleviation Program by Zeku County", June 23, 2009.

Implementation Office, 2007, "A General Plan of the Preservation and Construction of Sanjiangyuan Natural Reserve Area of Qinghai", In *A Project Handbook of the Preservation and Construction of the Sanjiangyuan Natural Reserve Area in Qinghai*, February 2007.

Lin Nan (translated by Zhang Lei), 2005, *Social Capital — A Theory on Social Structure and Behavior*, Shanghai: Shanghai People's Publishing House.

Liu Fengxian, 1979, "A Probe into Tibetan Sheeps' Daily Intake", *Chinese Journal of Grassland*, 02, 23–26.

Liu Shujie, Wang Wanbang, 1997, "A Study on the Yak's Intake during Different Phenophases", *Chinese Qinghai Journal of Animal and Veterinary Sciences*, 27(2), 5–9.

Maqin County Codification Committee, 2005, *Annals of Maqin County*, Xining: Qinghai People's Press.

The Historical Archives of the Tibetan Autonomous Region (Eds.), 1985, *Annals of Disasters — Snow Disasters*, Lhasa: Tibet People's Press.

World Bank, 2001, *2000/2001 World Development Report: Fighting against Poverty*, Beijing: China Financial and Economic Publishing House.

Xue Bai, 2004, "A Dynamic Study on Livestock Intakes in Native Pastures of the Tibetan Plateau", *ACTA Ecology of Domestic Animal*, 04, 21–25.

Yan Shoude, Gu Ling, 2005, "The Southern Pastoral Area in Qinghai Hit by Blizzard", *China Meteorological News*, December 14, 2005.

Yan Shoude, Gu Ling, 2006, "The Survival Test for Herders after Snow Disaster", *China Animal Husbandry Newsletter*, 03, 60–62.

Zhaluo, 2008, "Systems and Technology of Snow Disaster Prevention — An Anthropological Observation in the Eastern Tibetan Plateau", *Ethno-National Studies*, 05, 55–65.

Zhang Tao, Xiang Yongqin, Tan Jing, 2009, A Study on Chinese Traditional Concepts of Disaster Relief, Beijing: Social Sciences Academic Press.

Zhao Yandong, 2007, "Social Capital and Recovery after Disaster — A Sociological Study on Natural Disasters", *Sociological Studies*, 05, 164–187.

CHAPTER 12

Systems and Technologies for Snow Disaster Prevention: Anthropological Observations on the Pastoral Areas in the Eastern Qinghai–Tibet Plateau

ZHALUO

Abstract

Observations conducted on the rangelands on the eastern Qinghai–Tibet Plateau (found in He'nan County and Zeku County in southeast Qinghai) indicate that the following conditions result in heavy snowfall and snow disasters. The first factor to consider is the height of the foliage. If the foliage is short in length, this increases the possibility of a snow disaster occurring. Excluding natural factors, the undergrowth of foliage occurs because of improper use of the pasture lands set aside for winter grazing. Consequently, when the withered foliage is covered by the snowfall, the livestock are starved to death because of the lack of edible foodstuffs. Second, it is extremely cold after heavy snowfall. Coldness not only freezes weak livestock to death, but also starves healthy livestock, as it prevents the accumulated snow from melting. Third, the government's limited capacity to assist with disaster prevention and relief cannot improve the scarcity of food. Therefore, it can be seen that snow disaster risks are directly associated with the exploitation system of pastures and the public service level of the government.

The risks are both related to natural and human factors, that is, different ownership systems of pastures and the public service level of the government, which vary greatly over different historical periods. A more rational system and a better level of public service is crucial in order to reduce disaster risks.

Keywords: Pasture Areas; Snow Disasters; Nomadic Herding; Public Service.

The planet's "third pole", the Qinghai–Tibet Plateau, is the highest region in the world in terms of elevation. Due to the region's high altitude and certain special meteorological conditions, regular snowfall is a common climatic component of the Qinghai–Tibet Plateau all year round. However, in winter and spring, due to the heavy snowfall and extremely low temperatures, the snow may remain on the ground for a very long time without melting. Because the pastures are covered under a heavy coat of snow, it is difficult for the livestock to graze. Unfortunately, as a result of the cold and ensuing hunger, many livestock die of weakness and sickness, causing a significant loss to pastoralist households. For thousands of years, snow disasters have always been the foremost threat to the production capacities and livelihoods of the local herdsmen.

In order to prevent and mitigate losses caused by snow disasters, the local pastoralists have taken an array of countermeasures such as specialized production arrangements, and the promotion of techniques designed for disaster prevention and mitigation. Their overarching goal is to adapt as best as they can to the distinctive ecological conditions, as it is impossible for them to control the climatic conditions. In fact, after systematic inspection of the economic lifestyle of the nomads on the plateau, one can easily discern their acute concern towards disasters.[1] To some extent, it can be claimed that their unique nomadic lifestyle is built on these worries and concerns. However, this does not mean that there are no constant and long-standing rules governing their lifestyles and technologies. Conversely, these rules surrounding their lifestyle and technologies are subject to constant change, which in turn are dependent upon climatic and environmental changes as well as affected by the constant evolution of the human concepts of social and economic development. It

[1] Goldstein and Beall (1990).

is of interest to note, when comparing various historical periods, that the various measures and strategies taken to address snow disaster threats have often been quite contradictory to each other. It must also be noted that, despite the relentless efforts of the local pastoralists, they are still very restricted in their capabilities to effectively tackle the risks associated with snow disasters. Many of them are exposed to abject poverty due to the losses incurred as a result of snow disasters and have to rely on national and social relief aid. Therefore, in order to foster the development of pastoralism on the Qinghai–Tibet Plateau, as well as improve and boost the living standards of local herdsmen, it is necessary to constantly explore and improve the measures and strategies to help the pastoralists better prepare themselves for snow disasters.[2] The initial step in this effort is to investigate the systemic changes over the past 100 years, as well as to analyze and assess various technical methods previously utilized.

This process will begin via the analysis of two pastoralist villages: Mar Village and Geri Village. These two villages can both be found in the eastern rangeland of the Qinghai–Tibet Plateau. This chapter presents a historical inspection and analysis of the systems and techniques for snow disaster prevention in the two villages over the past 100 years. Mar Village is located in north He'nan (*rma-lho*) Mongolian Autonomous County, which is found in the Huangnan Tibetan Autonomous Prefecture of Qinghai. All the residents are Mongolians, who believe in Lamaist Buddhism, speak Tibetan, and are fully assimilated into Tibetan culture. Before the 1950s, Mar Village was under the rule of the local He'nan Mongolian Prince. Geri Village is located in western Zeku (*rtse-khog*) County, which is also in the Huangnan Tibetan Autonomous Prefecture of Qinghai. The villagers, historically part of the *dpon-'khor* tribe under the hereditary *Hor stong skor* (*chiliarch*, or *qianhu*), are all Tibetans. Both of the villages (the distance between them is about 120 kilometers) are located in the humid rangeland of the eastern Qinghai–Tibet Plateau, and the upper reaches of the Yellow River. The foliage here grows well most years, with the grass reaching 15 to 25 centimeters in height in most areas. On pastures with better temperature and moisture conditions, the grass can reach as high as 40 centimeters. This is in sharp

---

[2] Yu (1948).

contrast to the situation on the pastures in the central and western regions of the Qinghai–Tibet Plateau, where the grass does not grow very high and foliage in general is sparse. Yet, this area is affected by special geographical climatic conditions (it is the intersection between the warm and moist air currents from the south and the cold air currents from the north), and these two counties are frequently hit by large snow-storms.[3] According to related statistics, out of the 38 years from 1956 to 1994, there were 15 years in which snow disasters occurred in the south-ern pastoral areas of Qinghai Province (in essence, a 39% chance of a snow disaster[4]). As both the He'nan and Zeku Counties are part of the southern pastoral area, they both serve as a good sample for further investigation of snow disasters.

I Snow Cover and Low Temperatures: Threats in Winter and Spring

The existence of conventions and techniques for the prevention of snow disasters is dependent both on the local climate and the sociocultural conditions. In terms of defining what is meant by sociocultural condi-tions, it includes the following: societal type, societal influence and level of economic development (Figure 1). The foundation of how to respond to a natural disaster is based upon the accumulation of long-term observa-tions and personal experience. Backed up by their forefathers' accumu-lated observations and experience of the local climate and without the benefits of having a weather forecast, the herdsmen of Mar Village and Geri Village came to achieve a clear and definite understanding of why a particular snow disaster will occur and the intricacies behind the different types of snow disasters.

It is this author's opinion that the biggest threats posed by snow disas-ters are two-fold: the thick snow cover that follows them and the extremely low temperatures. Whenever heavy snowfall occurs, the

---

[3] It is pointed out that there are generally three large regions of snow cover on the Qinghai–Tibet Plateau, but annual snow cover varies greatly in the eastern part, which is the major region suffering from extensive snow disasters. See Dong *et al.* (2001).

[4] Sun and Wu (1996); Wen (2007).

Figure 1:   Female Herders in He'nan County.
Source: Taken by the author in Mar Village, He'nan County.

pastures will be covered by thick snow, this is a significant threat to the herders as it prevents the livestock from grazing and eventually causes them to die of starvation. Related studies indicate that if the livestock are prevented from grazing, from the fifth day, the old, the weak and the sick will die, by the seventh day fairly healthy livestock begin to die, and by the tenth day the majority of them will die.[5] On the other hand, the problems caused by the extreme cold are two-fold: It prevents the snow from melting, and at the same time directly threatens the survival of the livestock. According to the pastoralists' observations, the livestock lose weight rapidly in low temperatures and get sick easily. Modern science indicates that under low temperature conditions, livestock have to use their body fat to keep their temperature in balance and the severe cold may cause an excessive consumption of body heat, which leads to a rapid decline in the fat reserves of the livestock. As a result, those thin, under-weight livestock will be debilitated and even die within a couple of days.

---

[5] This is a conclusion drawn in accordance with the research conducted in the Inner Mongolian pastoral area (Gong and Hao, 1998); the results of the investigation in Qinghai Province are nearly the same (Zhou *et al.*, 2000).

Moreover, the special timing of snowfalls in those localities also con-
tributes to the frequent incidences of snow disasters. According to the
pastoralist respondents, snowfalls occur more frequently in the winter and
spring on the Qinghai–Tibet Plateau. However, unlike other places, a
distinct feature of the local climate of the eastern regions of the plateau
is that it snows early — and sometimes snow disasters occur even as early
as late autumn, but the snow season ends very late, so severe snow disasters will often occur towards the end of spring and in early summer.
Snowstorms frequently hit in late autumn and early winter, which signi-
fies to the pastoralists that they must move back in good time, to ensure
they utilize the winter pastures before wintertime and that it will be very
hazardous to stay in the pastures over summer and autumn. If the snowfall
in early winter is followed by a drastic temperature drop immediately in
its wake, it is a clear sign of what can only be described as the beginning
of a "nightmare" to the pastoralists because it means that it will be getting
much colder and the snow will not melt for a long period of time.
Consequently, the livestock may well die of hunger and the cold.
Compared to winter, spring is believed to be a more risky period because
of the relative frequency of heavy snowstorms.[6] To make things even
worse, the conditions on the pastures in spring are not as good as they are
in winter. After a whole winter's grazing, most of the foliage has been
eaten to its roots; and even if there is withered grass to feed upon, its
nutritional value is negligible.[7] Pastoralists have said that during this
time, even if the cattle and sheep graze all day they would still be hungry.
After a harsh winter, the livestock suffer from extreme malnutrition and
have only limited resistance to disease. As the pastoralists remarked, one
spring snowfall covering the grass for only two or three days can result in
the deaths of tens of livestock, and just one spring blizzard can leave

---

[6] According to the statistics on the number of days of snowfall in He'nan County from
1959 to 1980, there are on average 53 days with snowfall per year in He'nan County,
34.6 days of snowfall from January to May, accounting for around 65% of the snowfall for
the whole year (Local Records Compilation Committee of the He'nan Mongolian
Autonomous County, 1996, p. 184).
[7] Related research shows that the crude protein content of foliage in the grass-wither-
ing period (from November to the following April) is less than half of that in summer
(Qin, 2006).

pastoralists with no herd at all.[8] It is evident from this comment that spring is the most difficult season in the year for pastoralists.

Due to the heavy snowfall in early winter and late spring, the pastoralists are obliged to stay on the pastures for the six to eight months between early winter and late spring. Because of the considerable amount of time spent grazing on the pastures, this inevitably results in a shortage of foliage for the animals to graze upon.

How can one best prepare for the heavy snowfall and low temperatures in the winter and spring? Or more precisely, how can one address the scarcity of livestock feed and the damage done to the animals as a result of the fall in temperature that precipitates these incidents of heavy snowfall? Answering these questions is key to understanding how best to prevent the worst effects of snow disasters. Indeed, the systems and technical strategies of the people living in the Mar and Geri Villages that deal with snow disasters revolve around these two issues. However, it is interesting to note that the solutions devised in different periods are poles apart.

II Traditional Tribal Era: Taking Full Advantage of the Natural Resources

In traditional Tibetan nomadic communities, the tribes were both the basic political units and economic organisms of society (tribal members shared and owned the pastures). Generally, a tribe was composed of a certain number of "*ru-skor*". These served as the grass-root organizations of both economic production and providers of social mutual aid. Although tribal members grazed their herds on land privately owned by their respective households, the pastures — the most important means of production — was a collective asset of all tribal members (there were however, isolated cases where the tribal heads might own their private pastures). Therefore, the economic activities of traditional nomadic tribes were characterized on the one hand, by household grazing and private ownership of herds, and on the other, by organizational operation and collective ownership of pasture resources.

---

[8] Ekvall (1968, p. 31).

A small tribe under the jurisdiction of a Mongolian Prince at that time — the Mar Village community — was divided into five "*ru-skor*". They divided the pastoral areas into three seasonal pastures: the winter and spring pasture area, the summer pasture area and the transitional pasture area (which was located in between the winter/spring area and summer area). This final area was also known as the autumn pasture, though it was actually used in spring as well. Every year in late April and early May of the Tibetan calendar, when the weather got warm and the grass turned green, the Tibetan nomadic communities left the winter pastures where they had spent more than six months and moved about 30 to 60 kilometers northwards to the transitional pasture, where they would spend another two months. In early July, they would again move another 20 kilometers northwards, to the summer pasture. Two months later, they would return to the transitional pasture once again. Around 20 September, they would again return to the winter pasture, where they would remain until the pasture germinated the following year. The migration pattern of the Geri Village largely parallels that of the Mar Village. The main difference is that the seasonal pastures of the Geri Village varied greatly in elevation. Therefore, they were more conscious of the seasonal changes in climate. This perennial cycle of seasonal migration was not to seek better pastures; on the contrary, almost all of the summer pastures were meadows, and in terms of their makeup more "arctic-alpine", and thus, the conditions were more difficult. Rather, the pastoralist migration of the Mar and the Geri Villages can be understood as a strategic decision to move away from the winter pastures in order to better prepare themselves for the upcoming snow disasters and to ensure their economic security during the snowy season.

As mentioned above, one of the major impacts of snow disasters lies in the resultant thick layer of snow that covers over the pastures, which prevents the herd from grazing and thus results in the herd dying from starvation and the cold. The most common solution for dealing with the lack of foliage is to organize a reserve stash of foliage or fodder in advance. However, the nomadic pastoralists on the Qinghai–Tibet Plateau generally did not use the conventional practice of storing fodder, as the pastures on the plateau were generally sparse of foliage and thus mowing and collecting the grass was not easy. Although the pastures of the Mar

Village and the Geri Village were lush, the pastoralists there did not collect and store grass. The reason behind such seemingly strange behavior can be attributed to the fact that the herds were too small and therefore using labor to undertake such a task was deemed not worthwhile. However, considering the high mortality rates in herds after snow disasters, this rationale is not convincing. Robert Ekvall proposes an alternative interpretation. He believes that the absence of such conventions is because mowing the foliage would lead to the claiming of household land and exploitation, which was in conflict with their tribal concepts of having communal pasture areas for grazing.[9] Thus, it is very likely that a desire to preserve the public ownership of pastures, which was very important to the tribal members, prevented the pastoralists from mowing the land.

The pastoralists turned to another alternative. To avoid the worst effects of the snow disasters they tried to utilize the variable height of the natural foliage, so as to decide when to graze on a particular piece of land. Their experiences and observations led the herdsmen to the realization that the height of the foliage was directly related to whether a certain amount of snow cover would result in disaster. In the area where the foliage was tall, the tips of grass would protrude above the snow cover. As long as the animals could graze, even merely on the tips of foliage, they could survive. In contrast, if there was nothing to graze on, they would surely die. Based purely on these observations, the pastoralists were able to arrange their pastures according to the seasonal shifts. Those pastures in warm areas with excellent vegetation were used as winter pastures, while those in the areas of higher elevation and harsher weather conditions — where in summer there was usually enough foliage to graze on — were used as the transitional or summer pastures. Hence their pasture utilization system, as opposed to the strict nomadic system, was to set aside for the snow season a fully-grown pasture with possibly maximal grass height, where it was not to be used for grazing in summer. During the vegetative periods, the pastoralists left the winter and spring pastures and moved on to and grazed upon other pastures. They did this in order to give the winter and spring pastures enough time to grow sufficient

---

[9] Ekvall (1968, p. 35).

foliage. In this way, when winter came, they would have enough land to graze upon and built up a substantial store of foliage. In addition, this allows the grass to grow to its natural height, minimizing the risks of the pastures being covered by snow.

In order to meet the above aims, the pastoralists attached great importance to maintaining the collective pastures. Guidelines and related rules and regulations were established to ensure that the whole process of seasonal migration and land use goes smoothly.

First of all, the tribal members followed the principle of unified action during seasonal migration. In general, the winter and spring pastures were kept in areas of low altitude, warm in climate and with comfortable living conditions. Therefore, there were always some members of the nomadic tribes who wanted to postpone their migration away from them and return as early as possible. This was especially the case with the elderly and young children, who were very reluctant to leave the winter and spring pastures. However, for some people to remain on the winter pastures meant that a sufficient number of livestock also had to be left behind. For example, horses would be required for travel, and yaks for their milk. Moreover, the continued use of the land would certainly affect the ability of the land to recuperate. An additional concern was that if some members of the tribe were to stay behind, this might have a "domino effect" and encourage others to do the same. In order to address these and other problems, both the Mar and the Geri Villages had a collective consultative system, or more precisely a pastoralist representative consultative system. Its main task was to judge issues such as how best to distribute pastures, the timing of the migration and whether it is appropriate for people to be left on the winter pastures. In the Mar Village, these issues were negotiated by five elected headmen of the "*ru-skor*". While in the Geri Village, these points were decided by the "*khyigs-bdag*" — a specialized team composed of pastoralist representatives from the four "*ru-skor*" under the dpon-`khor tribe. When it was time for them to migrate, all members of the village were required to move within a specified time (usually two to three days), with no delay permitted. The Mongolian Prince would send pasture management personnel to inspect the winter pasture of the Mar Village. If any livestock (which belonged to the herders still staying on the winter pasture) was spotted after 4 May of the Tibetan calendar, the pastoralist who had violated this rule would be punished by having his herd slaughtered.

Second, they implemented a pasture inspection system. Under tribalism the various tribes were politically independent, therefore there were frequent incidences of mutual pasture raiding and seizing of land. Additionally, cross-border grazing on the pastures of other tribes occurred from time to time. In order to ensure that none of their land was stolen, the tribes implemented conventional pasture inspection systems. This meant that they patrolled the farthest ends of their pastures and expelled other trespassing pastoralists and herds. During more eventful periods, such as when there were disputes with neighboring tribes over the pastures, more tribal members would be recruited into these patrolling teams. It was required that each and every household present one adult male member of their family to the patrolling team. Those that could not provide a member had to pay compensation.

During the traditional tribalism era, two main methods were employed by the pastoralists to address the hazards associated with the severe cold. The first was to make every effort possible to ensure that the livestock were kept warm. For example, the winter settlements were established on the slopes or in the coves, which exposed them to the sun. The pastoralists of the Mar Village were not accustomed to building livestock sheds. This was not only because of the lack of building materials on the pastures, but also because of the pastoralists' lack of civil engineering technology. Importantly, because of the rules ensuring the fair use of pastures, there was little incentive for the herders to invest in creating well-insulated sheds. At the beginning of each seasonal migration, the camp sites of all "*ru-skor*" were determined by drawing lots; therefore, the annual locations of "*ru-skor*" were almost always different. Because of this factor, they simply used turf to build walls which would serve to ward off the cold wind. However, these livestock sheds lacked proper roofing, were in the open air, and thus, were not effective in preventing the low temperatures from harming the animals. Many livestock got sick or even died as a result of the cold temperatures at night. The other method they used was to improve and maintain the fat reserves and the weight of the livestock through careful shepherding. By maintaining the fat reserves of the animals,

they were able to make them more resistant to the cold. The diligent herders developed a range of livestock shepherding techniques, which were
sufficiently effective to ensure that the livestock were able to maintain
their fat reserves and weight, so when winter came they were able to survive the harsh weather conditions. In fact, the extent of herd loss in a
snow disaster has always been closely associated with whether the pastoralists have taken advantage of their experience and behaved diligently.
Hence, the number of livestock that died during any one of the snow
seasons was often held as a criterion to judge whether a herder was diligent
or not.

In short, the collective possession of pasture resources was conducive
to the unified management of pastures. Collective decision-making
within the grass-root organizations that decided on how the pastures were
used, together with collective supervision, prevented the arbitrary use of
the winter pastures. The private ownership of livestock maximized the
pastoralists' enthusiasm for looking after their livestock. Hence, this system was designed to take full advantage of the natural resources in order
to prevent snow disasters. For the pastoralists of the Mar and Geri
Villages, so long as they strictly controlled every process, the above strategies could be integrated in order to prevent a disaster. However, the herders were very clear about the obvious limitations inherent in this disaster
prevention system. For instance, they were not used to storing foliage to
be used in times of shortages, and neither was there any possibility of
them getting assistance beyond the community (e.g. government relief).
Thus, when the snow cover was particularly heavy and the temperature
extremely low, they were completely helpless. In the winter of 1954, it
snowed continually for more than 30 days and the average snow cover
reached 30–50 centimeters. At this time, there were also strong winds
and a drastic drop in temperature. The pastures were snow-covered for
days on end. At that time the newly established government of He'nan
County did not have sufficient capacity to offer relief. As a result, a large
number of the livestock were frozen or starved to death, with a mortality
rate as high as 50%.[10]

---

[10] Local Records Compilation Committee of the He'nan Mongolian Autonomous County
(1996); Shi (2003).

III People's Commune Era: The Introduction of Disaster Prevention Technology

Five years after the founding of the People's Republic of China in 1949, the governments of the Zeku and He'nan Counties were established. The establishment of the new regime gradually put an end to traditional tribalism and established the new socialist system, step by step. After nearly four years (from 1954 to 1958) of the transitional socialist reforms of the Mutual Aid Team and Production Cooperative, the Mar Village and the Geri Village were transformed into an integral part of the Renmin Gongshe (the People's Commune, or collectivism), and the previous tribes and *"ru-skor"* were replaced by production teams (*"gongshe"* or *"shengchandui"*). The new system was characterized by the public ownership of the means of production. In essence it meant that both the pastures and all the livestock previously owned by individual households were turned into collectivist assets (in a later iteration of the collectivist system, private possession of a small number of the livestock was permissible). Production was no longer conducted by individual families and the families were no longer the unit for accounting. On the other hand, unified planning regarding production and accounting was made exclusively by the collectivism and the production team, and the herders were supposed to complete the tasks assigned to them by the production team, with all labor being transformed into quantitative indicators (*"gongfen"*) and noted down in a *gongfen* book. At the end of the year the amount of *gongfen* determined a herder's personal income, which was calculated on the basis of the collective income. This form of ownership lasted for 27 years in He'nan County and Zeku County until the implementation of the Household Responsibility System reform in 1984.

Under the new system, although the form of ownership has changed, the mode of production was still a continuation of traditional nomadic pastoralism, with the pastoralists grazing on the original plots of pasture land, and still practicing their inherited traditional techniques for disaster prevention. However, in the face of the long-term shortage of products, the new local government officials believed that the high mortality rates of the livestock in winter and spring were unacceptable, and expected the pastoralists to undertake more initiatives to mitigate disaster losses. The proactive strategies taken may be generalized under the following two categories: The first was to adopt and indeed modernize, where possible, the effective techniques traditionally used by the pastoralists and their predecessors, and promote their use via institutional efforts; the second was to actively introduce external technologies, including better ways to cultivate wastelands and improved methods associated with foliage planting. One such method was the construction of "enclosed pastures with fences" (Figure 2).

1. Extensions of traditional techniques: Construction of stockyards and livestock sheds

In the traditional society, although everyone realized that the construction of stockyards and livestock sheds might increase the temperature at night and in winter, which was conducive to increasing the disaster-resistant capacity of the herds, only the tribal heads and a few well-off households were capable of building good livestock

Figure 2: Glimpses of an Enclosed Pasture in He'nan County for Disaster Prevention and Livestock Protection.
Source: Taken by the author in Mar Village, He'nan County.

shelters. During the collectivism period, the collective possession of the livestock and the system of grazing the livestock in separate herds and flocks resulted in a labor surplus in the production team. In the traditional society, at least two laborers were needed for each family to graze the herd and the flock separately; in fact, some households had such a small herd that the workload was very light. After the collective integration, the numbers in each herd and flock were increased greatly (generally speaking, 200 to 250 ewes formed one group, 400 to 500 wethers and one-year-old lambs formed another, 40 to 50 horses formed a group, 80 to 100 two- to three-year-old calves formed a group, 60 to 75 cows formed a group and 50 to 60 of the remaining calves formed the final group[11]). Where a labor surplus emerged, the excess labor could be allocated to two alternative activities, that is, the construction of stockyards and livestock sheds, or the reclamation of wasteland and the cultivation of vegetation. In addition, supported by the government's policies, the herders were allowed to cut down timber in the adjacent forests for the construction of these livestock shelters and they were sometimes provided with raw materials. The policy to increase and improve construction of the stockyards and livestock sheds undoubtedly had a significant effect on the likelihood of the livestock surviving the cold winters and snowstorms (Figure 3).

2. Introduction of new technologies: Wasteland cultivation, vegetation planting, and construction of "enclosed pastures"

The central cause of "natural death" in the winter and spring seasons, or death from a snow disaster, was the lack of foliage and the low temperatures. Any actions aimed at solving the problems caused by snow disasters should be focused on these areas. As a first step, common agricultural practices such as plant cultivation, foliage collection and storage were

---

[11] Data retrieved from an anonymous person's method for implementing the principle of distribution according to labor done (drafted on May 12, 1961) and the Local Records Compilation Committee of the Zeku County (2005, p. 564).

Figure 3: Interior of a Newly Designed Livestock Shed in the Zeku County.
Source: Taken by the author in the Geri Village.

introduced and extended to the wider community. The introduction of these agricultural technologies was largely a result of the ethnic background of local administrative personnel. In order to complete societal reforms and establish a new political and economic system, a number of administrative staff was sent to this area. Most of these mission-bound cadres were either of Han ethnicity from inland China, or of Tibetan extraction from the agricultural areas of eastern Qinghai Province. Regardless of their ethnicity, their rural background meant that they had a natural preference for the mode of production prevailing in the agricultural community. To them, the pastoralists were not proactive enough in addressing snow disasters, so they proposed that positive measures such as wasteland cultivation and vegetation planting should start. Additionally, foliage collection and storage should be undertaken. Under the guidance of the administrators, the pastoralists' patterns of disaster preparedness and mitigation (and even their lives) were subjected to a series of profound changes.

Looking back, Rgya-mtsho, a pastoralist from the Mar Village recalled: "*From 1958 onwards, the government mobilized the members of the communes and production teams to plant grass and develop agriculture. Farms were set up on the banks of the Yellow River, and members from my village were dispatched to these farms. As it was too cold to grow grain successfully, the farms had to be abandoned. However, activities such as foliage collecting and building livestock sheds and stockyards continued. An area of about 80 mu (about 5.36 hectares) in my village was reclaimed as farmland for oat planting. At that time, we had to spend one month each autumn collecting grass. However, most of the foliage prepared for snow disasters was fed to the cadres' horses and only a very small part of what was left was used for the livestock's winter feed. Given this, it is fair to conclude that grass collecting did not help much when it came to preparing for natural disasters. Therefore, the construction of livestock sheds and stockyards were common activities. The team leader made an annual check of the livestock sheds and stockyards, and arranged for laborers to repair the damaged buildings. In order to improve the pastures, and under the government's orders, we also undertook a number of water conservation projects such as drilling wells, water diversion and the building of water channels. It was the case that most of the materials and equipment were provided by the government. The water conservancy projects enabled us to obtain drinking water both for the people and the livestock, but at that time people did not do a great deal to protect such valuable assets. When the water channels were damaged, nobody made the effort to repair them. One by one, the water conservancy facilities were abandoned. In short, we were pastoralists, but over those years we often worked with the spades and sickles, just as the agriculturalists did."*

In theory the new technologies and methodologies were supposed to improve their ability to mitigate against disasters, however, in reality they caused a lot of damage to the pastures, as they did not pay attention to the local agricultural conditions when opening up new pastures. According to a piece of official data, from 1958 to 1960, a total of 572 million *mu* of land was reclaimed in the pastoralist areas (in Qinghai); even the good winter pastures within the six pastoralist counties were cultivated and over those years many more weak and emaciated livestock died of a severe lack of foliage in the winter and spring months.[12] In He'nan County, a total of more than 20 million *mu* of rangeland was reclaimed from 1959 to 1962, accounting for 2.02% of the available pastures in the county. Large areas of fine pastures were destroyed, which have not

---

[12] Niu (1993, p. 283).

recovered even 20 years after the cultivation was stopped.[13] However, the new technologies did achieve a certain degree of success on banks of the Ba-Chu River near the Geri Village in western Zeku County. This area has good irrigation and is located at the point of lowest elevation in Zeku County. Cultivated vegetation (including the annual and perennial types) has greatly increased unit foliage yield and facilitated the harvest of foliage and storage, which significantly improved the local herders' resilience to disasters. Therefore, when the mistake of reclaiming inappropriate pasture areas was subsequently corrected, the reclamation and vegetation planting in this area was not stopped; indeed, quite the opposite, it was encouraged. With the gradual expansion of the area used to cultivate vegetation, the Geri Village and other neighboring villages have benefited as their capacity to resist snow disasters has been significantly improved.

The pastoralists have mixed feelings regarding these new technologies. The practice of building livestock sheds and stockyard construction derives from their past production experiences and creating a foliage reserve is clearly helpful to ease the shortage of livestock feed after heavy snowfall. However, the pastoralists still remember that under the agriculturalists' guidelines, the physical condition of their livestock was particularly poor and during the winter and spring months the mortality rates of the animals were higher than when they used more traditional methods. All of this was ascribed to the public ownership of the means of production and an egalitarian distribution principle. Under such a system, the pastoralists' efforts to protect the pastures and the effort with which they managed the livestock was not linked to their income. Therefore, they lacked the enthusiasm in the operation and management of the pastures and the livestock.

A pastoralist named Jigs-med made the following remarks: "*Due to collective ownership, it was the collective that was supposed to take the losses. This had very little to do with individual households. People did not have a strong sense of responsibility for reducing the losses caused by snow disasters. Traditionally, the pastoralists would first move to the not-so-good pastures and*

---

[13] Local Records Compilation Committee of the He'nan Mongolian Autonomous County (1996, p. 266).

finally on to the better ones. This would enable them to fall back on good grazing areas in times of need. However, during the period of collectivism, the organization of the allocation of pasture lands was a complete mess and people went to graze wherever the foliage was lush. As long as they finished their assigned task, they cared little about anything else."

Moreover, activities such as the endless sessions spent studying political documents; meetings where there were public accusations in order to promote class struggle and other kinds of meetings where the herders spoke bitterly about their experiences also delayed the timely migration of the pastoralists. It was also pointed out in an official paper that many livestock which did not move to the summer pastures destroyed the winter pastures and harmed the (rotational grazing) system.[14] In addition, because the pastoralists cared for different herds and flocks in accordance with the arrangements of the production team, they were not familiar with the needs of the individual livestock. The previous intimate relationship between the herders and their livestock has completely disappeared, which prevented the herders from providing adequate, targeted care to the livestock.

In short, the poor physical condition of the livestock increased their risk of dying from snow disasters. Between 1954 and 1959, the eastern part of the Qinghai–Tibet Plateau was not hit by any snowstorms. However, they were not so fortunate in the spring of 1970. A snow disaster resulted in the death of 70,000 livestock in He'nan County and 154,000 in Zeku County. The two counties were hit by another snow disaster in the winter of 1974 and the spring of 1975, which killed a total of 130,000 livestock in Zeku County and 95,000 in He'nan County. The herder Dpa'-rdo made the following comments about that period: *"I was caring for a flock of 300 two-year-old lambs that year. It snowed continually from 15 October of the Tibetan calendar to the New Year. By the end of the snow disaster, only 30 lambs had survived"*. The new disaster prevention system was conspicuously vulnerable.[15]

Two snow disasters exposed the ineffectiveness of the system. One of the "Five Major Pastures" in China, Qinghai was an important livestock

---

[14]Niu (1983, p. 283).
[15]Xiao (1999); The China Society of the Qinghai–Tibet Plateau Research (1992).

producing area. It was the case that the safety (disaster resistance capacity) of livestock husbandry in this area had a direct impact on the national supply of livestock. Moreover, the development of new technologies in the area of pastoralist production had a direct bearing on national economic development. Therefore, the Chinese government attached a lot of importance to the exchange of disaster prevention and mitigation technologies among major livestock producing areas. Sharing knowledge in such a way allowed the herders to learn from others who lived in vastly different areas of the country.

As a result of this policy, the practice of *Küriyen* (that is, enclosed pastures) was introduced from the pastures in Inner Mongolia. *Küriyen* is a Mongolian word meaning enclosed walls. What is meant by setting up *Küriyen* is to enclose part of the pasture within walls (there are a variety of different types of walls according to the materials used, such as stone, clay and sod walls as well as wire fences — with all walls about 2 meters in height), with the aim of protecting the natural vegetation within the enclosure. This method was reportedly effective in disaster prevention on the pastures in Inner Mongolia. According to the official media, *Küriyen* had four major strengths. First, through protecting the natural vegetation growth and by setting up clay walls (or indeed other types of wall, such as those made by sod) in all four directions, the natural pastures could be protected from livestock trampling on it and therefore the vegetation could re-grow at a faster rate. Second, when the grass grew high enough, some of it could be collected and stored as dry green foliage. Additionally, seeds could be collected. Third, natural conditions permitting, through irrigation and fertilization, cultivation of some feed plants or quality foliage could be conducted to gradually achieve the integration of fodder and foliage. Lastly, emaciated livestock could be fed in winter and spring, which helped disaster prevention and livestock protection.[16] It is obvious that the rationale of the *Küriyen* technique is still to maximize the foliage yield, by preventing the disturbance or destruction of the vegetation growth by the livestock and at the same time plant foliage in suitable localities. In 1974, the *Küriyen* technique was applied and promoted in the Zeku County, where the Geri Village is located. A year later, in the

---

[16] News Bureau in Huangnan Prefecture (1974).

He'nan County, where the Mar Village is located, they began to promote the technique by following the practices of the Zeku County. According to relevant statistics, a total of 60,000 *mu* of pastures was fenced off in the Mar Village, while in the Zeku County, a total of 82,000 hectares of pastures was fenced off. Each head of livestock averaged 1.16 *mu*. According to the herders' assessment, if properly managed, *Küriyen* should have been an effective tool to help us protect the pastures, but at that time it was difficult for any measure to be properly implemented, even the best ones. Built with turf and sod walls, *Küriyen* was easily subject to erosion by the wind and rain. Moreover, it was not effective in stopping goats, sheep and other livestock which are good at climbing from getting in. Due to the poor management and maintenance of the *Küriyen* practice, the results were far from satisfactory and many pastures were damaged, in spite of the arduous work.

Küriyen construction did not yield the desired results. However, the success of one or two places has offered some useful pointers to the government authorities. First, the enclosed natural growth and cultivation method is not only helpful when it comes to restoring and rejuvenating the pastures and increasing their yield, but has also been shown to be effective in helping to enhance disaster resistance in the winter and spring months. The enclosed pastures later served as pastures for "disaster resistance and livestock protection". Second, the successful cultivation of perennial foliage introduced in *Küriyen* fostered a degree of confidence in the government authorities that they could improve the pastures. In the western Zeku County, along both banks of the Ba-Chu River, which is not far away from the Geri Village, more areas have been used for foliage planting. These areas are now the base for vegetation cultivation in that county.

IV Household Responsibility System Era: Integration of Property Rights and Government Relief

The Household Responsibility System Reform was implemented in rural and pastoral areas in 1979. As underdeveloped inland areas, the Mar and Geri Villages did not start the reform until 1984. The production and management systems have undergone further changes as outlined in the reform: The livestock were to be individually owned by the household; although collective ownership of the pasture is guaranteed by the law, the pastoralists, to some degree, were to have private property rights over their contracted pastures as the long-term contract policy allowed them not only the rights to exploit the land but also the rights to transfer their pastures to others. Another notable change was the divergence of the Mar and Geri Villages in their management modes of pastoralism: The pastoralists of the Mar Village adopted a sedentary way of living in 1976 and completely terminated their nomadic way of life. Thereafter, the herders practiced seasonal rotational grazing only on the pastures contracted to them in 1984 and according to the number of family members and livestock. Although the ancient mode of migratory pastoralism remained in the Geri Village, the pastures were also allocated to the herders' households by virtue of the size of their families. The reform in ownership and differentiation in management modes inevitably affected the herders' strategies and measures for disaster prevention.[17]

At the same time, other factors began to have an increasingly important impact on the pastoralists' mechanisms for disaster prevention and mitigation. First of all, since the 1980s global warming has brought about a degradation of the pastures and continues to cause the deterioration of the ecological environment in the eastern part of the Qinghai–Tibet Plateau, where the Mar and Geri Villages are located.[18] Second, as living

---

[17] Harding (1977).

[18] As Zhang et al. (1999) observed, the weather station data from 1961 to 1996 show that although the total precipitation in the southern Qinghai Plateau is fairly balanced, the precipitation in winter and spring is higher, while the rainfall in summer reduced somewhat, which resulted in an increase in the number of droughts in summer, as well as snowstorms in winter and spring. The study of temperatures at that time show us that the speed of the increase in temperature, in the period where the grass turns green, gets longer and longer each year. Moreover, the speed by which the temperature drops in the period in which the grass withers also gets faster each year. Therefore, the the speed at which the grass turns green was delayed but the speed at which the grass withered was accelerated. Thereby, the effective accumulated temperature in the grass growth period is reduced, and the effective grass growing season is shortened, leading to adverse effects on both grass growing and yield. The observational data from the enclosed pasture during 1988 to 1997 indicate that the height of the local grass generally decreased by 30% to 50% over this ten year period, and the foliage yield of the natural pasture lands has dropped substantially.

standards have markedly improved (especially the improved healthcare conditions and long-term social stability), the last few decades have seen a rapid increase in the population, which has almost tripled since the 1950s. There has also been a substantial increase in the total number of livestock, which has increased four-fold in the Mar Village and more than doubled in the Geri Village. The pastures which have already deteriorated as a result of global warming are even more strained by the large population increases. Third, due to the emergence of warmer winters, the snowfalls in the winter and spring seasons in the eastern pastoral area of the Qinghai–Tibet Plateau have significantly increased.[19] These changes expose the pastoralists to the higher probability of a snow disaster occurring and render the traditional systems, techniques and countermeasures completely ineffective. Thus, in order to adapt to the new changes, the local government authorities and herders have conducted a range of pilot trials in order to establish a new set of disaster prevention and mitigation systems, techniques and technologies. Although the relevant experiments are still ongoing, after more than two decades of exploration, the basic framework and a clear line of thought have emerged. First, the local authorities will try to trigger the herders' economic rationality through clarifying their private property rights and thus encourage them to use the pastures in a far more rational and long-term manner. At the same time, they have encouraged the herders to increase investment in producing more pastures and improving the lands they already have. The objective of this measure is to increase the foliage yield of the pastures. Second, with the initial success of the economic reforms, the local governments have gradually increased their capacity for snow disaster interventions (including their preparedness, preventive measures and disaster relief efforts). Hence, the government's assistance has become an important supplement to the pastoralists' capacity for addressing snow disasters. These changes, however, have not taken place

---

[19] The studies analyzing the information from the Weather Station of Zeku County during 1958 to 1994 show that there is an obvious relationship between the occurrence of a snow disaster in spring and the weather in winter. There were six warm winters from 1987 to 1994, which indicates that the climate change increased the probability of snow disasters occuring in the region. See Ren (1996).

overnight. In the early period of reform, although pastures were nominally contracted to individual households, the pastoralists did not formulate a clear concept of private ownership. As there were no strict physical or tangible devices to define the borders between different households, the herders did not confine their grazing strictly within their own defined pastures, but instead, often accessed others' pastures freely. On the other hand, the privatization of the livestock has resulted in herders' nurturing larger herds and flocks and pursuing higher profits. The pastoralists did not determine the size of their herds and flocks in accordance with the capacity of their pastures, but instead planned to utilize the pasture lands of others if needed. Therefore, the livestock population of most households increased greatly. Consequently, there arose a gap between the supply of foliage and the livestock population. Pasture degradation caused by the overuse of land was commonplace and the well-known phenomenon, the "tragedy of the commons", unfortunately occurred. Statistics taken at the time clearly show the tendency of rising mortality rates from snow disasters during this period. From 1984 to 1994, the annual average mortality rate of adult livestock in the Zeku County was 18%, with the highest rates approaching 27.18%. Hence, according to official records, it was the decade with the highest livestock mortality rates ever recorded.[20]

Due to the ongoing deterioration of the natural environment and the increased risk of snow disasters, the government is now aware that without the proper division of pasture lands, their usage will not be exclusive at all, and therefore private property rights cannot be protected. Because private property rights cannot be protected, it is unlikely that the herders will be willing to increase investment and preserve the pasture lands. Conversely, they will be incentivized to increase their livestock population and maximize their short-term benefits. Their focus on maximizing short-term benefits will result in the further deterioration of the pasture lands. Therefore, physically dividing the land into individual sections is the only way private property rights be effectively defined. The government tried to "deepen the reform", by demanding that the herders enclose

---

[20] Refer to the adult livestock's mortality rates in the Zeku County during 1970 to 1995 (Local Records Compilation Committee of the Zeku County, 2005, p. 139).

their pastures with wire fences. It encouraged this behavior by providing subsidies and special loans. Moreover, new policy initiatives have meant that the duration of contracts will be extended from 30 to 50 years. This will ensure that there is sufficient time after the initial investment, so that the herders will make some profit. After physically dividing the land by household, the government has also encouraged the herders to divide their own pastures into smaller seasonal sections with fences, so they can implement rotational grazing and allow enough time for pasture restoration. In addition, by virtue of good pilot results, the local government has asked every household to set aside a plot of land for use in case of disaster. The land would be used for disaster preparedness, livestock protection and targeting the potential hazards of increasing snowfall in spring. The average area of this land (by household) in the Mar Village is approximately 500 *mu*, where the pastures are relatively expansive. In the Geri Village, the figure is significantly smaller at only around 200 *mu*. If herders try to exploit these sections of pasture land, the government will intervene. A good example of this in practice can be found in 2007. Early that year, weather forecasts predicted that there would be heavy snowfall in spring (in the He'nan County). Hence, the government instructed the herders that the reserve pasture should not be used before 15 March. The government gave this instruction in order to ensure that the herdsmen would be well prepared for a possible snow disaster in late spring or early summer. This measure was well received among the herders. The pastoralists in the Mar Village believe that their reserved pastures may still be grazed upon even if the snowfall is as thick as 15 centimeters and can withstand a moderate snow disaster.

It is a compulsory requirement of the government that the herders cultivate foliage and reserve a certain amount of foliage in order to avoid the worst effects of large climatic changes. In contrast to the past and in order to avoid the destruction of the natural vegetation, the government prohibits the reclamation of grassland, in order to cultivate foliage. Instead, they request the herders to plant barley, oats and other plants for use in the livestock sheds in the winter settlements, when the herders move to (or practice rotational grazing in) the summer pastures. These plants are then collected and stored in autumn. It is required by the government in He'nan County, where the Mar Village is located, that each pastoralist household should cultivate foliage on an area of no less than 5 mu and at the same time store no less than 150 kilograms of feed. An example from the Geri Village describes a pastoralist named Bsod-nams who owns a flock of 40 sheep and a herd of 20. The government also requires each household to store a certain amount of foliage and feed, which should last for a minimum of 20 days. In 2006, this household stored 925 kilograms of foliage and 100 kilograms of feed.

Over this period of time, initial feedback showed that economic reform was successful and the revenue of the government at all levels had steadily increased. Because the western regions lagged behind other areas in terms of development, they were able to obtain financial subsidies from the central government and financial assistance from the economically developed coastal provinces. However, their dependence on this assistance enhanced the local government's ability to shape and change their disaster prevention system. Their first priority, among many others, was the construction of warm livestock sheds. Constant attention had been paid to the construction of livestock sheds since the People's Commune Era, and the livestock sheds at that time were mainly makeshift, made of clay and wood. Since the 1980s, the government has supported and extended three types of livestock sheds with better heat insulation. The earliest prototype used a plastic plate roof in order to address the shortage of timber on the pastures. In later models, the plastic plate was replaced by more solid synthetic materials. The most recent model of livestock shed is steel-framed and made with bricks. These sheds can fulfill two key functions: keeping vegetables in summer and keeping the livestock warm in winter. It has been reported by the herdsmen that if their sheep are placed within the livestock sheds they can survive without food for up to six days. If not, their life expectancy is shortened significantly, only surviving for three to four days. The government also provides herdsmen with annual subsidies calculated by proportion. Take for example the Blo-bzang family from the Mar Village who possesses a livestock shed of an area of 200 m², for which the family has invested 6,700 yuan. The government has allotted them 3,000 yuan worth of subsidies. When the author investigated the area in 2007, around half of all the herdsmen in the He'nan County had built livestock sheds. Besides this, the government also increased the proportion of expenditure on reserve foliage for disaster relief, which will be offered to disaster-stricken areas, in the event of a disaster. If the herdsmen are fortunate and there are no disasters that year, then in April, the foliage held in stock will be sold back to the local herdsmen at a low price.

Some herdsmen from the Geri Village follow an alternative route to development, which is rather representative of the new era. In order to halt the deterioration of plant life on the Qinghai–Tibet Plateau, the Chinese government invested a large sum of money in the "Three Riverheads (i.e. the Yangtze River, the Yellow River and the Lancang River) Ecological Protection Program". One of the key strategies in this program is to resettle many of the herders away from the most ecologically fragile areas, allowing these areas sufficient time to fully recuperate. The Geri Village, situated in the valley of the Geri River (a tributary of the Yellow River), is within the area designated for a resettlement program. In order to reduce the number of livestock in the area (mainly through imposing a grazing ban and/or advocating rotational restoration), the government resettled half of the pastoralist households (100 households) from the Geri Village to the Ba-Chu River region. This region had relatively little traffic and better climatic conditions. Moreover, it was the most successful area, in terms of foliage cultivation, in the era of the People's Commune. The government provided them with housing, livestock sheds and a small piece of pasture land. Additionally, every year each household obtains nearly 1,000 kilograms of foliage from the state-run cultivation base. Thus, through these measures, it is ensured by the government that they can still engage in small-scale livestock husbandry. At the same time, the government encourages them to develop alternative sources of income. This is reflected in the following examples of Blo-bzang and Sangs-rje. 41 year old Blo-bzang and his wife have tried very hard to adapt to this new way of life. He joined a construction team who paved an area of the road, while his wife got involved in raising sheep at home, planting vegetables and peddling goods at the side of the highway. Hence, the majority of their household income came from activities unrelated to livestock. Sangs-rje, a senior herdsman, has a courtyard near the highway. Taking this advantage of this fact, he has built a number of rooms to rent which has brought him a considerable amount of income. Although most people are still engaged in raising the livestock, they gradually became agriculturalists, as sheltered rearing liberated them from concerns about the impact of snow disasters. However, the changes in their lifestyles imply that they have been confronted by new challenges. For example, in order to get larger profit margins, they have had to learn more precise ways of calculating their costs, and thus have had to focus their attention on the market price of the feed, foliage and livestock products. Their way of life is fundamentally different now from that of traditional pastoralism. Collective mutual assistance, as well as migration in the snowy seasons, have gradually been reduced to a lingering historical memory.

In short, setting up pasture fences (including in the disaster resistance and livestock protection sections), building houses for the herdsmen, constructing livestock sheds, as well as cultivating and storing foliage, are summarized as the "Construction of the Four Matching Sets", which are the core elements of the new snow disaster prevention system advocated by the current government. The new disaster prevention system highlights the importance of government involvement, specifically, the government holds the responsibility of instituting a set of rules and regulations, as well as making it compulsory for the herdsmen to "insure" themselves (through the establishment of disaster resistance and livestock protection pastures). The government undertakes these responsibilities in order to minimize the risk of the herdsmen adopting a "leaving things to chance" mentality about the effects of a snow disaster. The privatization of the pastures and livestock may not necessarily bring about the effect of exploiting the full capacity of the pastures. However, it does stimulate the herdsmen's initiative to protect the pastures and attend to their livestock, as well as incentivize them to use the pastures in a sustainable way. This occurs because they are encouraged to control the size and population growth of the herd, which undoubtedly plays an important role in enhancing their resilience to the effects of disasters. However, an inevitable result of the privatization of pastures and herds is that some households are better at snow disaster prevention than others. The households with effective management practices and economic stability do not only possess good self-protection techniques, but also enjoy preferential treatment by the government (e.g. almost all poverty-alleviation projects require the herdsmen to provide matching funds to any government investment). On the contrary, the pastoralist households with poor management techniques are threatened by their inability to deal with the high risks of snow disasters. Moreover, privatization brought about a form of class distinction where the pastures were more than likely fall into the hands of only a few people. This particular issue brought about challenges in reference to social justice.

From 29 April to 7 May 2004, both He'nan County and Zeku County faced constant snowfall. The average depth of the snow reached around 20 centimeters and the pastures were underneath a thick cover of snow from about seven to ten days. As a result, in the He'nan County, around 30,000 livestock died, accounting for about 4% of the total livestock population. In the Zeku County, even more perished — around 34,000 livestock died. Although the livestock mortality rates have decreased significantly, the losses were still enormous. Dpa'-rdo, a herdsman from the Mar Village, reported that his household had 260 sheep and 100 lambs at that time. After the snow disaster, around 20 adult sheep and 60 lambs had died. In the same village, the household which suffered the most lost 70 yaks. Investigations by the authorities showed that the losses may well have been attributed to partial implementation of effective prevention measures, which occurred because of a lack of funds in many of the pastoralist households. In the short term, the modest subsidy provided by government was unable to cover such a large area. Therefore, improving and enhancing the capacity required in order to deal with snow disasters is still a major challenge for both the local government and herdsmen alike.

V Discussion and Policy Proposals

The distinct natural and geographical conditions found on the Qinghai–Tibet Plateau predetermines that snow disasters are an eternal challenge for nomads both in terms of their economic production and their way of life. Therefore, the methods of addressing snow disasters are inherent both in their social system and their production techniques.

The disaster prevention systems and technologies found in the tribalism era focused on sharing collective pastures and making full use of the natural pastures. This behavior can be seen as a reasonable choice by the local pastoralists, given their historical development which was affected by the local social and natural environment as well as a lack of intervention from outside sources. Snow disaster prevention systems and technologies were integrated into the nomadic culture, which lasted for thousands of years, fossilizing the nomads' understanding of, and reflections on, the relationship between human beings and nature on the plateau. However, there were obvious limitations inherent in the disaster prevention system prevailing in this era. When the disasters were too severe to endure, significant economic losses and even personal casualties were inevitable. Although the loss of both human life and livestock can be seen in the context of a wider battle between man and nature — which was seen as crucial for the effectiveness of the traditional system — the senseless loss of lives was a tragedy nonetheless.

The disaster prevention systems in the era of the People's Commune were characterized by the insertion of external practices, experiences and technologies. Although these out-of-date systems had shown some benefits, the introduction of new technologies widened the herders' abilities to find ways to prevent the worst effects of disasters. However, to some extent, the negative effects of the public ownership of the production means, as well as equalitarianism in income distribution, offset the positive effects brought about by the new technologies.

The market-oriented reform of the Household Responsibility System was a passive choice rather than an innovation. The changes in the environment and rapid expansion of human and livestock populations forced the herdsmen to use increasingly sophisticated techniques in the pastures. Moreover, the herdsmen even began to invest more, as a way to increase output. Fortunately, with the gradual increase of China's comprehensive national strength, the government takes disaster prevention and mitigation as an important component of the public services it offers, and the increasing involvement of the national government may, to a certain extent, make up for the inadequate capacities of the herdsmen.

As the government has already determined that it will build livestock sheds for every household in the future, the biggest problem that needs to be addressed is the lack of livestock feed in the event of a snow disaster. As mentioned above, the traditional methods based on managing natural resources have become inadequate. The worsening conditions found on the pastures were due to a mixture of the degradation of pastures, the increasing number of livestock and the settlement of the herdsmen on the pastures. Studies conducted by relevant government departments indicate that the pasture contract system and settlement[21] renders the grazing areas smaller, and the rational rotational grazing and seasonal pasture shift method impossible. The long-term repeated grazing and trampling of fixed pastures resulted in constant intense overgrazing. Thus, the foliage becomes incapable of regenerating and the vegetation found on the pastures ends up damaged. This damage results in the rampant growth of poisonous weeds, paving the way for the spread of harmful rodents. The pastures have been found to be in severe or indeed extreme degradation.[22] The change in ownership of pastures will inevitably trigger comprehensive responses. Therefore, the proper way of thinking when addressing any problem should be to take everything into consideration. It is the author's view that there are only two ways to solve the problem of insufficient feed: One is to restore the natural yield capacity of pastures and the other is to increase the output of the pastures through the cultivation of grass and foliage.

The most cost-effective way to tackle a snow disaster is to depend on the natural capacity of the pastures. There are two options available to achieve this goal. The first option is to allow the settled herdsmen to conduct nomadic grazing once again. Although rotational grazing is conducted by herdsmen on their own contracted pastures, experience has shown us that pastures that have been divided are particularly vulnerable to rodent infestation, and that rats, who are accustomed to inhabiting in the low grass areas, may also intrude into the adjacent tall grass areas. Thus, practicing rotational grazing on large areas of the pastures may be the only way the desired ecological effects can be achieved, for the most part. One feasible solution is to expand the area of rotational grazing by merging the pastures of different households, or even those of the entire

---

[21] The government has been encouraging the settlement of herdsmen because the fact that their homes are scattered across the pasture lands increases the cost of undertaking social and economic change (e.g. education, healthcare and cultural change). Furthermore, the development of the local community is hindered to some extent.

[22] Ma (2003).

village, and at the same time restore the seasonal nomadic migration. However, the contract system should be kept (as it is useful for resolving pasture disputes, and protecting the interests of the poor), and private property rights should be retained as well. The herdsmen could have their pasture lands combined in such a way as to maintain the individual's share. The carrying capacity of the pasture lands of each household should be estimated, and then each household may be paid or charged on the basis of the size of their herd and flock. On the other hand, where the pastures have deteriorated seriously, grazing should be banned through the government purchasing the right to use the pasture land. The cases where herdsmen are resettled is a case in point, with the pastures only to be used again once the land has been fully restored.

According to the current population, livestock scale and the carrying capacity of the pasture lands, the pastoralists need to be well prepared for snow disasters and cannot be satisfied by merely restoring the natural capacity of the pastures. The foliage yield of pastures also has to be increased. There are at least two alternatives. The first is that many years of experience has shown the herdsmen that most of the rangelands are not suitable for land reclamation and foliage planting, and random recla-mation can result in ecological disasters. However, that does not mean that they should give up on cultivation forever. On the contrary, foliage planting technology which does not destroy the original vegetation should be encouraged. In fact, related pilot trials have been conducted for many years, but there are still many technical problems urgently awaiting resolution. The direction of the future development of pasture husbandry is to foster a strain of foliage that is adaptable to the climate found on the plateau and the traits of the plateau's vegetation. Additionally, it will require them to explore various cultivation techniques and preservation methods for grass. Moreover, a technology-intensive foliage industry needs to be developed. The next step is to gradually settle the herdsmen in areas suitable for reclamation and cultivation, so that they can develop agriculturalist husbandry or other alternative sources of income in order to enhance their production efficiency. The replacement of nomadic livestock husbandry by agriculturalist husbandry is regarded as inevitable, because under the premise of a given amount of resources, population growth will inevitably lead to diminishing returns, while the increase in the livestock population will result in the excessive use of resources. However, the author believes that suitable areas are few and far between in the nomadic rangelands. Furthermore, it needs to be pointed out that high social costs are inherent in such practices, which may well cause drastic cultural changes. Whether the cultural adaptation of the herdsmen is successful or not will exert a direct impact on the stable development of the local community.

Bibliography

Dong Wenjie, Wei Zhigang, Fang Lijun, 2001, "Analysis of Climatic Characters of Snow Disasters of Pastures on the East Qinghai–Tibet Plateau", *Plateau Meteorology*, 20(4), 402–406.

Ekvall, Robert B., 1968, *Fields on the Hoof: Nexus of Tibetan Nomadic Pastoralism*, New York: Holt, Rinehart and Winston.

Goldstein, Melvyn C. and Cynthia M. Beall, 1990, *Nomads of Western Tibet: The Survival of a Way of Life*, Hong Kong: Odyssey Productions Ltd.

Gong Deji, Muling Hao, 1998, "Synthetical Indexes of the Disaster of Snow Cover", *Journal of Applied Meteorological Science*, 9(1), 119–123.

Hardin, Garrett, 1977, "The Tragedy of the Commons", In *Managing the Commons*, Garrett Hardin and John Banden (Eds.), New York: W.H. Freeman and Company.

Local Records Compilation Committee of the He'nan Mongolian Autonomous County, 1996, *He'nan County Annals*, Lanzhou: Gansu People's Publishing House.

Local Records Compilation Committee of the Zeku County, 2005, *Zeku County Annals*, Beijing: China Yearbook of the Counties and Towns Publishing House.

Ma Haiyun, Ma Chenghai, Li Zhiming, Kuantai Cairang, Gazang Duojie, Douga Jiabu, 2003, "All the Natural Grasslands of the Zeku County Contracted to Herdsman Households", *Qinghai Prataculture*, 02, 47–49.

News Bureau in Huangnan Prefecture, 1974, "New Achievements of 'Enclosed Pastures' in Zeku County", *Qinghai Daily*, October 1, 1974.

Niu Hongrui, 1993, *Historical Data on Cooperative Economy in Qinghai Agriculturalist and Pastoralist Areas*, Xining: Qinghai People's Press.

Ren Kejin, 1996, "Analysis on the Relationship between Warm Winters and Spring Snow Disasters in Southern Huangnan Prefecture", *Qinghai Meteorology*, 03, 23–26.

Qin Ningsheng, 2006, *Rebuilding Historical Climate Data and Research on Climate Changes in Qinghai Province*, Beijing: Meteorological Press.

Shi Guoshu, 2003, *Natural Disasters in Qinghai*, Xining: Qinghai People's Press.

Sun Wulin and Wu Yongsheng, 1996, "Snow Disaster Sequence Chronology and Climatic Statistical Characteristics of the Southern Qinghai Plateau", *Qinghai Meteorology*, 16(1), 3–8.

The China Society of the Qinghai–Tibet Plateau Research, 1992, "Resources, Environment, and Developments in the Qinghai–Tibet Plateau", *Proceedings of the First Symposium on the Qinghai–Tibet Plateau*, Beijing: Science Press.

Wen Kegang, 2007, *Chinese Meteorological Disaster Dictionary: Qinghai Volume*, Beijing: Meteorological Press.

Xiao Huaiyuan, 1999, *Rethinking Snow Disasters: Developments*, Lhasa: The Tibet People's Press.

Yu Xiangwen, 1948, *Social Investigation on Nomadic Tibet in the Northwest of China*, Beijing: The Commercial Press.

Zhang Guosheng, Li Lin, Wang Qingqing, Li Xilai, Xu Weixin, Dong Lixin, 1999, "Research on Climate Change on the Southern Qinghai Plateau and Its Impact on Alpine Meadows", *Acta Prataculturae Sinica*, 03, 1–10.

Zhou Lusheng, Li Haisheng, Wang Qingchun, 2000, "The Basic Characteristics of Heavy Snowstorm Process and Snow Disaster Distribution in Eastern Pastoral Areas of the Qinghai–Tibet Plateau", *Plateau Meteorology*, 19(4), 450–458.

Acknowledgments

On behalf of the Research Group of the Chinese Academy of Social Sciences, I would like to express my deepest thanks to the individuals and organizations who have contributed to the conclusion of this research project, "The Development of Tibetan-Inhabited Areas", and the publication of this book.

I am particularly grateful to:

The Chinese Academy of Social Sciences and the Beijing Office of the Ford Foundation for their long-term financial support;

The local governments of Gansu, Qinghai, and Yunnan Provinces, and the provincial Academies of Social Sciences for their coordination and assistance during our field studies;

Public service providers, village committee members, farmers and herdsmen, monks and laypeople, as well as local and non-local entrepreneurs, migrant workers, and merchants, for the abundant information they provided.

I would also like to take this opportunity to express my sincere gratitude to the Tibetan translators that assisted us during our field research as well as the English translator and the English proofreader of this book.

Zhu Ling
March 21, 2012

A Publication Funded by the Innovation Project
in Philosophy and Social Sciences,
Chinese Academy of Social Sciences

Index